Teenagers and Parents:
12 Steps to a
Better Relationship

by

Dr. Roger McIntire

<u>Fifth Edition</u>
Summit Crossroads Press
Columbia, Maryland

Copyright © Summit Crossroads Press 2016

Summit Crossroads Press
Columbia, MD 21045
410-290-7058
E-mail: SumCross@aol.com
http://www.parentsuccess.com

ISBN 978-0-9614519-4-3
Library of Congress Control Number: 2016908018

Contact the author at sumcross@aol.com.

Cover design by Earthly Charms, earthlycharms.com.

Dr. Roger McIntire is available for speaking engagements. His books provide excellent discussion material for parenting groups and may be ordered in quantity at sizeable discounts. E-mail sumcross@aol.com for more information.

We cannot prevent this world from being a world in which many children and teenagers are unhappy. But we can reduce the number of unhappy ones. And if we don't help, who else in their world will help them?

Excerpt from Albert Camus statement at the Dominican Monastery of Latour Maubourg (1948). Translation (here modified) by Justin O'Brien, 1961.

About the Author

D r. McIntire, father of three, taught child and adolescent psychology, behavior analysis and family counseling at the University of Maryland for 32 years. He has authored ten books including *Enjoy Successful Parenting, For Love of Children* and *Child Psychology* (a college text), and his books have also been published in eight other countries.

In addition to his work with families, he was a consultant to teachers in preschools, grade schools, high schools and colleges. Dr. McIntire's research publications (over 100) dealt with infant vocalizations, eating problems, strategies in elementary school teaching, high school motivation and college drop-outs.

Table of Contents

Preface

E ight to twelve-year-olds are often called "Tweens," so, I suppose, the "teenager stage" begins at about ten in the U.S. It blossoms early and develops rapidly probably because of so much adult experience—mostly second-hand—from TV, CDs, mobile devices, social media, Facebook, Twitter, YouTube, talk shows and movies.

Games are the electronic activity of choice with the preschoolers and grade schoolers, but the first addition to the games is likely to be some form of social media with an expanding group of internet friends. The average teenager in the U.S. spends over eight hours each day with computer companions, human or not, who pass along information, or misinformation, about life, sex, social skills, and almost everything else.

Before the next ten years rush past and our teenagers choose their next adventure with college, job or life, we parents want to build a relationship that lasts. But this internet obsession gets in the way. We want to tone down their attention to their little electronic windows and talk with us a bit more.

Chances for conversation (coming up in the first step) appear and disappear from one situation to the next. Your listening skills are crucial to building your moments of conversation with your teen and passing along these habits to your kids. What memories and examples of your style of parenting will your teenager remember and pass along to your grandchildren?

Robert Epstein ranked the 10 most effective child-rearing practices in *Scientific American* in 2010. He reviewed the scientific literature and interviewed many experts and over 2000 parents and their children. Top of the list was love (physical affection and quality one-on-one time together). Surprisingly, second was stress management by parents, of themselves. How they handled their own stress as it recycles through the family created the family atmosphere. Third was how Mom and Dad maintained their own relationship with each other, or with their significant other or co-parent. The top three add up to love and respect for your offspring, for yourself, and for your spouse or co-parent.

Of course, the top three determine a parent's disposition and in turn, the daily habits of child-rearing. The first ten years seem to require the most attention because the child's needs are so obvious. Five to ten-year-olds require lots of help. Once they reach ten however, they're starting to grow into teenagers and temptations multiply and everything becomes faster, more dangerous, and harder to evaluate. Sex, drugs, and cars become part of the adolescent years surprisingly early. To keep up, a parent must listen a lot.

All of the theories—about siblings, birth order, genetics, and early experiences—contribute understanding, but such past influences cannot be changed. Mom's and Dad's best opportunity to influence their teenager, really their only opportunity, is confined to the here-and-now—the present family interactions.

Many counselors believe that parents who hold back too much have a lasting negative influence on their children. One counselor friend of mine works with corporate administrators who suffer from depression. She said she often found that the root of the problem was an unfulfilled need for acceptance from their Dads. She added that every man longs for the day when his father says, "You're the son I hoped you would be."

Daughters have had the same longings, I'm sure, and Mom's acceptance is just as important as Dad's. But Dads may hold back on the gushier stuff just when it's needed most. Often called upon to be the heavies—*Wait 'till your father gets home!*—Dads may miss their opportunities to give deserved praise and admiration.

Social media can squeeze out the time for these important moments. Questions and solutions raised in this book come from both parents and their teens who were clients, regular readers of my column or website visitors. Common questions from the kids were reported by parents, "Can we talk?" "Can I quit school?" "What birth control is best?" "I want a sister. You have more eggs don't you?" Parental questions range from, "How can I deal with her tantrums?" to "What about his computer addiction, her Facebook obsession and their questions about alcohol, drugs and sex?"

The struggle to grow up is a confusion of emotions—a desire to break free from parental control is mixed with a desire for parental admiration and support. Of course, teenagers want to be on their own and different from their parents. And conversely, parents want their children to stay close to their example and be more like them. The compromise develops gradually in a mixture of granting greater independence and decreasing control.

Step 1: Listen Well

On the rare occasion when your teen interrupts his attention to his electronic window to ask, *"Mom (or Dad), can we talk?"* your answer needs to be a careful one. If you and your son or daughter have this part right, all the other topics in this book will be easier, and your adult experience will be available to your teen at a low price. So go slowly here and thoroughly review your conversational habits when talking with your teenager.

The next chapter will suggest ways to wean your teen from his computer companion, but first be sure you're ready to listen. Listening skills don't come naturally to most of us. But, with a little practice and extra attention, the skills will help you for the rest of your parenting years.

1. "What are You Saying About Me?"

Many people, especially teens, are most interested in themselves. They tune in to the parts of conversations that are about them, and they are a little less interested in the rest. The most important part of the conversation will be, *"What are you saying about me?"* Talks with our teens can go sour immediately when we parents think their *mistakes* are the most important parts while our teens, first of all, pay attention to the implied *personal evaluation*!

Ten-year-old Kirby: *"Mom, Carlin is still texting"*

Mom: *"Carlin, no texting at the table. It's rude."*

Carlin: (15 years old) *"Just a minute."*

Mom: *"No. Now I want to hear about your soccer game."*

Carlin: (mumbling and still texting) *"Have to sign off. Kid brother just squealed."*

Mom: *"Put that cell phone away. I told you before, it's rude!"*

This moment turns into an argument because a ten-year-old was making trouble, and Mom responded by adding the evaluation that Carlin is rude. When trying to set rules, leave the personal reasoning out—it distracts a teenager to argue.

Mom was right to ignore Kirby's intention of making trouble but adding the personal evaluation only turns talk into argument. Mom could have said, *"Stop texting at the table, Carlin and tell me how your game went."*

Let's give Dad a chance.

"You should have seen what happened in gym today, Dad."

"What, Donald?"

"Keith got in an argument with Mr. Effort, and they ended up in a real fight!"

"I'm sure it wasn't much of a fight."

"Yes, it was. They were wrestling!"

"I hope you didn't have anything to do with it."

"Naw, all I did was cheer."

"Cheer? Listen, Donald, you'll end up in trouble right along with Keith! Don't you have any more sense than to..."

Let's interrupt Dad here for a moment. Dad criticized his son's story: (1) he thinks Donald exaggerated because it wasn't much of a fight, (2) he thinks Donald might have had something to do with it, and (3) he thinks Donald should not have cheered.

Dad centered the conversation on what he disliked about his son's behavior instead of the story. All this happened in a 20-second discussion. Donald, like all teens, will resent the way his dad turned his story into a talk about his mistakes. In the future, Donald will drift further away and Dad will get less and less information.

Dad's style of continual correction puts Donald on the defensive. Donald only wanted to tell his story for the joy of it, without corrections that lead in other directions. Here's the first point of possible misunderstanding and conflict. A teen may extract a personal evaluation in less than a sentence. If the signals are negative, up come the defensive reactions before any useful exchange begins.

Let's back up and give Dad another chance to be more friendly and yet still communicate the possible consequences of the gym-class experience to Donald.

Dad's second chance:

"You should have seen what happened in gym today, Dad."

"What, Donald?"

"Keith got in an argument with Mr. Effort, and they ended up in a real fight!"

"How did it all start?" (Dad ignores the possible exaggeration, doesn't express doubt, and shows interest instead.)

"They just started arguing about the exercises, and Keith wouldn't give in."

"Hard to win against the teacher." (Dad's comment is a general remark about teacher-student relationships and it's not critical of Donald.)

"Yeah, Keith is in big trouble."

"Did they ever get around to the exercises?" (Dad shows interest in the story, not just in making points and giving advice.)

"Keith was sent to the office and then we tried these safety belts for the flips. Do you know about those?"

"I don't think we had them in my school."

"Well, they have these ropes..."

Donald may have a clearer view of the incident now, and he may understand the hopelessness of Keith's argumentative attitude. He wasn't distracted by having to defend himself when he told Dad the story. And now he's explaining something to his father. Dad's positive evaluation of Donald comes through in his respect for him and interest in what Donald is saying.

Teens are forever on guard to protect their fragile self-confidence. Carlin is on the lookout for Mom's opinion of him and Donald is on the lookout for Dad's criticism. We parents sometimes concentrate our efforts on mistakes, but our teens place that in second place, at best.

2. Slow Down, Use "It" Not "You" to Reduce Their Stress and Yours

Deliberately slow your pace of conversation so your child-teen can slow his. Even a sassy teenager is not likely to have your way with building thoughts into words and will become defensive when he's rushed or runs out of vocabulary.

Thirteen-year-old Marie: *"This terrorism business is awful."*

Mom: *"Well, you just have to learn to live with it. The world is dangerous."*

An argument has already started. Of course Mom didn't mean that terrorism is not awful, she just moved on (too quickly) and made her daughter the topic instead of terrorism (You just have to learn...) and missed the opportunity to agree with her daughter.

Mom is next in line for a "Yes, but...," an exchange leading to a louder argument because her pace is too fast. Now the focus has changed to winning the argument. Mom will make her points and Marie will struggle to stay even. Distracted now by the argument, there will be little help with anxieties about terrorism. Sons and daughters in this situation copy their parent's argumentative style of conversation that only looks for mistakes to correct. A simple conversation has turned into a competition.

Fifteen-year-old Teen: *"I've got so much homework."*

Mom: *"Sounds like...they gave you...a lot."* (Good remark. with a slow pace, and Mom only repeats what her teen said.)

Teen: *"How can I do all of this?"*

Mom: *"Well, why not start with..."* (Mom stops and remembers to avoid jumping in with advice.)

Teen: *"I'm not going to do any of it!"*

Mom starts to threaten grounding for a week if homework is not done, but she remembers to avoid punishment and instead says, *"You're really good at math, maybe you could just start there."* (Mom risks a quick-fix mistake but, mixed with the compliment about math, it's likely to be taken positively.)

Learning the "it-habit" instead of the "you-habit" can also reduce the stress of conversation by not centering the topic on your teen. When Dad gets his second chance he says, *"How did it all start?"* It helps avoid both the instant-evaluation-of-Donald pitfall and slows a conversation that could be going too fast. When a conversation seems threatening to your teen, try to look at the subject as an "it" instead of "you." This tactic avoids the trap of "attack, defense, and counter-attack." Conversation doesn't make a good competitive sport.

Mom: *Leave your baby brother alone, Justin.*

Justin: *I was just going to pat him.*

Mom's first impulse may be to say, "*I know what you were going to do, just stay away, you'll wake him!*" Her second impulse might be, "*I like to pat him, too. But it might wake him and he's tired.*"

Justin drops some crumbs from his potato chip bag.

Now Mom's first impulse might be to say, "<u>*You*</u> *are so messy! Look what you did!*"

But her second impulse might be, "*Oh, look what happened. Better pick those up before they get trampled into the carpet.*"

If Mom chooses her first impulse, she emphasizes Justin, the person. *You* will wake him, *you* are messy. If she chooses her second reaction to each event, she emphasizes a situation that *she and Justin* are dealing with together: *It* will wake him. Look *what* happened. It won't make a lot of difference to Justin on these two occasions. But over the long haul, Justin will end up with a very different message about himself and a very different relationship with Mom.

3. Careful When Teaching Lessons and Fixing Blame

The opportunities to "teach a lesson" and "fix the blame" are temptations most of us parents find hard to resist. But sometimes the benefit of getting more facts outweighs the "quick-fix" or the "make-them-sit-up-and-take-notice" approach. People who avoid instant evaluation and defuse confrontation with an objective conversation of "it" topics are easier to talk to. They are interested in the other person's experiences, not in placing blame or emphasizing mistakes.

Mom: *"How was art class today?"*

Amy: *"Oh, OK, what I saw of it."*

Mom: *"What do you mean?"*

Amy: *"Mrs. Clay sent me to the office."*

Mom: *"What did <u>you</u> do?"* (Attack #1)

Amy: *"I didn't do anything!"* (Defense)

Mom: *"<u>You</u> must have done something; <u>you</u> aren't sent to the office for nothing!"* (Attack #2, conversation going badly)

Amy: *"You never think it's the teacher's fault; you always blame me."* (Counter-attack, looking for a way out)

Mom: *"What kind of talk is that? Let's have the whole story."* (Attack #3, conversation almost destroyed.)

Amy: *"Oh, nuts!"* Amy stomps out. (Conversation dead)

Mom can do better by avoiding the personal evaluation by using the "it' topics.

Mom: *"How was art class today?"*

Amy: *"Oh, OK, what I saw of it."*

Mom: *"What do you mean?"*

Amy: *"Mrs. Clay sent me to the office."*

Mom: *"WHAT happened?"* (Emphasizes "what" instead of "you" <u>What</u> happened? This is better than, "What did <u>you</u> do?")

Amy: *"Tom ripped my paper."* (The conversation takes a new turn with Amy's answer to the "what" question.)

Mom: *"Oh, no!"* (Emphasizes sympathy rather than an evaluation of the upcoming mistake.)

Amy: *"Yeah, so I shoved him."*

Mom: *"And so she sent you to the office?"* (Mom's focus is on facts and sympathy instead of taking advantage of a chance to reprimand something that's already been reprimanded at school.)

Amy: *"Yeah."*

Mom: *"Then what happened?"* (Good "what" question that avoids "let's get to the bottom of [your mistake in] this!")

Amy: *"Well, for one thing, I'm behind in art again."*

Mom: *"Well, if you can stay away from Tom, maybe you'll catch up. What else happened today?"* (Mom adds a little parental advice and then on to looking for something more positive)

Too often we parents begin at the wrong end of the conversation. After our teen exposes a problem or troublesome topic, we often jump to the end in order to fix the problem. In our rush, the message becomes, *"Stop talking, you're wrong, I'm right, and I'll tell you what to do."*

Effective conversational strategies take time, but if they become a habit, the rough parts of family talk can become smoother.

4. Looking, Smiling and Other "Non-Verbal" Signals

There is more to conversation than what is said and what is heard. Folding arms, getting louder, and looking away all speak volumes. Looking is particularly important. For example, watching the TV, while holding your hand over the mute button, ready to restore the sound, may irritate your son or daughter more than a yawn. A teen will quickly learn these signals and may increase his aggressive style just to regain your attention.

Smiling can also be a big factor in getting along. One marriage counselor I know said she counts the expressions of support and agreement between husband and wife. If she notes less than six per hour together, she becomes pessimistic about the relationship. However, she counts smiling as one of the positive expressions. Actually she counts every smile as two in looking for six per hour.

A slump may also show an uninterested attitude. It's best to face your conversational partner. To accept your solution your teen has to stop thinking about himself and take up the courage to admit you could be right. Knowing how seldom he is likely to reach this opinion, sit up and show interest. Most talks with your teen will not reach a conclusion. That's OK, family conversation should not be a tennis game where every ball must be returned and every game scored and posted. Let it end as it so often does with your friend at work—additional understanding and support, but no answers. *Give* a nice day.

Practice these habits with another parent or a friend while you share a simple story such as getting the kids to school or helping them with homework. Begin with one person as the listener and one as the teller. Review the following guidelines for good listening.

Keep frequent eye contact. Look at your conversation partner most of the time. A teen expects a good listener to look at him/her. We don't like to feel unattended because the person we're trying to talk with is staring at the newspaper or TV while we ask a question. Teens feel that way too.

Smile at your kids frequently. It's a sign you found something good about your children. They appreciate it.

Use good posture. Face your teen while talking and listening. Use body language that says, *"I'm alert! I'm interested!"* A parent who slumps, looks away, or even walks away sends messages that discourage and insult the person talking.

Avoid criticism, ask questions instead. Use questions that continue the conversation by asking for longer answers than just *"yes"* or *"no."* *"How did it feel?"* is more likely to continue the talk than *"Did you feel bad?"* Emphasize *IT* questions instead of using *YOU*: *"How was it at school today?"* not *"How did you do at school today?"* Careful questions can help in a neutral, non-opinionated way, so the person asking the questions gains a better understanding of what happened and why.

Avoid solution statements and use reflective comments.
Re-word the last thing your teen said to show you understand what
he/she told you. *"Boy, I really hate that Mr. Jones for math!"* could be
answered with, *"He really annoys you"* or *"You get mad in there a lot, I
guess."*

Replace the temptation to give advice or criticize by reflecting
your partner's statements instead. Suggestions such as *"Why don't
you . . .?"* or *"Have you tried . . .?"* might make the story teller feel
inferior, resentful, and argumentative. You will get the whole story
by reflecting. Your listening helps because the speaker will clarify
the situation and his feelings.

Share your experience. Share stories and jokes, that helped
you learn about getting along in life. Be selective, avoid stories that
are too close to a sore point with your teen. If your son or daughter feels your experiences are not directed as advice to his or her
specific weaknesses, the tales can be enjoyed, and they will improve
the relationship.

5. Pass Up the "Quick-Fix."

Parents love to fix things, especially quickly! Parents, particularly
fathers it seems, can be too efficiency-oriented in their conversations with kids. If you told me you had trouble tying your shoe
because the lace broke, would you want me to tell you how to fix
it? No. As a matter of fact, it would be a bit insulting because it
implies you are a complete klutz!

Jumping in with a "quick fix" is often annoying because if Mom
or Dad jumps in too soon with advice, a teen may cancel his or her
next topic entirely—just to avoid more correction.

Better to jump in with a positive remark first. Identify and highlight the behaviors you like. Loving a teenager is not much without liking specific behaviors also. Mom and Dad's first parenting job is to find and compliment what is likable about their kids. Even when their teen feels obligated to brush them off, compliments will improve their self-respect. Repeat as needed. Learning is a process, not a single event.

6. The Real Topic May Not Have Come Up Yet.

Parental reactions that repeat what a teen just said often result in more information from a teen. Her first remarks are usually long on feelings and short on facts. Reflective remarks may encourage her to make up the shortfall. Also, a reflective remark can be satisfying to her because it says you understand.

Keep a regular time and place for basic talking such as a long dinner time or possibly right after school while they have a snack. Don't try to fill every pause, some silence is OK. Don't meet their expectation that you always have (pushy) advice to give. If parents jump in with early advice or opinions, their reactions could be way off target.

Reflective statements say nothing new and only repeat what your teen said in different words. Without adding anything new, this agreement keeps the conversation going and provides opportunities to get straightforward information without defensiveness.

Reflective statements also require a little creativity to avoid looking simple-minded or manipulative, but in small amounts these reactions can allow teens to continue *their* topic of conversation. Let's look at an example of reflective statements in action by a mother learning about her daughter.

Amy: *"Man, is that school boring!"*

Mom: "*It's really getting you down.*" (Mom is reflective and just uses different words for "you are bored")

Amy: "*You bet.*"

Mom: *What's getting you the most?*" (A good it-question starts with "*What,*" instead of, "*Why are YOU so bored?*")

Amy: "*I don't know. I guess it's the whole thing.*"

Mom: "*You need a break.*" This is reflective of "the whole thing (is boring)" and is a sympathetic remark that avoids, "There must be something wrong (with you)!"

Amy: "*Yeah, but summer vacation is six weeks away.*"

Mom: "*Got any plans?*" (Good, puts the conversation on a positive topic.)

Amy: "*No.*"

Mom: "*Hard to think that far ahead.*" (A reflective statement that just repeats "No plans" with sympathetic words)

Amy: "*Pam is looking for summer camps online.*"

Mom: "*Sounds like a good idea.*" Avoids the quick evaluation of, "Camp might be expensive...it might be too early to apply, etc." Immediate negative evaluations only discourage the search for answers at this early stage.

Amy: "*I might go online and look for some myself.*"

A complaint about boredom is a familiar remark to most parents. Although not much is solved about boredom in this conversation, Mom has a better understanding of her daughter's feelings and has avoided the temptation to "get something done" in this short talk. Indirectly, Mom said she has had similar feelings to her daughter's, and it's all right to have those. Most important, it's all right to talk to Mom about feelings without being criticized for feeling bored.

By allowing her daughter to direct the topic, information flowed to Mom, instead of from her, and she has a "ticket of admission" for next time:

"Say, did Pam ever get any camp applications?" or,

"Only five weeks left now; how's it going?"

Notice there is no room for adding old complaints in this approach. Avoid frequent criticisms such as, *"You shouldn't be bored,"* *"You don't plan ahead like Pam'"* or out-of-left-field complaints such as, *"You spend too much time on the computer!"* *"You never do your homework!"* and *"You have bad friends!"* Such criticisms are too broad and will be taken personally because they say, *"And while I'm thinking about you, another thing I don't like is..."*

Instead, encourage your teen to take the conversational lead and postpone parental topics. Later sections in this book will deal with those other complaints.

Help your teen explore alternatives. Reflecting your teen's statements can help him or her get to a point of exploring alternatives to a problem and taking action to solve it. When a parent sends the message, *"I heard you,"* and *"It's all right to feel the way you do,"* your teen is likely to go beyond letting out feelings to considering, *"What can I do about it?"*

A parent helps most by tuning in to her teen's level of feeling and energy. Is he looking for alternatives, considering a particular one, or just letting out emotion? Parents must listen with empathy and react appropriately to give support. If your teen is getting rid of emotion, a helpful parent reflects that. At other times a teen may be exploring the alternatives.

Megan: *"Those kids are always dissing me online. I don't know what to do."*

Parent: *"What alternatives are there?"*

Teens are creative at listing options when they are ready. But if no idea comes up, the problem may not be clear yet and your teen needs to explore more by expressing opinions and feelings.

Perhaps Megan is ready to try an alternative.

Megan: *"I'm going to tell those kids to quit bugging me!"*

Parent: *"How do you think they'll react to that?"*

Megan: *"They might stop, but if they don't I'll just ignore them from now on."*

Parent: *"Just ignore them?"*

Megan: *"Yeah, that works every time!"*

Well, the ignoring strategy may not work all the time, but Megan is now encouraged to take control and is working on her own problem—that's a step toward growing up.

Distinguishing different teen levels of emotion and energy and reacting with support requires practice and empathy. When in doubt resist the temptation to suggest solutions.

7. Suggest Solutions with Care.

We are always tempted to suggest solutions to our kid's problems: *"Why don't you . . ."* *"You should try..."* *"Don't be so . . ."* These statements are well intended, but they often strike the listener as pushy and superior. Most of us don't react kindly to suggested solutions that are too early.

If you told me you're frequently late for work because of traffic, and I said you should get up earlier or take another route, you might be offended. I was trying to be efficient giving quick advice, and we often just want to fix things—preferably quickly, but efficiency in conversation is for business meetings and TV shows—not family discussions.

Family conversation should be enjoyed; it's not a job to get out of the way so we can get on to the really important stuff. Teens need time to talk to you. As one lonely teen put it to me, *"If all they want is a project, why don't they take up a hobby?"*

Your teen may have her own phone but does she still resent your phone conversations with friends? Because they take too much time from her? Possibly, she may also resent the friendly, non-efficient nature of your conversation with your friends that doesn't come through when you talk with her. As an example of overcoming the temptation to fix things too quickly, look at the following conversation:

Sarah: *"Life is so depressing. People are so bad."*

Mom: *"I know it gets like that at times."*

Here's a good start. It may seem like a terrible start because the topic is so discouraging, but that's Sarah's choice. A terrible start would be for Mom to fall to temptation and disagree with her daughter right away by trying to "set her straight" with the solution: *"You shouldn't talk like that; there are a lot of good people in the world!"*

This correction is tempting but unnecessary—Sarah knows her remark is extreme. Also, it's somewhat dishonest on Mom's part because she knows Sarah is partly right. Since the statement has some potential for agreement, Mom's reflective statement takes the side that puts her closer to Sarah. Let's see how it goes:

Sarah: *"It gets like that <u>all</u> the time at school."*

Mom: *"There <u>must</u> be some times that are good at school."*

Not good, Mom's saying, *"You're wrong,"* and it's too early in the conversation for the implied disagreement, authority, and solution expressed in this nudge. Let's take that back and try again:

Mom: *"School's been bad lately, huh?"*

This is better because it's reflective without evaluating who's to blame; it keeps the conversation on a third entity where Sarah started it (not her fault; not Mom's). The next remark from Sarah is likely to be informative about what the problem is at school. Mom, if careful, will learn a lot and Sarah will *"get it all out."*

In most conversations between adults, the suggestions for solutions are left out completely. We don't end up a conversation with a neighbor by saying, *"So we're agreed you'll cut the hedge at least every two weeks!"* or, *"So don't go roaring off in your car like that, it disturbs everyone!"*

Be satisfied that most conversations with your teen, like those with your neighbor, will have no immediate conclusions or results. Leave out the closing comment in most of your conversations. If you try to be the "winner" in every talk, then you will always have to make someone a "loser."

8. Beware of Arguments for Entertainment's Sake.

Is the conversation just an argument for entertainment? The answer to this is particularly important when the argument is really about what your teen says, not what she does. Intentions are not actions, but they can produce entertaining arguments. Your teen may want a reaction from you or to convince you that you can't always control her. Some of your teen's behavior in school and other places are away from your influence and that could be one reason school and other outside activities are her favorite topics.

A teen's more obnoxious stories may be re-designed for your ears alone, just to push your button or get you to argue! Most of the time, your reaction should be plain vanilla, especially regarding abstract or distant situations.

When Todd's father first talked to me, he described Todd's stories about rude remarks he says he made to his teachers. These stories always resulted in a sharp reprimand from Dad.

Dad's typical reaction was: *"You better watch what you say, those teachers work hard to help you and you just give them trouble!"*

Then Todd came back with: *"Dad, you don't know, they don't care about me, they're just in there for their paycheck!"*

Then Dad countered with: *"Well, you'd better listen to them if you want a paycheck of your own someday."* The argument is a destructive one, each looking for weaknesses in the other, no winners, no progress. But there is a little entertainment for Todd.

Todd said he didn't like these arguments, but that's questionable because he always came back for more. In fact, his mother told me, *"I just don't get it. I think Todd deliberately stirs up his Dad."*

Of course, Todd didn't intend to insult his teachers. That was too dangerous. He just *talked* about insulting them, maybe to relieve frustration, or to stir up a little excitement at home, or both. Being only 14, Todd might not even know he has a habit of putting down teachers at home, and no idea *at all* as to why he does it. If Todd's parents want a change, they need to work with the behavior in front of them, not the threat of what he does, or could do, at school.

We need new topics for Todd and his dad to talk about, and they need to be worked out in advance. If Dad has some good topics in mind, he and Todd wouldn't be so easily drawn into verbal fencing matches.

With new topics and Dad on the alert for chances to compliment and encourage Todd for reasonable conversation, the family airways will improve. The best habits for parents are ones that help them stay alert to see and react to the best behavior of their teenagers.

Reflecting a teen's statements can help move him toward exploring alternatives and taking action to solve a problem. It helps when a parent sends messages, "I heard you" and "It's all right to feel the way you do." Then your daughter or son is likely to risk talking about possible answers to questions like: "What can I do about it?" or "What would help?" A parent helps most by tuning into the teen's level of feeling and energy for the problem.

Is your teen looking for alternatives, considering a particular one, or just letting out emotion? All of these purposes are good. A parent may listen with empathy and react appropriately to give support. If her teen is just venting emotion, a helpful parent reflects that and does not give or push the teen to look for answers.

Lori: *"Mr. Factors is a terrible math teacher! He won't even let you ask a question."*

Mom: *"Questions are important in math—to get the problems straightened out before going on."* Good. Mom stays clear of who is right, Lori or Mr. Factors.

Lori: *"Sure. How can I learn if he won't answer the questions?"*

Mom: *Does he ever review?"*

Lori: *"Oh, sure, he reviews, but it's so fast nobody knows what he's talking about."*

Mom: *"Why don't you go in after class?"* (Whoops, Mom just took a superior view here. Lori may counter with, *"That won't work"* or *"I tried that."* Let's give Mom a second chance)

Mom: *"Why does he go so fast?"*

Lori: *"Who knows? What a jerk."* (Lori's voice is lower now, running out of steam for this topic.)

Mom: *"Hmmm."* (always a good response in tricky situations)

Lori: *"Some teachers are so hard to deal with."*

Mom: *"Hmmm, Yes."*

You may feel impatient with Mom in this conversation. Why

doesn't she help? Couldn't she at least encourage Lori to go in after class? Or encourage her to speak up insistently in class?

If this is the third complaint about Mr. Factors, Mom might give some of that advice, but on the first round she should pass up the temptation to give advice and just let her daughter know she's on her side. How can her daughter feel comfortable and spontaneous in bringing up sensitive topics (at this age, they all seem to be sensitive) and venting some steam if Mom always takes a shortcut to a solution and "quick fix?"

Conversation doesn't make a good competitive sport.

Step 2: Yes, You Should Look at Your Teen's E-mail

1. Computer Companions

With the principles of Step One in mind, talk to your kids about social media when the chance comes up. Notes in their personal diary may be private, but notes sent online by e-mail, Facebook or otherwise, are not.

Anyone (even parents) can see any note a teen sends. Geeks with a little computer savvy can copy them, use them, anywhere. You might as well spray-paint them on a fence downtown or, if they go even a little viral, then on the town water tower. You need to see what they type and read what comes back.

Teenagers average almost nine hours each day using online music or videos, TV, or "chatting" according to a 2015 report by Common Sense Media. Tweens, ages 8 to 12, average six hours a day, reports Jim Steyer, the director of the study. Over 2600 teens were interviewed. Kaiser Family Foundation's 2010 study said the average then was five and a half hours for tweens, over eight hours for the 11 to 14 group and nine for the 15 to 18 year olds—more than the daily hours of school. The trend is definitely up. But 25 percent of kids say their parents know little of what they watch on TV or do in social media.

On the positive side, schoolwork online is a growing demand for a teenager's digital attention. Yet 25 percent say their parents know little of what they watch on TV or do on social media.

Mom: *"Jason, are you still on that cell phone of yours?"*

Jason: *"Yeah, I'm talking to Mark."*

Mom: *"Mark, who?"*

Jason: *"He's my fellow fullback on the J-V soccer team."*

Mom: *"Well, get off and come to lunch."*

Jason: *"Just a second."*

Mom: (A minute later) *"Jason, come now!"*

Jason muttered "gotta go" while texting, then he shoved his phone in his pocket and went into the kitchen.

Mom: *"I'm starting to think that phone was a big mistake."*

Jason: *"Mom, Mark's a friend. We were just talking over the game."*

Friends are an important part of life and social media has become the connection of choice for teenagers. Parents need to be careful in setting limits because many teens "talk" with friends a lot more since the social media has become so popular. Time spent socializing has gone way up. But Mom is right to worry about how much time is OK, yet the time chatting with friends is not a waste.

A study by the Pew Research Center reported a lot of flirting on the net by teens but three-quarters said they never dated someone they only met online. However, of those who had a steady friend or partner, 38 percent expected to "hear" from their partner every day. Eleven percent expected hourly check-ins. Forty-eight percent had resolved arguments online and 70 percent had conversations that made them feel closer.

Among 12 to 17-year-olds in the U.S., 95 percent are online. Three out of four access the internet by cell phone or other mobile device and 20 percent said they have received unwanted sexual solicitations.

In 2016 we have over 800,000 registered sex offenders in the United States. Seventy percent of our teens will accept "friends" regardless of whether or not they know the person making the request. Only 25 percent of 12 to 17-year-old victims told their parents of the sexual predators they met on line. Only 10 percent of victims of cyber bullying told their parents.

Girls are more likely to be harassed online with unwelcome flirting and 69 percent said that social media gives too many people a window into their private lives.

2. Uses and Abuses of the Electric Window

Computers and hand-helds have become the gadgets of choice and sometimes trouble for teens socializing with friends, surfing for informative sites, doing school work or playing games.

Socializing. In my childhood, the family telephone was just off the living room. No one in my neighborhood had a phone of their own unless they lived alone. My end of the conversation could be (and was) heard by all. If Mom answered the phone and it was my girl friend she handed me the phone while holding up five fingers. I had five minutes to talk. Everyone listened, it cost money not to be squandered and "time online" was a continual subject of argument.

Thankfully, the good old days are gone, and now we all have phones that can do almost anything. Yet they can also be very pri-

vate and time limits remain a problem. Children and many adults
have to learn what is rude and when to turn off the gadget.

The internet may establish a fear of missing out that keeps
a teenager up to the wee hours not only because he might miss
out but also because he might fear missing anything, says Sherry
Turkie in her review of high-tech gadgets in the lives of teenagers. Her book is *Reclaiming Conversation. The Power of Talk in a Digital
Age.*

But something is missed, Turkie says. Phones may also separate
people. One dad reported his time with his seven-year-old on a
school field trip. He realized that while texting and sending photos
to friends, he had ignored the opportunities to talk with his son.

Surfing. The library and encyclopedia have been replaced for
many students with a hand-held that can search quickly through
many sources. But while a trusted librarian can keep a student on
track, a search engine can go in many directions and the sources
presented are not always friendly or in the best interests of the
student. The trust a young student has in a discovered site may be
greater than his trust of parents and teachers. It is important to
keep the lines of communication busy with discussions of the latest discoveries of your student's surfing.

School Work. Most schools now presume students have a
computer device on hand and assignments often require some
surfing. It's an opportunity for parents to stay up-to-date with their
son or daughter's work.

Games. Playing games has become so mesmerizing that walking into traffic or a construction site is becoming a danger, especially with *Pokeman* getting so popular.

Is addiction the right word here to describe these rapidly
growing habits?? Alcohol addictions will be defined in **Step 9** as

persons whose drinking habits produce excessive absenteeism from work or school and complaints from friends and family.

How does an electronic addiction measure up to that definition? Excessive absenteeism could extend to times when your teen is at school but mentally absent because he is texting friends or cruising the web. Complaints from family and friends would include times when a teenager is absorbed in his computer or mobile device and paying no attention to present friends and family. I think the definition of addiction fits.

The Pew Center study reported 78 percent of students interviewed said the most acceptable way to break up is face-to-face, more than any of the other ways, social media or phone or texting.

We already know alcohol-related car accidents will still be the biggest killer of our teens until they pass college age. Now we can add multi-tasking to the reasons for the fatal crash.

3. Who is Tweeting You Now? The Dangers of Facebook, E-mails, Tweets and Texts.

Ninety-five percent of teens in the U.S. are online. Also, three out of four access the internet by cell phone or other mobile device. Teenagers who fear being embarrassed often feel safe when tweeting, texting, or posting on Facebook. It allows more time to think over a potentially embarrassing faux pas and it also allows them to be unidentified.

Nevertheless, it is also a danger to your teenager because unidentified people could be sending your offspring scams or worse. How old is the author of the next e-mail exchange with your teen?

One father said his son had objected to his father invading his online privacy. Then the son was arrested for distributing pornographic materials on the net. His son had found pictures of younger girls not quite dressed and in provocative positions. He sent them to "friends" on the net, one of whom was a detective posing as a teenager. This son was arrested. If convicted, his record could follow him the rest of his life. Keeping up-to-date on your teenager's internet activities could be a very important parental habit. Since we all know that anything online can be seen by anybody, this is not a privacy issue.

4. Friends, Bullies and Meanies All Chime In On the Net.

Bullies often prefer social media because they not only have a victim but also an audience. Not just to admire them, but to add to the victim's embarrassment. Be a frequent companion when your son or daughter is on the net.

"Let's look it up on google," your teenager may say. Stay well informed with what your son or daughter is looking up on the internet by working with your teen on one screen. Make a habit of asking them to show you what was interesting, frightening or bullying. Let your child-teen have the computer seat while you watch and the two of you talk over what is presented. Of course, you can't always watch but, as a frequent visitor, you will be more informed.

5. No Internet Privacy for Minors— Too Many Predators.

At some family times, the social media should be off limits. For example, dinner times should not be times when one person is staring into his or her lap at a little window. Keep the family table clear of these distractions.

Blocking some sites as off-limits can help, but how do you

block the sites she or he will hear about tomorrow.? Time limits can be useful, but sometimes, to stay up-to-date, you need to sit next to your teen to learn what is going on.

Mom: *What are you doing on your cell phone?"*

Fifteen-year-old, Marie: *"Just texting a…friend."*

Mom: *"Who's the friend?"*

Marie: *"Mom, do you have to know everything? Just a friend."*

Mom: *"I just wondered."*

Marie: *"Don't I get any privacy? Do you need to know everything?"*

Mom: *"No, but the net is used by dangerous people. I don't want you to get into trouble."*

Marie: *"I'm doing my own private texting—it's nobody else's business."*

Mom: *"Nothing is private on the net, it's the business of anybody savvy enough to cut in and read your stuff."*

Marie: *"Oh, Mom, nobody cares. I'm just talking to Jim somebody. He's not even in my school."*

Mom: *"Wait, where does this friend live?"*

Marie: *"Mom, I don't know. Around here somewhere, I guess. Leave me alone."*

Mom: *"How old is he?"*

Marie: *"How should I know, stay out of my private life."*

Mom: *"This is on the internet, so it's not your private life."*

Marie: *"What's the big deal? We met in this chat room I follow."*

Mom: *"The big deal is you're talking to some boy (or man) you met in a chat room, you don't know his name, his age, or where he lives."*

Marie: *"Just bug out."*

Mom: *"No, I can't bug out. Don't text this person again. And if he sends you a text, please show it to me."*

Of course this is not the end of this problem Mom needs to stay up-to-date on this conversation. If Marie remains cagey and secretive about "Jim Somebody." Mom should be nosy until she's satisfied that Jim is a legitimate friend. Minors shouldn't have privacy on the public internet, there are too many predators.

Marie needs to learn that social media is not private. There is a record of everything. This is not a telephone where businesses inform you when your conversation is being recorded. Online, it is always possible to keep records, and they can be reviewed for any purpose. Marie's access to the net should remain limited until she is mature enough to be more careful.

The most important part of managing your high-tech teenager is to be available—available to talk and listen to your teen, to discuss his or her concerns, and to provide your adult perspective.

6. The Consequences of Being <u>Busted!</u>

Caught shop-lifting or driving under the influence, very few people, even adults, would understand the circumstances, the lawyers, and a lot of other details you don't see in TV shows. Because of these vague aspects, your teenager might not have a clear understanding of the likely consequences for not-quite-innocent internet behavior. This lack of understanding can keep the deterrent aspect of our justice system from having its best effect on your teen.

Teens are likely to belittle a parent's warnings of consequences, and they may be partly right that they will get off easy that first time. So if short-term consequences are mild, emphasizing the long term ones may sound pretty weak to the young and short-sighted.

At the moment of temptation, would a teen know that a conviction of a drug-related crime would exclude certain rights for the <u>rest of his life</u>? For example, he would never be able to get a private pilot's license for flying an airplane!

Unfortunately, many of the consequences require long-term

thinking—not a familiar task for a teenager. The shadow of a conviction lasts a long time in these days of high-tech data banks. The system never really forgives you. Everyone gets to know and your teen gets to keep no secrets. The information given on job, school, and loan applications is easily checked and you can't just "not tell them" anymore!

Parents should do their best to dispel the magical thinking and the self-serving delusions that are short on facts. Internet "friends" who may tempt your teen into trouble will always be short on facts.

For example if you're between 15 and 20 and arrested for some internet activity or for some traffic violations, would he know the possibility of waiting in jail? Would he know who is responsible for fines and expenses? How much do lawyers cost? Who has to pay?

In the long term, a conviction can also limit your future opportunities—job and credit applications will explore your record and financial institutions will bring it up. Will a conviction jeopardize a college loan or a job application at a computer programming company? Teens need to know what they have to lose.

95% of teens
in the U.S. are
online today.

Step 3: If Their Computer Is On, Avoid Shortcut Parenting

With so much competition from TV, CD's, mobile devices, social media, Facebook, Twitter, U-Tube, talk shows and movies, chances for a talk with your teen may become precious. When the opportunity comes up, here are some reminders.

The first priority in parenting should be finding things to highlight about our kids. If Mom or Dad zero in on the shortcut of looking for the obvious mistakes, blunders and bad behavior, they may miss the gems and successes. Reprimands are easier to think of and compliments take more time. As we parents react to what our teens do, messages accumulate every day about what we like and what we don't like. If you are on the lookout for bad behaviors your messages can overwhelm the less frequent expressions of love.

This can be one reason some growing daughters and sons become alienated from the family and would rather go outside with friends or stay in their own rooms with their social media. Often it is the likelihood of criticism, "put downs," and corrections that drives them away.

A habit of saying "I love you" is not much without frequent
messages that say "I like you." Finding behaviors to like are the
main business of being a parent. Your habits are contagious and
your attention is the main part of the family atmosphere. If looking for mistakes become the routine, parents might not like the
parenting job and look for ways to shorten the time spent. The
family atmosphere follows that mood. Teenagers will respond in
kind, recycling the wrong attitude through the family.

Teenagers sometimes engage in a conspiracy—almost uncon-
sciously—to convince you that you are having no effect. But don't
be misled. Your influence may not show up in the short run, but
your reactions do make a difference. Don't give up. Watch a certain
behavior for a few weeks to test your influence and notice how upset they get when they feel ignored. Attention, praise, and general
encouragement are handy rewards. They should be used often.

Vague expectations about what good behavior is and specific
descriptions of bad, lead to unbalanced parental messages that
say "I don't like you" more often than they say, "I like you." Bad
behavior may attract most of the attention because the "good" behavior is not spelled out well enough to be easily noticed. Getting
down to the specifics of good behavior leads to many advantages.

For example, parents who are alert and praise the small successes that are the parts of larger accomplishments send clear
messages about behavior. The kids develop and improve with
small, easy steps instead of becoming discouraged by reprimands
for small mistakes.

Developing a great parent-teen relationship should be a part of
every day. Teens long for the joy and safety of it; and parents take
satisfaction and pride in it. Your relationship is developing from a
mixture of your understanding of what's going on, your messages,

rules, listening, and your example. Consistent strategies are key ingredients in cultivating this relationship.

Basic heredity and personality will still show through in a growing family, but a review of daily events can often be useful because a parent can plan to withhold reactions, and deliberately provide a positive model. The best outcome would be that we all get what we deserve and improve our behavior as a result. Of course, out in the real world of your teenager, some justice is done, but undeserved rewards do occur and satisfaction only happens to a degree.

1. One-ups and Put-downs of Shortcut Parenting.

Put-downs and one-ups disrupt useful family conversation. They give too much attention to winners and losers. Then parents have a tough time getting any information about the temptations and troubles the kids are facing.

Where does shortcut parenting lead? Both parents and teenagers may have verbal habits and attitudes that can turn an otherwise valuable conversation into an argument.

Put-downs are tempting parenting shortcuts to get Mom's point across, but they are often too vague and personal. For example, vague complaints are sometimes triggered by a particular infraction, "Only ignorant people use that language." Of course he knows you're talking about a particular (usually four-letter) word, but, for impact, this parental objection is expressed as an insult of the whole person.

Better to avoid the general put-down and focus on the present mistake. "Don't say that word in our family; it's rude, abusive and as an adjective to "car" it doesn't even make sense. It sounds as if you don't know enough language to express yourself."

I agree this is still a put-down but, focused on the specific behavior with some extra explanation, it is more constructive. This will not immediately take care of the problem, but at least your teen may search for other words next time. When he finds them, let him know you are impressed.

One-upmanship is also a bad habit. It usually comes near the end of a conversation when we decide to declare ourselves the winner. We often like to see starts and ends where only a continuing process of change exists. For example, as parents we hope to persuade our children to avoid bad habits by not starting them. No smoking, no drugs, no alcohol.

Conclusions on the end of these conversations are better left off. "So I don't ever want to hear that you..." is better replaced by a reason, "Once those brain cells are gone, they don't re-grow."

These discussions will continue beyond the age of 20. The best help will be your example and your reasoning against the bad habits. Statistically, smoking kids come from smoking families. Alcohol abuse breeds alcohol abuse—regardless of Mom's and Dad's rationalizations or excuses for their own behavior. Teens copy better than they listen.

Here's another example.

Dad: *"You can't quit school. You won't get anywhere without an education."*
Teen: *"They don't teach anything I need to know."*

Now Dad could remain inflexible, stay with put-downs and disagree, saying his son needs to learn the basics and doesn't know what needs to be learned. He could also go with a one-up. *"Your mother wouldn't have the job she has today if she had quit, and I wouldn't be teaching without my extra schooling."*

A better approach might be to look for agreement. Certainly there's more to learn since we were in school. Maybe he is right about what he needs to know, and it's time to look to the school for a better menu. Just working out what else needs to be learned may help him start learning it, whether the school decides to teach it or not.

All candidates for public office know it's dangerous to admit they are not perfect, right, efficient, and the best. But candidate strategies are not productive in family conversation.

Parents can easily slip into office-candidate modes with their own children, but unlike political campaigns where only the candidates are judged, at home everyone is in for the long haul and everyone is a player on stage. This makes a big difference.

Conversation should not be a game. In games, for every winner, we imply there is also a loser. If parents play to win, the games will be short because parents have more practice putting everything into words. Sooner or later Mom and Dad will not be able to find a "loser" who wants to play.

"How was school?"

"Same old thing."

Mom has a choice right away. She could say, *"Come on, something must have happened."* Mom's score is up one, daughter's is down one. Or Mom could leave the score at zero saying, *"Gets pretty dull in the middle of the year."*

"Yeah, everybody's going nuts having to stay inside all day—even for soccer practice."

Now Mom could say something else agreeable and understanding, *"This weather has certainly been awful."* Or she could play to win, *"Well, at least you have more time to get your homework done."* Mom's score is up one but her daughter's alarm goes off. Here comes Mom's favorite topic and criticism. Her defenses are activated. Parents can easily slip into this shortcut mode. One Mom told me,

"I don't have all day to blabber; she needs to spend more time on her work, so I have to steer her in the right direction when I have the chance." This is a parenting style reserved for speaking to children, of course. We know the conversation will end soon, and we want to wrap it up with our point.

Better to forget about the ending and let most conversations explore situations without conclusions. Neither side wants instructions anyway.

A disadvantage to adversarial games with children is that losers quickly become non-risk takers. Then creativity goes down and conversations increasingly become defensive and short. Sometimes both sides end up just attacking and defending.

Often parents suspect that these confrontations have become a habit and an entertainment. They are inefficient encounters for a teen looking for the satisfaction of dominating at least in a conversation at home.

You don't have to be drawn into these tennis-game conversations. It isn't necessary to return every argument with a retort. Take your time with reactions as you would with an adult. Just, *"Hmmm"* or *"Ahhh"* is often enough. Avoid the personal comments as much as possible and encourage your offspring to think (and talk) like an adult.

With the time-limit ignored and the score left at zero, future talks will be frequent, more productive and probably more interesting.

Parenting shortcuts often come up short. They can make us feel we are protecting and disciplining our kids when we are actually giving no specific help or instructions at all.

"You need to try a little harder to be nice at these family gatherings."

"Your manners were terrible, and you should be nicer to your cousins."

"You had better shape up and make an effort, Jeff."

Mom's well-intended advice to Jeff is of little help. Trying harder, showing better manners, being nicer, shaping up and making an effort are not specific. They could strike a teenager as magical ideas.

These general directions leave enough loopholes to allow Jeff to avoid any new effort and still have room to defend himself later. Better to be specific and say, *"When your aunt asks you about school, stop and answer her."* Better yet, *"Stop and tell her about your science project."* The specific suggestion is no longer magical, and if Jeff takes the advice, he can be more pleasant next time.

Sometimes we engage in magic to avoid direct confrontation and sometimes because we have no answers. We only know we want things to be better. One Dad said to me, *"He knows what I mean. I don't have to spell it out for him."* Vague criticism makes it easy for Dad but it is confusing for a teen.

"Jeff, you had better start acting right."

"What did I do?"

"You're always fighting with your sister."

"She starts it."

"Well, you'd better learn to get along."

Not much information in this exchange. What is "acting right?" What strategy should Jeff learn to "get along" besides the one he has already selected—blame the problems on his sister?

Better to quit this game of teen-parent dodge ball and be specific, *"Jeff, when your sister calls you names, tell her you won't talk to her when she does that and then leave."* Will this advice solve the problem? Probably not, but a specific plan gives Jeff a little more control and Dad a way to be truly helpful.

Separating sister and brother is sometimes necessary but

doesn't teach much. It just satisfies Dad (or Mom) with a temporary stop to the arguing. Dad's guilt is relieved because he has "done something" about the problem.

Often it's our definitions, or lack of them, that get us into trouble. *"OK, you can ride your motorbike out on the road, but be careful."* What does "be careful" mean? Go slow? The whole idea of getting on the road is to go faster. These two are going to have another argument about the motorbike. Mom should be specific or refuse to let him use the road.

To make real progress, Mom will need to identify the actions of her son that will directly contribute to a better adjustment. Usually this requires coming up with specific and clear alternatives to bad behavior.

The best advice you can give your teenagers is not spoken but shown. Your example is the best control you have in arguments. If you lower your voice they will lower theirs, and you'll have a better chance to get your suggestions across to them.

Girls and boys need any encouragement we can give, and the most useful encouragement will be your time—time with homework, time for talking over career plans and time for looking into the prospects after high school graduation. Don't be discouraged by a teenager's apparent lack of enthusiasm for these topics. Kids often feel obligated to act independent (I don't need any homework help) and competent (I know all about those college programs).

It's a parenting pitfall to become discouraged by the apparently indifferent attitude of a teen and leave him or her short on helpful conversation about these topics.

When your school asks for volunteers for field trips or away games, encourage Dad to take on the opportunity. It will give him a chance to learn more about his children, and it will set a standard for students who need the male example.

In those conversations at home, remember that often a teenager's number one fear is embarrassment. Avoid beginning with a question you know they can't answer, *"How are you going to learn if you don't pay attention?"* Start with information they might want, *"Here's a flyer on that golf scholarship in Virginia. What do you think? Maybe we should drive down and take a look."*

Don't be too busy for mealtime talk. Mealtimes can provide a snapshot of general family happiness, but many families have given up the tradition. Breakfast is either nonexistent or taken on the run in the morning rush. Lunch takes place at either school or work. Shawn eats by herself in the evening also, in front of the TV. Her big sister snacks and sends text messages to friends. Dad and Mom eat supper while watching the news. Little time is left for serious talk.

Without mealtime practice, parents and kids forget how to talk to each other. Family conversation is reduced to sound bites. Parents try to get in their points and the kids mimic the latest patter from TV sitcoms where zingers have been memorized in advance. Big mistakes can result.

Mealtime talk is often replaced by other rushed conversations designed for a purpose. Joey at 15 years old can talk at a breakneck speed if he thinks talking fast and acting impatient will get an "OK" when a slower pace might produce a "no."

Joey: *"Dad, Ross and his family are going to the school football game tonight. Can I go?"*

Dad, looking at his e-mails: *"Ah, what did your mother say?"*

Joey: *"She said it's up to you."*

Dad, still looking at his computer: *"OK, as long as you stay with the family."*

With more mealtime practice Dad might have recognized Joey's devious use of "family" and asked, *"Who did you say was going?"*

Joey might have said (still in the rapid fire mode) *"Ross and some of his family."* And then with a very painful face, *"Dad, he's waiting on the phone."*

Dad, knowing Joey's impatience, might have said, *"Let's talk it over. Do you mean Ross's brother is driving?"*

Joey would say, *"Dad, I don't know who all is going. Anyway, Ross's brother is a good driver, can I go or not?"*

A teenager's view is on the short-term, but Dad should have paid attention to more than going to the ballgame. Certainly Joey's idea of what makes Ross's brother a good driver is not enough.

Dad missed all this and while the consequences were serious, they were not tragic. Ross's brother was arrested for driving under the influence, and it caused a family row. Dad said Joey had mislead him, Joey said he hadn't. Little was said about drinking and driving.

Are you too busy for a slow pace? Most of our social habits are learned from our parents' example and will not be learned by the kids if we are too busy to sit down and take time with supper. *"They've got to learn to shift for themselves,"* one Mom told me. What choices will they make and who will teach them to "shift for themselves?"

Sit down with the kids for at least one meal every day—deliberately use a slow pace, no newspaper, no TV, no mobile devices. This is a great time for family stories. Avoid starting remarks with "you," don't try to steer the conversation, don't try to "win" and, oh yes, don't expect changes in the first month.

The crucial question confronting parents is not whether rewards, punishments, encouragements, and discouragements will be used to influence a teen's behavior. In day-to-day living that influence is inevitable. The question is whether parents will have time enough to plan some of these consequences so that their teen will be encouraged to learn what needs to be learned while growing up.

The emphasis on the defects in the person will act as a punishment. Jovial and approachable people never seem to punish. They seem to have a rule that says, *"When mistakes happen, emphasize outside events."* To the extent that we must correct, contradict, reprimand, and punish, we risk losing this friendly air.

Selecting behaviors for positive attention is the main business of being a parent. Your habit will be contagious and the whole family atmosphere will be more positive.

If looking for mistakes becomes the routine, parents may become unpleasant, and they may not like themselves when doing the parenting job. A teenager will respond in kind and avoid the family situation when possible.

The parental habit of looking for mistakes can preoccupy a parent's view of the family situation. Even pre-teens may pick up the habit. They may not criticize parents directly, but siblings will be fair game.

Once the habit is learned, it will develop into a game of "Who can find the most mistakes in whom? The situation makes a sad family and is not conducive to developing friendships.

Friends should appreciate and support each other's strong points. The friendship is doomed to be an unhappy one if they dwell on or make fun of the vulnerable spots. Eventually I won't like myself when I am with them. I won't like the "me" they draw out. I am not likely to come back.

2. Placing Blame and Giving Credit

Positive communication promotes more comfortable and informative conversations. But through the processing and maneuvering in a family, it may go beyond conversation to the complex negotiations of parenting. This development creates dangers in placing blame and giving credit in parent-teen negotiations.

We usually give credit for successes, but for mistakes and failure, we distribute the blame in one of two ways: For *our own* mistakes we usually choose "outside blame" that finds the explanation in circumstances outside of ourselves. This makes us unfortunate victims of situations outside of us, *"It was so noisy in there, how could anyone think or be able to do the right thing?"* "Outside blame" also includes people, *"I was too distracted because people were coming so late!"*

When it comes to the mistakes of *other people*, we are tempted to use "inside blame." *"What* (inside condition) *makes him so inconsiderate, so clumsy? Why doesn't she pay more attention? What was she thinking of?"*

Inside blame is a dangerous parental habit. It leads parents to frustration because their teen is viewed as "having" (inside) an almost unchangeable character.

Outside blame leads parents to look for problem *situations* instead of problem *kids*. With a good understanding of a problem situation, you have a chance to support a workable solution, and that, in turn, gives your teenager a new chance. In order to plan reactions to problem situations, a parent needs a clear view of what's happening. Using inside blame with your teen doesn't help because it makes assumptions about what is going on inside.

Nick: *"Dad, can you drive me to soccer practice now?"*

Dad: *"Just a minute, Nicholas, I'm listening to your mother."*

Nick: *"Oh great, if I'm late for practice, I won't get to play on Saturday."*

Dad: *"Just a minute!"*

Nick: *"We need to leave right now!"*

Dad: *"A minute ago you were watching TV, now we have to drop everything and rush".*

Nick: *"Forget it. I just won't go."*

Dad: *"You just said ..."*

Nick: *"I mean, I'll just skip Saturday, too."*

Dad: *"Just get in the car, OK?"*

Nick: *"OK, if you insist."*

Dad: *"What!?"*

Later, Dad says: *"Nick is so selfish. He sits around watching TV, then demands immediate service because he's late! And then, he blames me for insisting he hurry! His switching the blame drives me crazy!"*

Mom: *"Maybe he is selfish, but we could try a rule that says all rides require a 5-minute warning before take-off time. And any time he tries abusing us like that we should just say, Well, if you really don't mind not going, OK!"*

Dad: *"You're right. Soccer is less important than giving him the message he can't twist us around like that."*

Mom: *"It might not always come out perfect, but at least we will take back a little control of the situation."*

Instead of fixing the blame inside Nick (he's selfish), Mom suggested they try changing their reactions to Nicholas when he makes a demand. It could be he's doing it for attention and even an argument about his demanding nature could be rewarding.

The complaint that Nicholas is *"too demanding and selfish"* refers to real actions of Nicholas, but also implies the problem is part of his nature. The result is that the blame has been put inside Nicholas, and his parents may believe that any change can only come from there.

The *"Why?"* of a teen's behavior is best answered by changing *"Why?"* to *"What happens next?"* Nicholas makes an inconsiderate demand and then what happens? His ride comes through *and* any disruption is blamed on Dad for not cooperating on demand. What different consequence could be planned? The answer is not always simple and obvious, but Mom starts at the right place by looking for a solution instead of blaming Nicholas. This approach is more productive than giving up and just labeling him "selfish." The new focus may lead to a plan to support Nick's considerate behavior and to exercise caution in reacting to his little traps.

Parents can be on the lookout to give credit for the good accomplishments of their son (or daughter), but they often feel these opportunities are few and far between. The problem may be partly due to the way behaviors are described. If good behaviors are only vaguely defined, they are less likely to occur and be recognized. Deciding just when to support a teenager may not be easy:

Matt (age 13): *"I got my room cleaned up."*

Dad: *"Great!"*

Matt: *"I didn't pick up the parts to my model because I'm not finished yet"*

Here's a crucial moment for Dad. His choices are: continue support for what was done; after all, half a loaf is better than none, or hold out for a higher standard and only give credit when the whole job, with the model put away, is done and the credit is due.

A definition of what is acceptable would help. Doesn't Matt have the option of leaving one on-going project out? Matt's parents will have to make this judgment of Matt's progress and potential, but the parental habit here should be to err to the side of encouragement—there are few circumstances in adult-rearing where there is a danger of an overdose of support.

Another concern for Dad is what kind of credit should he give? "Outside credit" may be "no credit" (support) at all for Matt: *"I guess the mess finally got to you. Even you couldn't stand it any more."*

So Dad may give the credit to Matt's environment for driving Matt to do the right thing, But also, Dad shouldn't take the credit himself by saying, *"Well now, didn't I tell you that would be better?"* Dad should send the credit directly to Matt for getting the job done:

Dad: *"Well, you still need the model out; you would have to just about wreck it to put it away.* <u>*You*</u> *(not me, and not other influences) have it looking really good in here!"*

3. Look for Needs Instead of Blames.

Recognizing the priorities of needs can sometimes explain the otherwise puzzling fate of some rules. For example, I worked with two very different sisters whose reactions to cleaning up their rooms were very confusing.

Michelle needed to be constantly assured that her parents thought she was capable and successful, and she tried hard to be cooperative and helpful. Her sister Susan, also seemed to value her parents' approval but wanted prolonged attention and companionship more than praise.

A rule that reminded their mother to praise both daughters for keeping their rooms nice worked well for Michelle seeking confirmation of a job well done. Since attention ended when the rooms were done, attention-seeking Susan procrastinated in doing her part just to keep the cleaning going on and on. Susan prolonged the room-cleaning chores for the attention she received—even negative attention would do—while our more goal-directed Michelle worked hard for the confirmation of her success.

Mom may want her daughters to clean up their rooms to keep the place looking nice, but does she have to be right on top of them while they do it? The reason may be that while she thinks having a nice room is the point of the clean-up (a long-term goal), the daughters' priorities may be quite short-term—one wants assurance that she is contributing (doing it right); the other wants attention for doing any work at all!

Mom has *two* strategies to work on. One strategy Mom carries out deliberately—encourage them when they clean their rooms; the other strategy is an unintentional one of giving unusual attention to Susan's procrastination. So Susan *slows up* for attention, but Michelle *finishes up* for praise.

The solution for Michelle and Susan's mother came with the insight that Susan needed attention at the end and long after the chores were completed. This attention did not need to be in the form of praise for room-cleaning; it just needed to continue in order to show Susan that finishing the room didn't finish Mom's attention.

It would be a mistake to conclude that Michelle wants to please Mom and Susan doesn't. Or that Susan wants to aggravate her mother. These conjectures about sinister Susan would only lead to more nagging and a sour turn in Mom's relationship with Susan. Mom is the adult and *she* has to make the special effort, after room-cleaning, to show interest in Susan.

4. Avoid the Temptation to Increase Blame as They Grow Up.

As children become teens, blaming them is increasingly tempting for parents, *"They're old enough to know better!"* This habit can distract parents from looking for a chance to give personal credit when it is deserved. For example, you might know a teenager who is moody, disrespectful, rebellious, or cynical. This might be a "long-standing habit" (inside blame) and his parents may think, *"That's just the way he has always been."* But even older teens act the way they do partly because of the way they expect to be treated— because of what has ordinarily happened next.

Teens may be disrespectful because the only time they are taken seriously is when they act disrespectful, or their bad behavior may produce an entertaining argument, or their bad talk may seem more "adult" than saying something pleasant. Even some adults believe that!

When a disrespectful teen turns happy and cheerful, adults may pat him on the head and tell him he's a "nice boy" but otherwise ignore him. The usefulness of bad behavior in this situation is not lost on a grumpy teen.

Showing respect for your teen by asking for his opinion, showing confidence in his abilities, and doing a good job of listening will bring out an improved form of respect in return. This strategy, an example to be modeled, encourages an attitude that will replace "disrespectful."

Dad: *"It's too early for a garden outside, but we could start seeds inside. What do you think, Nick?"*

Nick: *"What good would that do?"*

Dad: *"Later, when you plant them outside, they would have a head start."*

Nick: *"Even melons and stuff like that?"*

Dad: *"Even melons. Let's do melons."*

5. "I Always Felt I Was Not Quite Good Enough."

Many parents have told me that while they were growing up, their parents always pointed out the room for improvement. *"I always felt I was not quite good enough,"* was one father's comment to me while telling me he wrote a letter to his mother every week throughout his adult years until she died. But each letter was criticized for leaving out some detail. *"I wish she had just once said that she appreciated all the news; she never wrote me, she always called and pointed out some person or subject that had been left out of my latest letter."*

It is a shame that many never experience such deserved appreciation. But the greater tragedy is that while a parent holds back compliments, the kids become discouraged with the task and resentment sets in. It takes courage to overcome the disadvantage of parents who have been too stingy with their compliments.

A parent's short-term job is child-rearing, but the long-term goal is adult-rearing. To reach that goal, children need examples of how adults handle their responsibilities and accomplish their tasks. But the kids are not adults yet, and left to their own inclinations, they may miss their chances to learn. They need a lot of time just following along while the adults show them the ways of the world.

Leaving a child out of the daily demands risks the loss of the adult example and parental instruction. The skills missed leave a void where a feeling of pride and usefulness could be developing. Protected from this education, they will feel less useful and less valuable.

Of course all members of the family need some times when they have it their way. But the productive learning is more likely when the adults do the leading. In *The Gesell Institute's Child Behavior,* you are advised to *"try to provide, so far as you can, the kind of situation in which each kind of child can feel comfortable and do well. But don't try to change him or make him over."* The advice is good except you are not yet told what the "kind of situation" is. The best situations will be ones where children learn by adult example and adult instruction.

The advice from the Gesell book also includes a caution to avoid trying to make your child over. It's a little confusing since we are working for some change. So just how far can we go and not be accused of "making him over?"

The way in which a child grows into the independence and competency of adulthood varies from family to family, and we all know that the extent of success varies also. We could probably agree that, ideally, child-rearing should be a process of gradually expanding responsibility and independence. Unfortunately, we have all seen many families where the children go through a long period of severe limits followed by an abrupt and risky freedom at about the age of 17 when the American teenager is sprung from the nest to go to college or work.

Mom: *"I need some help with dinner every night. Neal, could you set the table for everyone each night?"*

Neal (age 5): *"Do I hafta? Make Dawn do it."*

Mom: *"No, since she turned 9, Dawn makes the whole dinner on Tuesdays and lunch on Saturdays. You can set the table."*

Neal: *"I'd rather make a meal like Dawn."*

Mom: *"OK. Let's work on a few meals together, maybe we could start tomorrow night. But for now, set the table. That will be a great help!"*

I am sure Neal isn't completely happy with this new chore, but with the proper appreciation, he will have an additional feeling of worth and ability. Dawn is learning she can take care of herself and Neal needs to learn the same.

Once away from home, our offspring-now-sprung will have to learn to make meals as well as car payments. They need to avoid the pitfalls of credit cards and checking accounts, and leave time to enjoy life, but not too much time. We had better get started now teaching some of these complications of life.

Most children-turned-teenagers grow up late, painfully, and abruptly, but they grow up. Unfortunately, the newspapers tell us about many young adults who do not cope well with their sudden plunge into independence. As a result, many "children" come back home to live a few more years in the nest—not always a welcome idea to parents.

Mom: *"Neal [age 12, now], maybe you could balance the checkbook each month this summer."*

Neal: *"What? I don't know anything about that!"*

Mom: *"Now's the time to learn. Maybe you should earn a "service charge" for the job."*

Neal: *"I'll try. But don't get mad if I get it wrong."*

Coping well with the demands of bank accounts, budget management, and the need to plan a future beyond the end of the month requires a great deal of practice at the younger ages.

While parents usually talk to their offspring about the demands of the outside world, it is easy to forget to allow practice with as much of that reality as possible. As soon as reasonable, children need experience with the freedom to make decisions on their own and reap the consequences of those decisions.

When they are successful, the protection of the family nest can make sure that the success is recognized and encouraged. The failures can be learning experiences with the consequences softened by parents. A long period of safe trial and error is possible for children whose parents allow for it.

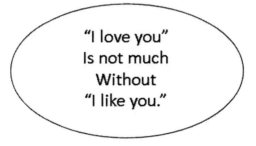

Step 4: Games Both Teens and Parents Play

When a teenager puts his electronic entertainment aside, he looks for entertainment somewhere else. Maybe an argument with mom or a conflict with a sibling will provide a fun game.

"Don't play games with me!" an aggravated parent will say. But everyone plays a few games, and the best way to deal with a game is to recognize what your teen's purpose is in the game and how you want to play it.

Game 1: "Referees Are Fun."

Steven: *"Mom! Mark won't turn down his music!"*

Mom: *"Mark, turn it down. Steven needs to get his homework done."*

Mark: *"He's not doing his homework, he's just goofing around with it."*

Steven: *"Mom! Mark still has it too loud!"*

Mom: *"Steven, it sounds OK to me now."*

Mark: *"Mom, Steve came in and turned off my music!"*

Steven: *"Mom, Mark pushed me!"*

Mark: *"To get you out of my room, I have to push."*

Mom: *"You two cut that out! Mark, get out here right now! If I have to come in there..."*

In this game, Mom is referee. You can almost hear someone yell, *"Hey, Ref! Call those penalties and control the game!"* It's safer than regular conflict because you can count on Mom, the Ref, to call a halt to the escalation. By the way, as all basketball and soccer mothers know, referees (I was a soccer referee for 20 years) are usually wrong 50 percent of the time from each player's (or parent's) point of view. So if you lose, you can always blame the referee—what a nice way to pass time or procrastinate on doing homework!

Why don't adults play this game? Sometimes they do, of course. It's just that the third party (the referee) can't be counted on to keep the game going or to intervene when the conflict gets hot. Once the referee leaves the game or fails to play the role of protector, the players have to quit or play by their rules.

Most referees are tempted to coach now and then and parents are no different, *"Mark, why don't you let Steven do his homework and play your music later?"* Suggestions are usually resented because the game would be over.

If the suggested solution is rejected, Mom could always end the game by removing the source of the conflict—Mark's music or Steven's selected place for doing homework. If Mom remains stern, she might insist the boys use one of her solutions. The danger here is that if Mom is not stern, her solution will only become a new source for more "fun and games."

The resolution can't be perfect for the kids. But Mom's goal here is to get herself out of the referee role and give responsibility back to the boys. The less-than-perfect solution can be fixed any time the brothers want to fix it. Many of these games become much less troublesome to parents when they identify how the game is being played and change their reactions to give control back to the teen players.

Game 2: "I'll Bet You Can't Make Me Happy"

Here is a game that also pulls parents into the problems of their teens when teens should be taking responsibility.

"Mom, what can I do? I'm bored."

"Why don't you finish your art project?"

"I've done most of it, and it's not coming out right."

"Well, how about helping me with dinner?"

"That's just work."

"Well then, you might as well get your homework done."

"I don't have to do it yet"

"Well, why don't you..."

Many parents recognize this conversation as one that has no end. There's continuing attention from Mom as long as no suggestion is right.

Suppose old hard-headed Uncle Harry and his friend, Al, came over and started this game with Mom? She would probably make a few suggestions, and then since they are adults, she would think it was time for the old coots to entertain themselves!

Parents can't win the *"I'll-bet-you-can't-make-me-happy"* game, but after a few suggestions, they can pass the responsibility back to "the kids."

Game 3: "My Problem is Your Problem"

This is a common game of young teens that will develop in the later teenage years into *"It's Your Fault Because You're My Parent(s)."* As with many of these games, frankly stating the fair truth may stop the game and allow some real progress.

"This homework is due tomorrow, Mom!"

"Well, you'd better get at it, Tyler."

"Where's some paper?"

"In the desk."

"I already looked there."

"Why don't you try upstairs?"

"Mom! It's supposed to be down here, could you go look?"

"Hold it, Tyler, your homework is your responsibility. Don't make it my problem."

This game has a little of the flavor of the *"I'll-bet-you-can't-make-me-happy"* game. In both cases parental attention looks suspiciously like the reward that's prolonging the game, and it's time to put Tyler on his own for awhile to search for solutions.

Game 4: "You're the Parent, Let Me Tell You Your Job."

Alan: *"I'd like to take those self-defense classes, Dad."*

Dad: *"Good exercise. And it could come in handy."*

Alan: *"Well, the ones I want to take are in Freetown."*

Dad: *"Freetown? That's almost an hour from here."*

Alan: *"Sam is in the class near here, and I don't like him."*

Dad: *"I can't drive 2 hours every Saturday because you don't like Sam."*

Alan: *"You're supposed to help me. There's no other way."*

Dad: *"You could take the lessons here."*

Alan: *"You're the Dad. You're supposed to take me!"*

Dad: *"Alan, I'll be glad to take you to the lessons here, but I have a life on Saturdays, too. I'm not driving to Freetown, wait an hour and then drive back."*

Alan's game brings up the important notion that Dad has the right to be selfish at times. Alan's tactic of telling Dad his responsibilities isn't working, and he may change the game to:

Game 5: "If You Serve Me, I Won't Make You Feel Guilty."

Alan: *"David's father drives him to Freetown."*

Dad: *"Well, I don't have that much time."*

Alan: *"Time for your own son?"*

Dad: *"Alan, don't start that. You know I spend a lot of time with you on our projects."*

Well, this is not going well for Alan and if he doesn't think of a good argument fast, he's going to have to take lessons locally. Alan may have to start yet another game:

Game 6: "I'm Not Responsible, You Are Guilty for My Mistakes."

Alan: *"Well, don't blame me if I get in a fight with Sam."*

Dad: *"What?"*

Alan: *"You're making me take the lessons here, so if I get into trouble it's your fault."*

Dad: *"Alan, you are responsible for what you do. If the situation with Sam is that bad, maybe you should skip the lessons."*

Alan is almost out of ammunition for this argument and he is in danger of having to show responsibility and consideration for Dad. He can't have his own way, and like the rest of us, he resents having to compromise and make some extra effort to get along. What tactic is left?

Game 7: "You're Not Right, Because...Because."

Alan: *"Dad, it's not that far over there."*

Dad: *"It's the other side of the interstate!"*

Alan: *"The lessons here are not as good."*

Dad: *"You haven't tried them yet."*

Alan: *"They might cost more money here."*

Dad: *"Call and find out."*

Is Alan going to call now? Probably not. Before he agrees to do that, he may ask Dad to make the call, bring up Sam again, and he may get out a map to show Dad he's wrong. Eventually, Alan will realize Dad is not driving to Freetown.

The key here is Dad's firmness for his own welfare without attacking Alan with, *"You're inconsiderate, irresponsible, selfish, etc."* Dad sticks to the issues, *not* Alan's personal traits.

Game 8: "If You Really Loved Me, You Would Serve Me."

Here's a game that is similar to the *"My-Problem-is-Your-Problem"* game with a little extra pull on the guilt strings of Dad or Mom.

Michael: *"Mom, I need those shoes!"*

Mom: *"Michael, I told you. You have a pair of running shoes—one pair is enough."*

Michael: *"But these are different. Matthew's mom got him a pair."*

Mom: *"I said one pair is enough—it's too much money."*

Michael: *"Matthew's mom said they're worth it for <u>her</u> son!"*

Mom: *"Michael, don't run that guilt trip on me. I'm the one who bought you the first pair, remember?"*

Calling Michael on his attempt to blame his mom for his troubles will not stop this argument, but when Mom recognizes the game, she can keep the proper view of the talk and not let her *son* get control of *her* emotions.

If the reasons (current consequences) for the game are hard to find, possibly some chain or group of behaviors is performed before the consequences occurs. For example, complaining about school only results in a parent's suggestion of what to do about homework, which provides an opportunity for procrastination about it and then a game of *"I-haven't-got-this,-get-me-that."*

The school complaint may be a secondary means to a teen's

goal—getting his parent tangled in the homework responsibility. Consider a teen who fights and complains about his siblings in order to get his parent to referee and then separate them. He now has a short entertainment entitled *"Referees are Fun,"* followed by getting the room to himself.

Game 9: "I May Do Something Bad!"

"I may do something bad" is a game where a teenager *talks* about wild intentions because of his parents' intense reaction. When you suspect this game, you can try to inhibit your strong reactions to his verbal description of his intentions and concern yourself only with performance. These are important strategies to work out in your planning sessions and in your parent support group. Without a strategy, your teen may find it easy to "get through" to you by making a remark about some absurd behavior he has no intention of performing.

In the *"I may do something bad"* game, getting a teen to "talk right" sometimes becomes the goal of Mom or Dad and part of the power struggle with their teenager. Little talks may become unproductive, because if your teen starts to lose he can always say (promise) what is being demanded without having to carry it through. Threats may be made, voices raised and your teen may get a good "talking to," but he will only learn to say what is necessary to avoid any genuine discussion of controversial topics.

Game 10: "You're Just Not Perfect!"

Here's a game played by both parents and teens. Parents will push for perfection while hoping to produce a stronger motivation in their teen:

Mom: *"Sandra, don't forget to practice your flute before dinner. I think you could be professional some day."*

Sandra: *"BORinnng! I'm sick of it. Why are they so particular about the way you hold it?"*

Mom: *"Don't start arguing. Just get in there and get busy."*

Sandra: *"I think I'll work on the computer for awhile first."*

Mom: *"You were so excited at first and now you don't practice for days. What happened?"*

Everyone starts projects that later falter. Why would Sandra procrastinate on practicing her music when she was so excited about it at first? Why would she keep missing practice by letting the hours go by? It's time to support smaller steps far short of "professional" and Mom needs to be content with Sandra's less than perfect dedication to the project rather than risk giving attention to the procrastination.

If the goal of music lessons is enjoyment of music then the little steps along the way are the ones to encourage; the pursuit of perfection was never the purpose. Has her attitude toward music been raised? It's hard to know. All one can do is support the activity and set a good example through interest. Since progress toward a concert debut was never the point, why not join in her interest and forget perfection? Often you may be accomplishing more than your teen would like to admit.

Sandra can play a version of *"You're-just-not-perfect"* also. Her purpose may be to belittle her parent's influence or power, or she may just have a negative attitude. The habit can fool a parent into thinking nothing is getting done:

Sandra: *"These art museums are boring."*

Mom: *"Some of these paintings are very famous and beautiful."*

Sandra: *"They're all old pictures of old people."*

Mom: *"But look at this one. Can you see how the artist used light and dark to show how the light comes from the candle?"*

Sandra: *"I could do that."*

Mom: *"And look at this one. Look how some things are made to look far away and some closer."*

Sandra: *"They're just smaller."*

Mom: *"But they are just the right sizes, and a little less clear."*

Sandra: *"I guess."*

Is Sandra getting a new appreciation of art? Be careful in concluding that Sandra's museum trip is a waste of time just because she thinks your place to go was not the "perfect" one. Remember, sometimes kids feel an obligation to make you believe you are having no effect! Later on, when Sandra encounters other art or tries out her own painting skills again, you may get a better indication of the usefulness of the museum trip. Keep your own spirits up on the museum trip even if things are not going perfectly, and guard against copying your teen's gloomy attitude. More may be getting done than you realize.

Regardless of your approach to teen-rearing, or adult-rearing as I like to call it, the question of whether anything has changed in the mind of your teen will remain partially unanswered. All parental efforts will seem only partly successful. Teenagers, seeking proof that they are persons in their own right, want it that way!

1. Listening During the Game.

Good parental listening skills are crucial to handling games that teens play. All the rules of Step 1 apply here. When the conversation starts, look at your son or daughter rather than a TV screen or newspaper. To deal with any of these games you need to focus all of your attention on it. Turn and face him or her so that there is no impression that you will miss what's really going on. These physical aspects of your attention let him or her know that you're paying attention and are not likely to be fooled by some game.

Feedback of what your teen just said is a good habit during these conversations. Let your teen know that you heard what he or she just said by repeating it. Avoid suggesting solutions in these games. They only lead to *"make-me-happy"* or *"my-problem-is-yours."* Also, suggesting solutions makes you sound superior and tempts your game-player to counter with something different just to stay even.

Take up the habit of asking questions in a form that is not threatening and don't try to "win." Parents who frequently try to win by getting their son or daughter to *say* they'll try harder, be more responsible, or not be bad any more, may feel some progress has been made. But every time you make a winner you also make a loser and the next conversation is likely to be more confrontational as your teen tries to improve his or her record.

2. Taking All that "Guff."

One obvious characteristic of a teen's "bad disposition" is that it generally reduces parental demands. Yes, a parent can take on a threatening pose that implies punishment to silence a teen or keep him from acting up. Your teen learns and uses the same idea, but since he is a less powerful figure he must use threat in a more subtle way.

I have named a teen's threats and lack of compliance "Guff" or "Guff Control" because some parents I have worked with said they had a habit of giving in rather than *"take all that guff."* Your teen might use guff to put you off and to get out of undesirable requests for work. But his behavior may also be a result of the fact that the request is *just* work; that is, he is using guff to avoid a job because the job itself doesn't seem (to him) to pay off.

By this time you may be getting a little tired of the idea that everything has to pay off. But remember that what is meant by "pay off" in many cases is just an honest expression of appreciation, admiration or encouragement when something good or helpful is done. Frequently material rewards are not necessary. In your job you probably do many things because you believe that it is the right way to do it or that it will please someone. You did it for some reward that had meaning for you, not necessarily money.

Guff control is usually a reaction to too little pay off, and it is continuous because it attracts some attention on its own. Now if it also works in getting out of some requests, we are well on the way to building ourselves a new problem.

Why don't you try guff with your boss? Because it wouldn't work, I imagine. And also with a good boss, it never occurred to you to use guff because there *is* consistent support for doing the job—pay, appreciation, or some combination of both.

So Sam, at 14, usually engages in guff and his parents try to bring about some effort from Sam by coercion. He avoids that effort—if he can—because it is straight coercion without a recognizable (to Sam) encouragement.

When Sam is using guff, he often exposes the situation quite well by saying, *"Oh, why should I do that anyway?"* The statement is pure guff intended to stop a request from Mom or Dad, but, incidentally, it asks a very good question: *"What does Sam get out of it?"*

One difficulty is that attempting to coerce behavior is much easier than planning and providing support—as any boss could tell us. Providing reasonable, positive consequences requires planning and sometimes a new point of view that at least includes opportunities for more social approval.

3. Watch for a Chance to Encourage Something Better.

When the game stops, what activity will fill the gap? The kids will practice something else. We can watch for a chance to reward good behavior. Practice allows trial and error in the family where parental encouragements can consistently motivate more practice and emphasize the benefits of better behavior. If parents know what is happening and what they want to happen, then they can apply this fundamental law of learning: *"You learn what you do!"*

Anyone who has ever tried to play a musical instrument, improve in a sport, or raise teenagers knows that just talking about it is not enough. Reading, lecturing and memorizing rules can help, but real practice is crucial! Even golf has helpful hints and rules to learn, but all golfers know the only way to improve is through practice. And all golfers know players who still search for the magic gadget or secret technique for success while they avoid practice time. The notion applies equally well to social behavior, controlling anger, getting along with siblings, homework, tooth-brushing, and money management!

So helping a teen listen and pay attention to advice is not enough, he will have to try out your instruction, test your rules, and then, if the consequences and encouragements are there, he will learn. The progress itself—the result—will have to come from practice. Here is an important role of the family—to provide a place where successful practice is supported and mistakes receive only constructive reactions—not a likely experience in the outside world.

4. Careful Messages for Daughters and Sons.

Parents show their expectations of gender differences in their questions and opinions of teen behavior. A bias in these expectations can reduce the self-confidence of a girl interested in an area traditionally "masculine." It can also delay development of social skills in a boy if he is excused from social obligations because he's "a naturally immature boy." The bias can slip in early, be on the lookout for it. Note the gender biases in the following table.

Teen #1	Teen #2
Are you happy?	Are you successful?
Are you acting right?	Did you win?
Is your homework perfect?	Is your homework done?
Is your hair attractive?	Is your hair combed?
Are your shoes shined?	Where are your shoes?
Don't eat too much.	Don't eat too little.
Sleep, you look tired.	Sleep, you act tired.
Exercise to look better.	Exercise to be stronger.
Have friends.	Do sports.
Be friendly.	Be competent.
Be attractive.	Be productive.

In spite of the recent emphasis on gender equality, our expectations of boys and girls differ; boys and girls develop different capacities and motivations, and the world has different expectations of them. Whether the characteristics are inborn or learned, I'm sure you needed no extra hint to recognize that Teen #1 was a girl and Teen #2 was a boy.

We often emphasize different values for boys and girls, and different aspects of growing up, partly out of consideration for them and partly out of our desire to prepare them for a world we know still has sexist expectations. Sometimes our emphasis is in the best interest of our teen, sometimes not.

Parents usually react to a boy by directing him toward success with the tasks at hand and by placing less emphasis on social relationships. Usually we encourage girls to succeed socially and give only the necessary minimum emphasis to the task at hand. Pressuring boys about being winners and girls about being charmers produces stress that will be resented. It also risks a reaction by your teen of proving your values wrong, *"I don't have to win* (or be perfect), *and I'll prove it, I'll quit!"* A parent who pushes for a perfect student or a perfect charmer may end up with a school or social dropout.

The job for parents and teachers is to carefully separate fact from prejudice. Teens need to be encouraged to try many skills, develop interests and abilities into strengths, and enjoy successes. The sources of sex differences are in both the environment and our heredity. Records of school problems with boys reflect these differences.

The parent's role is to avoid unrealistic expectations and unfair limitations created by gender stereotypes while remaining alert for opportunities to help teens learn by practice. Taking a risk and trying out new tasks may be influenced by your teen's self-confidence, partly acquired from parents. Gender biases of parents will partly determine how much practice a teen will risk and, in turn, how much encouragement a teen will experience.

"OK," Mr. Effort said, *"Everybody make two lines at the side of the exercise mats. If you want to practice the standing exercises, get in the line near the windows. Those who want to practice handsprings, line up over here."*

Donna's friend: *"Come on, Donna, I'll help you with the flip."*

"Flip?"

"The handspring. Com'on I'll help you."

"You can get hurt doing that."

"You can get hurt getting off the bus!"

"Naw, it's mostly boys over there. Anyway I'm not very good at that sort of thing."

"OK, but I'm going over. Mr. Effort said I'm getting pretty good for a girl."

So Donna's friend went to do handsprings and Donna started for the floor exercises. Floor exercises were boring to Donna, but she felt safe with her own gender and safe from embarrassing mistakes.

Donna's expectation of herself determined what she practiced, and her expectation grew from many seeds planted by parents, teachers and experience. She was given a choice and she decided to practice merely what she did best—a habit many of us have. She was intimidated from trying handsprings perhaps because of adult implications. Or perhaps she has learned from experience that she doesn't have the athletic ability for handsprings and could be hurt trying. Certainly kids have the right to apply their own common sense!

But if her timidity came from cautions and lowered expectations suggested by adults merely because she is a girl, then she has been tempted away from her potential, and another opportunity to gain self-esteem has slipped by.

Did Mr. Effort really tell Donna's friend she was pretty good *"for a girl?"* Or was the sexist qualification added by a girl who has become wise to the ways of the world? Whether spoken or presumed, she's a strong person to focus on the encouraging part of the remark and continue her practice.

Let's look at a male example:

Teacher: *"Today I want to check the sketches of plants you began out-*

side yesterday." The art teacher starts to visit from desk to desk.

Jim: *"Hey John, let me have one of your sketches to show Mrs. Aesthetic."*

John: *"Use your own, Jim."*

Jim: *"Com'on John, I only need one. I threw mine out when we came in yesterday—I'm no good at this artsy stuff."*

John: *"Do another. She won't be here for a while."*

Jim: *"I told you, I'm no good at this artsy stuff!"*

John: *"You don't even try, Jim."*

Jim: *"Oh yeah? I'll see you outside!"*

Has a boy like Jim, who says he's no good at "artsy stuff," been sold on his own weaknesses by a prejudiced society? Is he "no good" because he lacks potential, or has he been convinced he's "no good" by the same sexism that might have told Donna to stick with floor exercises?

5. Encourage Enjoyment of Success.

Dad stopped to pick up his two teens from school.

First Teen: *"I got my math papers back today, and I got more right than anyone!"*

Dad: *"Wow, that's great. I hope you'll have time this weekend to study so you can keep ahead of the others."*

First Teen: *"Oh, I can keep ahead of them easy."* (Does the competitive attitude tell you this person is a boy?)

Dad: *"Just knuckle down to it and you'll get it."*

First Teen: *"I have another decimals assignment tonight."*

Dad: *Well, if you want to stay at the top, you have to keep at it."*

Second Teen: *"Mrs. Brown said we have to choose a final project for home economics: a cooking or sewing project."*

Dad: *"Cooking can be fun."*

Second Teen: *"My friend Jennie is doing cooking, but I'm better with sewing."*

Dad: *"Wouldn't you rather be with Jennie?"*

Second Teen: *"I guess you're right."*

Regardless of the sexes of these two students, one is encouraged to be concerned with success, while the other is encouraged to be comfortable.

Questionnaires about adult attitudes toward children tell us that the person in the math class is likely to be a boy, and the one who is encouraged to worry about friends before projects, a girl—at least her dad is treating them that way. There is no mistake here, merely an example of common family conversation where parents should be sensitive to their own reactions. Then they can encourage each teen to develop his/her very best potential, without too much concern for fitting into common molds.

6. Tiger Mom.

In *Battle Hymn of the Tiger Mother*, Amy Chua, AKA Tiger Mom, put aside her interest in her two daughters and replaced it with days filled with music practice and homework hours designed to see that her teens avoided the disgrace of a getting a "B" in school or music. Success was all that counted.

What did her teens think of that? We don't know because Mom never asked and probably didn't care. When they balked at doing their daily hours of violin and piano practice before completing hours of homework perfectly, she browbeat them with threats, "You can't stay in this house if you don't listen to Mommy."

Chua's "Battle hymn" is a no-nonsense approach to teen-rearing that leaves no doubt who is in charge and who is setting the goals and the daily agenda for each teen. A's in school and first place in violin and piano are the only acceptable grades or outcomes. Mommy knows best and the smaller person's interests or thoughts on the matter are not important and shouldn't be part of the selection of activities which are to be practiced until perfect.

The essence of tough Chinese parenting, according to Chua, is this demand for all-out effort in teen endeavors. She is not native Chinese. She grew up in the American Midwest so she might not be completely correct in her description of what goes on in China.

Tiger Mom wants prodigies no matter how her teens might suffer. Instead of "Tiger Mom," I think "Bully Mom" would be a better description.

If Chua were training high jumpers in track, she might focus her effort on a few with great potential. She would see that some of us are just too small or have legs too short. Even with great pressure from Chua, we will not be "successful" by Chua's standards. In her daughters' cases, we don't know if they have "legs too short" or just need more pressure from their mom who has the confidence of a parent but not the common sense.

Another disadvantage of the Tiger-Mom approach is that the teen's view is entirely discounted as if her teens have no idea of what talents they have or which activities deserve extended practice. What if Chua's daughters had talents in other areas not of interest to Mom?

This happened when one daughter finally quit violin lessons. Mom was very unhappy. She had no idea if her daughter was gifted in music let alone the violin specifically. If her daughter was interested in playing guitar would things have worked out better? I doubt Mom ever asked because there are few trophies or concerts for guitars. Tiger Mom thought she would have no chance to be proud.

Chua does offer some useful observation. For example, she says western parents often give heaps of praise when a teen's accomplishment is close to nothing, This habit reduces self-esteem because real accomplishment is viewed as no better than a casual attempt. With nothing to strive for, a teen may have no reason to try harder. Some of us locals could learn from Chua's suggestion of holding off on undeserved praise. But Chua would hold off on almost all praise because she's never quite satisfied.

If Mom's routine reaction to her teen's interests is negative, and she has no respect for anything outside of the preferences of her adult friends, she may say, *"Put that guitar out of your mind and get to work."* If her daughter fails to impress others after hard work, her daughter may not try again. Instead, her daughter may wander into bad habits and become a victim of the fanatics and predators that troll the troubled waters of the teenage years.

The best parental strategy will include supporting the desirable, ignoring the tolerable, and reacting with logical, mild, and consistent reprimands to the intolerable. This plan will give a teen a good model to follow as well as a way to learn. They will become more competent and pleasant people. Even Tiger Mom may come to like them!

How will others treat your teenagers? Most people will not treat your kids any better than you do! You set the tone for your friends and relatives on how you want the kids treated, and the adults tend to give them the same respect and have the same expectations you present. These other adults will also react to the collection of skills, presumptions, and attitudes your teens have acquired *from* you. In your school years, *your* expectations were partly acquired from *your parents'* attitudes and the foundation of your self-concept was begun. Now you are passing along that information—those assumptions about the good in yourself and the good in others—modified by the valuable experience you are willing to share.

From that, your teen will develop an expectation about how others will perceive him. This becomes a self-fulfilling cycle of expectations because he or she has acquired a pattern of attitudes, assumptions, and habits that will be *re*created in new acquaintances, and repeated from the same experiences he left behind.

Most people won't treat your teen any *worse* than you do, either! People model each other, and their reactions tend to create their surroundings. Each of us cause some people to fade away and others to draw closer. We feather our own social nest.

Your teens will pick up your model of how you treat each person. They will pick up your attitude, disposition, and the nature of your appetite for life. Then they will be off to create their own social environment by reacting in ways you would find familiar. Without giving it much attention, they will present a certain model to others—your model, modified by their experience.

Teens copy
much better
than they
listen.

Step 5: Careful With Punishment. It has Great Disadvantages

Punishment is a tempting strategy when bad behavior demands immediate reaction, and the long-term relationship with your teen is temporarily less important. But punishment doesn't deliver the needed information about what a teen needs *to do.* You can't make a garden just by pulling weeds; you have to grow something, plant something.

The family needs to be a place where training through trial-and-error is encouraged and guided. This is the opposite of what is created when punishment is used.

You're too easy on the kids! Let me have them for a week. They'll shape up after a couple of swats from their Uncle Harry!" Nancy and Martin are a sister and brother team who started their game when they were five. Now in their teens, they know all the buttons to push to get the reactions they want. They're still playing their game of *"Let's-see-how-much-we-can-get-away-with."* They either conspire to work their parents up or they bug each other and get parent attention as a bonus. Any suggestion to Nancy or Martin by their parents that they do *"something useful"* is rejected, perhaps because that would mean the game would be over.

1. Ten Reasons Why "Get Tough" Advice Is Off Track.

Most of the relatives, including Uncle Harry, think they could fix the Nancy-and-Martin problem with stern talk and extra punishments—restrictions or removed privileges. Uncle Harry thinks he would somehow use punishment more effectively and more consistently than Nancy's and Martin's parents.

Reason #1: Uncle Harry's Hard-Line Approach Will Be, Must Be, Inconsistent.

The first problem with Uncle Harry's use of the straight punishment rule is that even Uncle Harry cannot, *and should not,* be consistent with it. Punishment would be too inhuman without the inconsistencies of warnings and threats.

If Uncle Harry's reactions could be as consistent and as quick as, say, an electric shock from a wall outlet, he might make some short-term progress.

Wall outlets and lamp sockets will consistently punish us without warning; they don't hesitate because we look cute trying to be "devilish." They don't think we've had a bad day or haven't been reminded lately of what will happen if we mishandle them. We get none of this consideration, and we are careful not to mistreat outlets and lamp sockets.

But Uncle Harry is not a wall outlet. Out of love and sympathy neither Mom, Dad, nor Uncle Harry can resist preceding punishments with the warnings and threats and so the game begins.

When the kids were younger, spankings might have been used. But you can't spank the big ones and anyway, even spanking would have to include lots of warnings.

Parental consistency is always desirable and basic to learning. The lack of consistent reactions, on the reward side, leads to confusion and slows the pace of progress. The inevitable inconsistency of punishment brings on additional problems. Remember that "mean" teacher you had in school? Mr. Meany, or maybe it was a Ms. Meany, used punishments, reprimands, sarcastic remarks, putdowns, and embarrassments whenever the kids deviated from the desirable, and sometimes even when it seemed the kids had done nothing wrong! I bet you hated that class!

A student's greatest fear is to be embarrassed. With "Mr. Meany," you just couldn't be sure when you might trigger an embarrassing reaction. *All* behaviors (even volunteering right answers, suggestions, or questions) were reduced because you and your friends just wouldn't risk it. Not surprisingly, most "mean" teachers think the students in their classes are not very smart.

When punishment is uncertain, students become very cautious, especially when they are around the teacher who punishes. Around other people, bad behavior may increase to let off the oppressed steam or just to somehow even the score for the whole day.

Parents also can fall into the "mean teacher" trap, and their kids may learn to behave whenever Mom threatens them or looks mad. As Mom realizes this works, she may increase "looking (and acting) mad" to include most family moments. Parents in this pitfall soon find that "looking mad" won't do, and they have to act "really mad." Now Dad and Mom have been pushed up a notch toward becoming behavior problems themselves!

So for Nancy and Martin to grow into happy, independent,

productive adults, they need alternative activities that make the "*Let's-see-what-we-can-get-away-with*" game unimportant. Mom and Dad need to catch opportunities to encourage the kids. They also need to sharply limit punishment and use alternatives such as allowing the kids to make amends for mistakes as we do adults.

Carrying out all of this is more difficult and requires more planning than hard-headed Uncle Harry's idea of "*thrashing it out of them.*"

Reason #2:   The Punishment Trigger is a Parent's Exasperation, Not a Teen's Behavior.

In most parenting situations, punishment is a dangerous practice partly because it may be more related to the frustrations and moods of a parent than to a teenager's mistakes. Frequent use of punishment, when Dad or Mom have had it "up to here," usually results in a teen more interested in his parents' signals of where "up to here" is than his own rights and wrongs.

So Martin and his sister become manipulators who know that as long as they don't push too far, they're safe. They can predict punishment better, but still not perfectly, by watching their parents' emotions rather than adjusting their own behavior.

So Uncle Harry's punishment is inconsistent because it will be related more to his frustrations and moods than to the mistakes of the kids. If Dad or Mom use Harry's idea when they have had it "up to here," Nancy and Martin will only be interested in that frustration point as their signal to ease up just short of the boiling points of Mom and Dad.

Reason #3: Punishment will be Imitated.

We usually think of a teen's imitation of parents as very specific. "*Look at the way he walks, just like his Dad.*" "*Look at the way she does her hair, trying to be just like Mom."* But copying Mom and Dad is more likely to involve social habits. How does Mom handle situations when things don't go right? What is Dad's solution when others don't do what he wants? If Dad gets frustrated, how does he react?

We all know how quickly kids will pick up those words of frustration when Dad hits himself on the kitchen drawer, but they also pick up the cues on *how to react* when things go wrong. Kids may get the message that the punishments used by Mom and Dad are good ways to deal with people.

The imitation of punishment will be included in the rest of your teen's social life. How should he handle friends when they don't do the "right thing?" A parent becomes a role model for punishment. *"It works for Mom, maybe it will work for me when I feel like it."* In any case, the most natural reflex to punishment is to give some back.

If it is not possible to punish his parent, your teen might turn to others.

So there's the possibility that your teen will pick up some cues from your behavior about what is the appropriate reaction to unwanted behavior. If your daughter frequently criticizes and yells at her baby brother, a careful observation of her parents' own reactions might discover a clue as to where a daughter's reactions come from.

Teenagers make a lot of mistakes, being led into errors by peers, forgetting chores and commitments, indulging in unhealthy foods, and wasting time, to mention a few. When parents see so many errors, they may find it difficult to be accepting and look at the long run. But the goal of teaching how to react to others may be more important than correcting the mistake itself.

Reason #4: Punishment is Insulting, Belittling, and Lowers a Person's Self-Esteem

The emotional put-down of punishment distracts the victim from learning about the desired behavior. The punishment act, itself, is childish and belittles the significance of the victim. Isn't that why *adults* are so insulted when punishment is tried on them? So we all learn that the only possible ages for punishment are from 2 to 18. Before that, it's called abuse; After that, it's hopeless.

Once a teen's value of himself goes down and the fear goes up, a new disadvantage develops for learning. Much of the teenage years are a trial-and-error process. The discoveries of "how to get along" come from a lot of guesses. How much guessing will a frightened person risk? Once your teen becomes discouraged and engaged in self-degrading thoughts, parents and teachers know learning will be slow.

In my college course in animal learning, students had to teach their own pigeon to perform tasks by rewarding small successes. The first task was to get the pigeon to peck a disc by rewarding it with seeds, first for stepping toward the disc, followed by putting its head toward it, then touching it, and finally pecking it.

Sometimes students had trouble with the project because their pigeon was too scared to even move in its cage. If it had been handled roughly or it had escaped and been chased down before being put in the learning cage, it was too upset to do anything! Pigeons that won't do anything can't be taught anything! The student stared at the pigeon waiting for a chance to reward success. The pigeon stared at the student waiting for a chance to get out! Punishment can produce the same impasse between teen and parent.

Reason #5: Punishment Encourages Stressful Behaviors.

Punishment will encourage bad habits such as nail-biting, hair-twirling, and *"safer obsessions"* like video games and TV. These *"escapes"* are very stubborn habits maintained by their usefulness for avoiding contact with the punisher. Whenever encouragement and reward are low, these stress behaviors will increase. If the stressful behavior attracts some parental attention, then we are in a vicious cycle with a new long-term problem.

Reason #6: The Power Struggle.

Punishment will tempt your teen to resist his parent's intimidation; the struggle takes over the family airways leaving little time for positive interactions and learning. A parent can "win" the power struggle, but, again, for every winner a loser is made!

The power struggle of punishment can spread to all family members. As others pick up the habit, a competition develops, *"Who can 'outdo'* (put down, criticize, reprimand, catch more mistakes of) *whom?"* It ruins the family as a nurturing place where learning is encouraged through practice—*with* mistakes.

Reason #7: Punishment is a Short-Term Trap That Can Last Forever!

The *parental* bad habit of using punishment can be stubborn because it produces short-term results. For example, when Martin aggravates his Aunt Hazel, she may keep him in line by finding fault where he is vulnerable, *"That music is terrible. Your hair is a mess! Your face is breaking out again."*

With each of these insults, Martin's obnoxious behavior is temporarily interrupted while he defends himself, Aunt Hazel has released a little tension, and maybe Hazel has "taught Martin a lesson" or at least evened the score.

The long-term disadvantages of Hazel's punishment habit may go undetected because they will grow slowly. Martin will start the bad escape habits, he will feel worse about himself and about Aunt Hazel, and *he* will try to use punishment himself.

These two people are developing a poor relationship where Martin annoys Aunt Hazel just to get even and Aunt Hazel boils over now and then to gain temporary relief from her allergic reaction to him. Martin will learn when to let up a little, and he may also learn to imitate her insulting style just to gain more control.

Reason #8: Discrimination.

A teen subjected to a parent or relative in the *"I'll-get-even-with-you"* game learns the signals well. Innocent chaperones and teachers become fair game until they learn how to insult or scowl miserably enough to get control. An additional social problem is that no adult around a teen like Martin likes to be forced to act mad or abusive and would rather avoid him, partly because they don't like the person they must become to keep control.

Parents suffer the most from the frequent punishment policy, and their teens may suffer less because they learn to adjust to people who will play their game and those who will not.

We all develop discriminations and act differently with different people. But when punishment is used, we do our best to avoid the punishing person altogether. The negative, critical and threatening boss may have a reputation as a hard-liner, but the employees will duck and dodge her as much as possible. And they'll give no extra effort. Who wants to please her?

The relationship that develops is one in which two people only barely tolerate each other because they are forced to. A teen may like to escape such a situation because of the possibility of being punished, and a parent may want to be away (at work, at meetings, or just out anywhere) because of the uncomfortable parental reactions that seem to be called for in the situation.

Reason #9: Relatives Will Go Home, Parents Will Be Left Behind.

When Uncle Harry leaves, Mom and Dad are left with the long-term side effects of punishments that were too severe and too frequent. Your teen's solution may be to stop responding altogether or, at least, to respond as little as possible. The situation has produced a kind of success, your teen *is* quiet.

Even if the adults try a better approach later on, Nancy and Martin may refuse to risk coming out of their shells. The biggest wish of these kids is to get out—out of the room, out of sight, out of the house, if possible. Wouldn't we all rather dodge the punishment? With punishment you have to find your teen; with praise, your teen finds you.

With repeated experience, the situation preceding punishment signals a need to withdraw. The signal could be a classroom, a house, a time of day, a particularly dangerous person, or a combination of these. Once experiences have taught these signals, the mere termination of punishment is not likely to be effective immediately, because a teen in these circumstances will be unwilling to take risks to find out if danger has passed.

Uncle Harry and Aunt Hazel will leave behind other unintended effects. Activities and behaviors that explore new opportunities for learning may be reduced because they now seem dangerous or potentially embarrassing. Often an uncle's opinion of your son or daughter is better understood than the specific reasons for punishment. The details of why he was so angry are smothered in the emotion, fear, and desire to suppress the memory of the whole experience. The lack of understanding combines with the fear of risking any more punishment, and we are well on the way to stopping all progress in this situation.

Left on their own with Harry's punishment advice, parents will be tempted to increase punishment when the kids don't seem to get the message. But punishment gives too little information—it only tells you one of the things *not* to do, nothing about what *to do.*

To reverse Uncle Harry's effects, a reduction in punishment must be accompanied with an increase in opportunities for genuine encouragement. Very minor events can act as punishments for a timid teen. Simply interrupting him at dinner may silence him for the whole meal. A verbal snap from his sibling may accomplish the same thing. It will require many isolated one-on-one moments with generous parents showing great tolerance and support to draw him out.

Many of Uncle Harry's threats will very likely be of the one-shot nature if his stay is longer than a week (perish the thought). As the punishments fail to produce results, he may opt for larger punishments such as canceling a trip or party. Usually one-shots are too late and produce the most resentment and argument with the least amount of change. Since parties and trips are infrequent, Uncle Harry feels he has to threaten a lot just to milk as much influence as possible from the upcoming event. Once the party or trip is over, a new threat will have to be dreamed up, or, if Harry's gone, the parents will be left with that job.

The one-shot leaves parents with the dreary task of sorting out threats, bluffs, and final conclusions. In the process they are likely to fall into a negative reinforcement habit (see next page).

Reason # 10: Punishments Can Lead to Divorce.

Any person being punished has one thought in mind, *"Get away!"* Teens could plan running away or withdrawing if running away is impractical. And yet the conflict and confusion are intensified because your home is their most important source of security.

So don't talk about divorcing your teenager. This ultimate consequence is too disturbing and implies that your love for your teen can be easily traded away. Your love and loyalty should have a higher price tag and should not become part of bluffing or bargaining.

Whenever punishment is used, we are counting on some other aspect of the situation to keep our teen within range for deserved punishments. Either the doors must be locked, literally or figuratively, or the rewards from parents are enough to overwhelm the unhappiness. No matter how effective punitive measures may seem in the short-run, parents risk losing their teen. One reason punishment strategies usually don't work on adults is that adults can leave.

2. Negative Reinforcement.

Isn't negative reinforcement the same as punishment? No, it's more subtle but also more common. The purpose of regular punishment, as everyone knows, is to reduce or eliminate bad behavior. Negative reinforcement is not punishment for mistakes, it's punishment for <u>failing</u> to do the right thing! The threat of a consequence for failing to meet someone's expectations is a common experience in a routine day.

Why do I make dinner for the kids at the same time every night, use their favorite plate, prepare only certain foods? Is it because they watch for their chance to support my "good" behavior?

No, the answer here usually begins, *"Well, if I didn't do that, the kids would complain and make a lot of trouble."*

When it is the *lack* of performance that produces bad consequences, it's called negative reinforcement. As long as I avoid unwanted dinner plates, unwanted food, delays, and don't disappoint my little masters, *I avoid* their nasty behavior.

Parents also use negative reinforcement. For example, as long as the kids don't act up or fight, *they can avoid* their parents' angry reaction.

The difference between regular punishment and negative reinforcement is important because the threat of negative reinforcement is always hounding the child-teen. It has a continuous nature to it and, if not tested, the fear can continue long after the threat has passed.

Punishment in its consistent form, even with all its faults, is easy to understand: *"If I do the wrong thing, I'll get bad consequences."* Negative reinforcement has all the same faults as punishment with the added confusion of an obscure rule: *"If I fail to do the right thing, I'll get bad consequences."*

Mom: *"Zac, did you pick up your clothes?"*

Zac: (Watching TV) *"Not yet."*

Mom: *"Did you put your dirty clothes in the laundry?"*

Zac: *"No."*

Mom: *"How about the mess in the living room?"*

Zac: *"OK, as soon as this is over."*

Mom *"Take those dishes out, too."*

Zac: *"OK"* (Remains an intimate part of the couch.)

Mom: (She's used no punishment so far, but now she reacts to Zac's *lack* of action.) *"Zac, I have had it! Now turn off that TV and get these things cleaned up!"*

Zac: *"OK, OK, don't have a cow about it."* (Mumbling) *"Gee, who knows when you're gonna blow up, anyway?"*

Mom: *"What was that?"*

Zac: *"Nothing."*

Part of Zac's and Mom's problem is that Mom's strategy is the use of negative reinforcement. If Zac fails to perform (enough times) and Mom asks him (enough times) then Mom gets mad. Mom may also support and compliment Zac if he cleans things up, but Mom's exasperation limit and Zac's fear of her are the main factors at work in this situation.

At times, the distinction between punishment and negative reinforcement may seem like a word game. Could we simply say that Mom threatens punishment for Zac's sloppiness? She could use that strategy—dock his allowance when he leaves his clothes all over, for example. But her reaction is negative reinforcement because it is triggered by the *lack* of behaviors and occurs at a non-specific time. Zac is tempted to continue to procrastinate, delay, and test the limits while Mom is driven to using "mad" as a motivator.

Negative reinforcement does not produce a happy situation. If you do most of your activities everyday just to avoid someone's flack, you're probably unhappy with him or her (all spouses know who I'm talking about). *Positive* reinforcement is needed for a good relationship.

Dad: *"Did you take the car in today?"*

Mom: *"Yes, it just needed a tune up."*

Dad: *"Great, thanks for getting it done; that takes a lot off my mind."*

Dad used the positive reinforcement idea, but in the next minute he slips to negative reinforcement:

Dad: *"Did you get the little dinners I wanted for lunches?"*

Mom: *"Didn't go by the store after work."*

Dad: *"Hey, how am I supposed to work all day without lunch?"*

(Here's a reprimand as negative reinforcement for Mom's failure to do the right thing.)

Mom: (Borrowing from Zac) *"OK, OK, don't have a cow over it. I'll get them tomorrow and I'll make something good for you to take in the -morning."* (Mumbling) *"Gee, beam me up, Scotty!"*

Dad: *"What was that?"*

Mom: *"Nothing."*

Children have a better chance finding positive reinforcements everyday because parents and teachers know kids have to be encouraged. But negative reinforcement is probably the more common experience for us all even if it is a less popular term. It occurs when a behavior is used to <u>avoid</u> a consequence: Make your bed or Mom will be mad. Do your homework or the teacher will embarrass you in front of the class. Be home on time or Dad will be furious. Even though the intentions in these examples are to motivate, they sound like—and they are—threats.

For a teenager, the situation requires an effort to avoid the threatened outcome. He might want to escape the situation altogether as with punishment and he could try to run away but usually he will try to deal with it.

We're all familiar with the dark cloud of negative reinforcement produced by past bosses or parents and the escape we, at times, wished for. We recognize it when we hear someone say, "Well, if I didn't do it, I'd get so much flak..." If your day is filled with such efforts to stay out of the line of fire, you probably have leaving on your mind.

If most of what your teen does is an effort to avoid punishment or embarrassment, he or she will find it hard to be happy but won't have the resources to leave.

A marriage held together by one spouse hopping from one task to another trying to keep the other spouse from getting mad is an example. This unhappy situation may last for years, and it doesn't make a pleasant home environment either.

Even with the threat removed, a teen (or spouse) may be afraid to risk ignoring an old threat actually removed long ago. It will take some time and courage to test the new situation.

So here's a possible resolution: Every day, find something to compliment, appreciate, and support. Translate some old negative reinforcement into its flip side—the positive encouragement for what should be done instead of the criticism for failures. Gush a little, even if you have to be a little corny. Tell your teen you noticed when he makes a successful effort—cleaned up some dishes—said something nice to his brother—got ready for school without complaints about clothes and lunches.

This "behavioral smile" is contagious; the kids are likely to copy your effort and the new style will recycle through the family. Keep it up—even a spouse can pick up the habit!

One-Shots. Negative reinforcement in combination with an upcoming, one-shot event is a tempting strategy to try to get the kids to do right. *"If you don't stop complaining all the time, we'll just give up going to the beach this summer."* or, *"You had better show me you can get along with your brother or I won't sign you up for soccer this year."* Because the threatened events happen only once or, at most, once a year, they can't be a part of *repeated* practice—unless we add a lot of nagging, *"Remember what I said, treat your brother nice or no soccer!"*

The threats for not acting right sound a lot like negative reinforcement with all its bad baggage, so nagging sets in to try to use the future one-shot event to get a little cooperation now.

Also, going to the beach is a singular future event not likely to be repeated for some time. Mom and Dad may repeat the *threat* many times since the vacation itself will only happen once. Of course, your teen needs to learn that you mean what you say about the beach or about soccer, but the consequence is so far off that any outcome may seem arbitrary.

So after all the argument, you either take the kid to the beach anyway, or you hold to your threat and don't take her/him. The first choice seems too lenient, but the second is too tough because it says that overall, he/she has been a bad kid. This one-shot consequence has no winners and little chance of a satisfactory outcome.

This situation is gloomy for the family and for the event when it finally comes. It's like holding off the enemy in battle with only one bullet; you have to do a lot of posturing, bluffing, and threatening. Once you use your bullet, you are an ogre for not allowing the beach or soccer or you are a patsy for giving in! And then the next day, you will need to threaten with a new bullet.

A better strategy is to allow yourself and your family the enjoyment of individual events without trying to use them to limit bad behavior or produce good behavior. Instead, choose some smaller event that can come up more frequently, something not so severe, that has a positive side to emphasize. For example, instead of threatening to ground your teen next semester if grades don't come up (an unmanageable threat with an "only once" character to it), possibly each good grade on any test, quiz or paper could produce a guaranteed 2 weeks of regular "going out" curfew privileges. This procedure has the advantage of being a consistent and repeatable consequence while a parent emphasizes the right habits. It is not negative or severe, so parents don't need to feel guilty and inconsistent. Also, it is logically related to the need for study time.

A very repeatable consequence makes it much easier to refrain from nagging. The repetition does the reminding. Nagging on the problem can stop, and the airways can be opened up for more pleasant family talk.

3. Why Would Anyone Use Punishment?

With all these discouraging problems, one might wonder why some parents continue to use punishment. Even the choice of punishment should diminish when it is unsuccessful. So when a parent's action (punishment) doesn't get the desired result, why don't they just quit?

The answer is that in the very short term, punishment produces some results. If Mom punishes Fred for using bad language by grounding him, Mom's punishment behavior is reinforced by its immediate effect of interrupting Fred's bad behavior even if only temporarily. So Mom is tempted to use it again.

Parents, particularly American parents, hurried by schedules filled with job and family responsibilities, often hope for the "quick fix." Punishment may seem to fill the bill, but we seldom try it on adults. Instead, we use one of the following alternatives.

4. Five Alternatives to Punishment.

A large investment firm reneged on an announced $1.3 million dollar profit a few years ago because an accountant left off the minus sign—it was really a $1.3 million dollar *shortfall!* How did the firm's president discipline his accountant for the $2.6 million dollar mistake? To his disappointed stockholders he said, *"Well I guess that's why they put erasers on pencils!"* With adults, we usually get on with fixing the mistake. We deal with unwanted adult behavior every day, but like the accountant's president, most of us gave up punishment of the straightforward kind long ago.

The culture we live in continues to provide some punishment—"logical consequences" we sometimes call them—and the courts hand out punishments for the larger transgressions. But logical consequences and court sentences are usually long delayed and given only for repeated bad habits and big mistakes. So for unwanted *adult* behavior what punishment alternatives do we use?

Every day, adult mistakes receive *very kind* reactions. Even blowing your horn at a poor driver's mistake is considered too aggressive. Often we just allow the person to make amends, or we ignore the mistake altogether. If we control the situation, we might try to make it less likely that he will repeat the mistake: *"The boss should give better instructions. He should put up more signs about how to use the printer!"* After more instruction, the boss may use warnings: *"Anyone caught putting their sandwich in the printer will be ..."* Then, if that doesn't work, maybe, punishment. Since punishment has so many disadvantages anyway, let's get on to a more adult way of handling problems.

Alternative #1:   Making Amends.

Making amends is the number one strategy adults use to handle bad adult behavior. If you come to my house for dinner tonight and spill your drink at the table, you don't expect me to threaten punishment by saying: *"Hey! What do you think you're doing? You're so clumsy! Now pay attention to what you're doing, or I'll send you home!"*

What nerve! Treating a guest like a child. What happened to "the benefit of the doubt?" You expect to be allowed to make amends; you expect me to belittle the problem, you even expect sympathy. *"Oh, too bad. No problem, I'll get a cloth."* You say, *"I'm sorry, let me get that. I'll take care of it."*

Isn't adulthood nice? Even with big mistakes, we would rather have the offender try to fix the mistake than punish him. At what age did you, and our innocent accountant with the 2.6 million dollar mistake, earn such consideration? Why wasn't *he* punished? Because it wouldn't help and it would look as if the investment firm was a simple-minded company, naive and heartless. After all, mistakes happen.

Two-year-olds, teenagers, and accountants who make mistakes, accidental or not, should be allowed to make amends. Not that our accountant could make up for his mistake in this century. Your teen deserves the same respect. It is only fair to assume he or she is doing his or her best.

Remember the movie about a troublesome city teenager whose life was popping with mistakes that he could never see coming? His parents punished him, hoping he would avoid future "accidents." At last, in exasperation they sent him to the country to live with relatives. We saw our teen toil the whole afternoon, making amends for a clumsy mistake, spilling the milk can, before supper—cleaning up the spill. Finally finished, he went into dinner, justified, un-criticized, and with an experience that motivated him to be more careful.

At home he would have been restricted or physically punished and belittled, and he would have lost practice at making things right. Though the movie lesson was unrealistically easy and quick, the message was a good one: our teen learned by making amends and cleared up his guilt; the adults maintained a healthier relationship with him in the bargain.

Grandma: (Sitting down to dinner) *"Whoops, now I know what I forgot at the store—coffee! But we have juice, how about that?"*

Mom: *"Don't worry about it; juice is fine. We'll get the coffee tomorrow."* (Mom belittles the mistake)

Grandma: *"At least I'll get out the juice."* (Grandma makes amends)

Nancy: *"I accidentally erased our list of names and addresses from the computer today."*

Grandma: *"What! Didn't you put it back from the flash drive? I was looking for that for half an hour this afternoon. You're so inconsiderate at times. Don't you have enough sense to..."*

Mom: (Interrupting) *"Nancy, after dinner, find the right flash drive and reload the address file, OK?"* (And then to Grandma) *"I can get along without the coffee until tomorrow if you can, so don't worry about it."*

Grandma: *"What? Oh, ah, yes, OK, OK. If I get a break on forgetting the coffee, I guess Nancy gets a break, too. And, Nancy, could you add the names on the outside of my phone book?"*

Alternative #2:   Ignoring.

Ignoring behavior eventually decreases it, especially if our teen was acting up to get attention. If a parent can tough it out and hold back attention for bad language, our teen may go on to something else. The problem here is that in the short-run, *more bad behavior* is more likely rather than less. This bad behavior has been a part of a habit to get some entertainment or attention from Mom and Dad. Now his parents plan to cut that off. For example, no more attention for bad language.

If the usual amount of swearing will no longer work, what should our teen do? He may escalate the volume, frequency, or foulness of the talk. At the "higher" level, parents may break the new rule and punish this outrageous behavior. If that quiets things down, parents may return to the ignoring rule only to go back to punishment when the assault on the ears again reaches pain threshold. The process builds up a new level of bad behavior. Escalation is a very common problem because the natural childish ("teenish?") reaction to failure (to get attention) is escalation.

Ignoring means consistently overlooking relatively unimportant, undesirable behaviors and paying attention to other aspects of a teen's actions. When Tim shaved his hair nearly to the middle of his head, his parents felt it was within his personal grooming choices to do so, but when he slapped his younger sister, they reacted strongly. Their different reactions to these very different behaviors keep the priorities straight and reduce unnecessary criticism.

When you react to the behavior of your teen, keep the overall family atmosphere in mind. Sacrifice family atmosphere only when necessary. If an action has a low priority rating, it doesn't deserve your time and energy, nor a lot of family disruption.

You may want to ignore behaviors that occur only occasionally as well as others that come under your teen's growing sphere of control, for example: keeping a messy bedroom, using poor grammar, wearing strange outfits and unusual hairstyles. A parent's greatest influences on these daily habits will not be by way of arguments and consequences, but the model they present. Some behaviors are part of passing stages that will be outgrown, and therefore they are easier to ignore. When your teen invites a friend to visit, the bedroom will be spruced up to *their* level of tolerance. Unwanted grammar, language, clothing, and hairstyles are probably temporary, fluctuating with peer and media influences.

One 13-year-old, I know, sprayed her hair to stand up six inches above her forehead and wore glaring makeup, but she was a good student with pleasant social skills. It was a tribute to her parents' ability to overlook extremes of grooming and focus instead on her *important* actions. Extremes of personal care will probably change toward the norm when a teenager wants to fit into a different group or workplace.

Alternative #3: Adding Something Good to the Ignoring Plan.

Mom and Dad need to have a plan to encourage good behaviors and be alert to the first opportunity to work the plan! Ignoring the unwanted behavior *and* planning to encourage *specific, likely,* good behaviors will produce better results. The message needs to be clear: *"Now that's a good way to handle that." "I liked hearing about your report on the Civil War battle. You're learning about interesting things." "I noticed you helped clear the table after supper. That was great!"*

"Catch 'em being good" means recognize, praise, or reward the good behavior you see. Perhaps you remember as a teen thinking, *"When I make mistakes everyone notices and I get in trouble, but a lot of times I do well, and nobody says anything."*

To prevent unwanted behaviors, parents need to "catch 'em being good," not just when the desired behavior occurs, but when a behavior in the right direction comes along. Actions that are improvements and a step forward need the most encouragement, recognition, praise, and reward.

Research tells us that catching people when they come near to appropriate behavior is a more efficient learning technique than punishment for errors. Considering all the possibilities for error, a teen isn't much closer to learning an important skill just by being told, *"Wrong!"*

Which choice is more likely to produce positive results?

1. Teen has no friends. You can:

   a) discuss the importance of having friends, or

   b) listen and encourage any socializing in the family and outside it.

2. This young adult pouts and sulks. Would you:

   a) tell him to stop being a sourpuss?

   b) ignore pouting and talk pleasantly when he is sociable?

3. He/she has no outside interests. You can:

   a) require your teen to choose two activities of his/her choice and insist on participation for a half-year, or

   b) you can be available to listen for his/her interests.

In the first example, discussing friendship will be pointedly painful to your teen, but listening and socializing in the family will provide practice and build confidence for your teen to reach out in other situations.

In example two, reactions of anger to pouting will give attention to poor behavior and possibly encourage it with an argument about its justification. The better plan is to support the less frequent, appropriate, pleasant interactions.

In the third case about outside interests, both choices are helpful for a teen who needs to develop activities. Insisting on some selections takes authority, but that may be an ingredient needed to get things started.

Alternative #4: Using the Cost of Inconvenience.

Many little inconveniences may seem trivial, at first, but when put into practice they may be extremely effective. For example, if Dad has to put a penny in a jar on the kitchen table every time he loses his temper, it may seem like a trivial act for someone with plenty of pennies. But if the rule is strictly followed, the inconvenience of having to stop, get a penny, go into the kitchen and put it in the jar can be a very effective consequence. Pennies are unimportant but the behavioral "cost" makes this consequence work.

Many psychologists use the principle of inconvenience as a strategy for removing or reducing smoking in adults. The heavy smoker is instructed to keep an exact record of his smoking throughout each day. He carries a little notebook wherever he goes and writes down the time, to the minute, when he takes out a cigarette, and the time he puts it out. He may be asked to note the situation as well, including who was with him and what he was doing. Some psychologists also ask for the cigarette butts to be saved and brought in for counting. These tasks may not seem like consequences as we have discussed them so far, but they are consequences of a most useful type. They are costly in time and many a smoker is just too busy to make all those entries and save butts, so he takes a pass on having that cigarette.

Such a self-administered procedure requires a very cooperative and trustworthy subject. I have found the cost-of-inconvenience procedure useful when smokers referred to me have been told by their doctor that their health or even their life is at stake! They usually *want* the process to work, and they can be counted on to try hard. The procedure has not worked well when used on people who *"feel they should cut down"* or quit for the children's sake. With these less motivated subjects, it takes a stronger procedure than raising the cost of inconvenience.

Sometimes teenagers can be enthusiastic about a record-keeping procedure. One mother reported that her 19-year-old son, Damon, continually disrupted the family by "checking things." On some evenings, he insisted on checking as many as 70 things before going to bed. Damon checked to see if the back door was locked. He checked to see if the light was out in the basement. He checked to see if his pen was on his desk, and if his dresser drawers were completely closed. Some of this would have been reasonable, but the situation got out of hand when he checked the same thing for the fifth or sixth time in the same evening!

At first his checking was examined for the possibility that it was an attention-getting behavior. Some progress was made by reducing Damon's parents' attention to the excessive checking and increasing conversation time before he went off to bed. The most effective procedure was beginning a record of every item checked, the time it was checked, the result of the check, and what could have happened if the item had been left unchecked. The procedure involved so much writing and decision-making that it was nearly impossible to check 70 things each evening.

Because of the work and inconvenience of the procedure, Damon began to pass up items that were not so important, and he made a special effort to remember the ones already checked, or look at his record, so that he didn't have to do it again! The number of times Damon checked things soon was down to a level that was only a little unusual instead of disruptive to the family.

The same principle of inconvenience can be used to increase a habit. For example, good homework habits can be influenced by how convenient it is to get started. If there is a place to do homework with little distraction that is well supplied with paper and such, then we have a better chance of getting some homework done.

Dianne: *"I'm not going to practice this stupid violin any more, it's too much trouble!"*

Mom: *"Just another ten minutes, then you can quit."*

Dianne: *"Phooey."*

Dianne's practice is best done in intervals that keep frustration to a minimum, but once Dianne begins, Mom hates to let her quit because it's such a hassle to get her to start again. Maybe Mom could do away with some inconveniences associated with Dianne's "re-starts." She could help Dianne get out the music, set up the stand. Then while Dianne checks the tuning, Mom could turn off the TV and get everyone else far enough away. If some of the inconveniences could be done away with, maybe Dianne would practice more frequently.

Mom: *"Let's set up a special place for you. How about in our bedroom? We're never in there when you need to practice and it's away from the TV and your brother. You can leave your music and stand out, and it won't be disturbed."*

Dianne: *"OK, but I still think all this practice is stupid."*

We have not solved the violin problem by just finding a place for practice. Dianne is going to need more encouragement than that. Mom needs to visit the practice situation a lot, comment on Dianne's progress, and help the instructor find practice pieces that interest Dianne. But a place to practice easily, without frustrating start-up time, is a step toward making good practice convenient.

Alternative #5:   Consequences, Even Time-outs, Must Give Way to Modeling.

Sometimes the bad behavior demands a reaction. We don't let adults get away with just anything and teens becoming adults shouldn't be misled that anything goes either. What alternative is there when bad behavior should not be ignored and making amends or hoping for opportunities for encouragement is not enough?

For young children, time-out is often a good solution but may not be appropriate for teens—especially older teens. We all know the drill of putting a child or teen on a chair or in his/her room for a little "cooling off" as a kind of punishment. The procedure can work well if the threats, arguments, and other verbal decorations that often precede the time-out can be kept to a minimum.

Mom: (Liz throws a toy at her sister.) *"Liz! We don't throw toys. You could hurt someone. That's One!"* (Liz throws again.) *"Liz I told you, that's Two"*

Liz: *"I don't want it!"* (Liz throws again.)

Mom: *"OK, that's Three,"* Mom takes Liz to the kitchen chair and deposits her there.

Mom is doing well with her younger one. She doesn't talk much during the count which could lead Liz to act up more, she doesn't make a lot of threats, and she corrects the behavior in a way that can be used frequently—no dramatic punishment that requires a big build-up.

Time-out for young teens means spending a short time in a quiet place, alone, after inappropriate behavior. It can be very successful. The separation of younger teens from others interrupts overheated verbal and physical reactions with a calming-down period. When your teen has regained emotional control, she or he can discuss what happened and plan changes. The time period that is most helpful is long enough to break up unwanted behavior and tempers, but short enough for everyone to remember clearly what happened and want to plan other reactions. Just having time-out for a minute or two is effective; a long time-out is not necessary, nor helpful.

This alternative cuts off fighting between siblings and helps a parent regain perspective and control, instead of escalating a problem situation. Parents who try time-out find it prevents them from using physical and verbal punishments they regret later.

When parents react with punishments, they frequently prevent discussion and planning for changes. Because of bad feelings, the bad behavior is likely to occur again. But after time-out, each person involved in the problem has a chance to tell his/her feelings and make suggestions. A parent and teen can practice the listening and understanding, and gain experience planning for a change. Time-out sets the stage for a new beginning.

When Mom returned from shopping, she noticed lipstick on the kitchen wall. Mike had been talking on the phone instead of watching his younger sister, Tina, the wall artist.

Mike: *"But I have to talk on the phone to my friends sometimes. It drives me crazy to watch Tina every minute. I shouldn't have to watch her this much! How could she do that? Mom, you've raised her all wrong. I'm not going to clean that up. I have to leave to go to the mall with Bill."*

Mom: *"We're going to have to talk about this now."*

Mike: *"I can't stand it! It's not my fault, and Tina should have to clean it up! Mom, you can't make me do this."*

Mom: *"Mike, I'm getting mad and you're upset too. Cool off for five minutes in your room, and then we'll put our heads together to work this out."* (Mike stomps out to his room.)

When the two get together after cooling down, it's more likely they will be able to make a compromise. Perhaps Mom, Mike, and Tina can do the wall cleaning together. The baby-sitting needs more planning and incentives. Mike needs some specific activities to do with Tina while baby-sitting, and he can be given extra time with his friends for doing a good job. When you try to reach a solution, if either you or your teen find you can't be reasonable, extend the time-out until all persons can contribute to the agreement.

Dad was proud of his intelligent daughters, but when the girls fought, he couldn't tolerate it. Joy and Bonnie started kidding around and then sparring in the upstairs hall. When a framed picture hit the floor, Dad ran to the stairway and shouted for them to stop, *"Joy and Bonnie, you go to your rooms and we'll discuss this in 15 minutes if you're ready to talk reasonably!"*

Dad's girls are almost adults; it's time for them to find ways to keep their playfulness from escalating to breaking up the house. Dad's discussion with them as near-equals may help them share responsibility for controlling themselves as they reach for adulthood.

For a teen who is almost an adult, the time-out method will seem more and more childish. After all, except for long time outs in prisons, you seldom see it used in the adult world. Your example, on the other hand, will always be an influence to your teen even in the decades to come.

Both parent modeling and family identification help a young person keep direction. Mom said, *"In the Weiler family we try to think of and respect everyone in the family and outside of it. I expect you to live up to the Weiler standard."* Of course Mom's actions must follow her words. Family sayings get across things parents consider important. My father was fond of saying, *"With all thy getting, get understanding."*

The following examples I have heard show how modeling and positive consequences work together. A parent who wanted a teen to read books turned off the TV and began reading an exciting adventure novel aloud with her teen. A mother who wants her daughter to be honest can ask, *"Whose money is this under the kitchen table?"* instead of just pocketing it. When a father noticed shoes accumulating by the front door, he put his in the closet, and soon his teen's were not at the front door either. The power of what we do is surprising; it's natural for members of the family to observe and be affected by it. Imitation occurs every day.

A teen with whom I worked developed a problem controlling anger. He started fights when classmates teased him and felt
bad about himself later. His parents needed to demonstrate and
describe their methods of controlling anger in their lives. Mom
shared a story: *"I was driving to the post office today and when I changed
lanes, another driver honked a long time at me. I guess he thought I slowed him
down. I felt mad and thought about pulling over and shaking my fist at him.
But I said to myself, 'I'm angry, but I'm in control—not him. I'm not going to
let him make me do something dangerous.'"* Sharing family experiences is
an important part of modeling.

Try this modeling exercise. Bring family members together to
make lists of each other's actions. Each person writes everyone's
name, including his/her own, on a piece of paper. Ask each person to list the most positive action of each member of the family
after each name. Which family members work hard? Which ones
have the most interesting stories, are creative, dress fashionably, use
good manners, tell jokes or funny stories? Add actions that come
to mind, but keep them on the positive side. This is not a gripe session.

After everyone has written a list, exchange sheets and ask someone to tell one of the answers on the sheet. Talk over these answers
briefly but move right along to the next person and answer. The
idea is to have people think about the positive actions of the ones
they live with and encourage these activities. If someone is getting too few items or items too unimportant, add some during the
discussion to even the totals.

The last part of this exercise is a discussion in which people
pretend they are other members of the family. Let people choose
their roles, and everyone can guess who is pretending to be whom
as the discussion goes along. Select a discussion topic such as,

where should we go on the next family outing? The purpose is merely to see how alike we are and yet how we each have a different view of others. Also, we may gain a clearer understanding of how much of our personalities are a function of those we live with.

Allowing a teen to make amends, use time-outs, ignore some things, look for something good, or watch your own example, *all* require diligent effort. Contrary to the easy magical advice from aunts, uncles, or some professionals, being a parent can be downright hard work. So make sure you eliminate rules about trivial behaviors before you start any of these plans. Here's an exercise to start the habit of keeping the rules appropriate and on target.

5. Use a Behavior Checklist in Your Planning Sessions.

Planning sessions have a dangerous tendency to turn into general gripe sessions. Although complaining can be therapeutic for parents, they often jump around from one problem to another without concluding a plan for any particular problem.

So a planning session needs an agenda that will focus on effective parental reactions to a particular situation. The session should also produce an overall understanding of what is going on when the specific problem is encountered.

The purpose of the checklist is to do a complete "walk through" of a problem. You may not always need such a complete analysis, but for the purpose of becoming alert to the possible aspects of behavior, this exercise will include all the steps.

First select a behavior that will be the problem under discussion in this session.

Create a checklist that shows specific behaviors, punishments, and alternatives you could use. As you create your checklist, think of the behavior you want. What would you have done if the wanted behavior had occurred instead of the unwanted action? Would you have reacted positively just as you reacted negatively to the error? Was any part of the desired behavior done before the mistakes were made? If so, what encouragement did you give? This list will be helpful when talking over a behavior with your teen. A sample list follows on the next page.

Fill out a behavior chart. A short outline of the chart is presented below. You will not yet have a record of the behavior as described in the last part of the chart, but you can put down your own observations as you remember them to answer those questions.

A Sample Behavior Chart

Fill in a chart, with the answers to these questions:

1: What is an objective description of the behavior problem?

2: What usually happens next?

3: Where would you place the possible blames and/or credits?

4: At what age would you expect an average teen to do what you are hoping will be done in this situation?

5: How could you allow more practice?

6: When do things happen? (Keep a record)

Review this check list for consequences as you consider possible reactions to the behavior. Pose each of the following questions in the planning session:

1. Is the problem big enough to bother with?

Remember even a "No" should indicate a strategy—a strategy to eliminate nagging yourself, or your teen, about the problem.

2. Am I attempting too much at one time?

A tempting pitfall in parenting is to try too many changes at once. Don't attempt to control eating, piano practicing, bed-making, and doing homework all at once. Concentrating on too many plans leads to mistakes and too much "policing." Think small. Begin with one rule at a time.

3. Can the behavior be guaranteed without the management of consequences?

Some behaviors can be made impossible by engineering the environment and that strategy is sometimes easier than using rules. For example, keeping sharp knives in a high cabinet or assigning a special kitchen drawer of utensils for a son or daughter's cooking.

4. Have we thought of all the consequences that could be maintaining the behavior?

A good way to separate consequences is to consider what we *have now?* What usually happens when the "bad" behavior occurs and what happens next? What usually happens if she performs correctly? If we select a new consequence, how should we set up *the practice?*

5. Is the consequence a one-shot?

The one-shot consequence is a rule that can only work once. A parent uses a promise of something good or threat of something bad in the *future* as a consequence for a *present* behavior problem. Whichever way the consequence is stated, threat or promise, it has the same disagreeable characteristics: it is not repeatable, it tempts parents to use repeated threats and will probably be somewhat arbitrary in the end. And then we need to start a new threat.

6. Is the consequence too severe?

Be sure that your selection of a consequence is not a reaction to one case of bad behavior. You want something that can be used repeatedly. The real test will come after things have settled down. The main feature of your plan that will help you will be that you have planned to reward good behaviors reasonably and react to bad ones reasonably. So don't make plans when you're still angry over a mistake.

7. If ignoring is the plan, are we prepared to handle the resulting escalation of the bad behavior?

And what good behavior will we be on the lookout for, give attention to?

8. Is the expectation reasonable?

Your expectation may be reasonable but still much more than your daughter has ordinarily been doing. She was cleaning her room and now you want her to vacuum and dust the house. Remember we need to start where *she* is, not where you *wish* her to be.

9. Is the consequence too weak?

What can be done if your teen just doesn't seem to care about the new consequence? It could be that you are not sticking to the rule and he really doesn't *have* to care. Or possibly he has too many freebies available or too many alternatives (If I can't go out, I'll watch TV!).

Are you starting with a behavior simple enough so that rewards can occur—even on the first day?

10. Review this Check List for Alternatives to Punishment.

1. Could you use the adult reaction to adult mistakes, *making amends?*

2. Is it possible to first try *ignoring?*

3. Could we help him or her to see us as a *good model.*

4. Have the other possibilities presented in this been considered: *"Catch 'em being good," Changing the convenience* of the behavior, and *"Time-outs."*

You can't make a
garden just by
pulling weeds. You
have to grow
something.

Step 6: Help with the "Boy Problem" and School Work

1. The "Boy Problem."

Of course, both girls and boys have problems. But, as a group, boys have more problems with social media and many other things.

The Southern Regional Education Board studied 40,000 typical high school students, not stars and not low performers, in 2002. While 84 percent of girls said it was important to continue schooling after high school, only 67 percent of boys agreed.

Boys are five times more likely than girls to have accidents with bikes, sticks and baseball bats. Later on, they are four times more likely to have trouble with the law. In the U. S., boys cause most teen driving accidents and get most of the traffic tickets. They also have lower grades in school and are more likely to drop out. Boys have shrunk to a minority in colleges, medical schools, and law schools. Although girls were rarely even allowed in these institutions a century ago, now, for every 100 male college graduates there are over 140 women graduates. The genders are different and there is a "Boy Problem."

By 12th grade, 44 percent of girls have become proficient readers but only 28 percent of boys have reached that standard. Only
41 percent of boys said they "often" tried to do their best work in
school, compared with 67 percent of the girls.

Now that the "male chores" of the farms of 1900 have become less needed, girls have an advantage. Girls make an earlier
contribution to the family, particularly in the domestic chores. As a
result, they enjoy early appreciation and are better prepared to care
for themselves.

Parents tend to cave in to flack from boys while resisting any
flack from girls. Insisting on girls doing their chores and homework develops their skills as well as their enthusiasm for work
done successfully. Boys may receive less encouragement from ex-
asperated parents or because boys dodge the work altogether, and
they fall further behind in the experience department.

Dads are particularly vulnerable to competition with their sons
and hold back on compliments for chores well done for fear of
appearing weak.

Support your school's active projects in home improvement,
financial management, small business management, mortgages,
stock markets, computer management, applied science, and tracking diet and exercise. These projects encourage both boys and girls
to be proud of their abilities right now. Even abstract subjects can
include practical applications.

College applications may not ask about these "non-academic"
skills, but schoolwork should help your son or daughter with concerns now, at their present age. "Someday you'll need this," is not
enough. They need a good answer to, "What good is this (homework, project, learning, work) now?"

One source of the gender difference may come from the trend

to single-parent families. The year 2000 U.S. Census said one-third of our children were raised in single-parent households, up from only one in 10 in 1960. These children were five times more likely to be raised by single Moms than single Dads. Girls will have a same-sex role model while the boys may be looking to teachers, relatives, and media for guidance part of the time. Whatever the sources of influence, the differences between boys and girls in school are worrisome.

Going from father to grandfather, I went from girls who have the highest grades in school and are the least likely to need school discipline, to boys who are most likely to be disciplined and six times more likely to have trouble with the law, with driving, with alcohol and drugs, and six times more likely to go to prison later on.

Is all this genetic? Some of it must be but there are positive, and negative, contributing factors from parents and grandparents.

Many parents, teachers, and counselors believe girls are more socially skilled at an earlier age and therefore may attract more support, acceptance, and admiration than their brothers. Boys on the other hand, seem to want only to be competent and be admired for it. They seem to shun the gushier praise.

Parents shouldn't be misled by a son's bland reaction. To prove they are not easily influenced, boys often fend off sincere praise in the years when they need it most.

The lack of enthusiasm from a son may lead parents to conclude that compliments and admiration don't work so they should lay off the positive approach. This is a deadly mistake.

Parents should not be misled by short-term rebuffs because the long-term results are more important. The temptation to let boys go their own way, with discipline for only the big blunders and a trickle of support for the successes, is destructive to skill development in boys.

Dads are particularly vulnerable to taking up this strategy and come off looking as if they never completely approve of anything their son does.

A strange effect of sexism in our culture is that girls sometimes show better adjustment in childhood than boys possibly because they make an earlier contribution to the family, particularly in domestic chores. They enjoy early appreciation and are encouraged to do more.

While "protecting" a boy from drudgery, parents can run the risk of driving their son to find other activities that show he can "do something."

Threatened by his perceived "worthlessness," he will cast around for a way to show off—what will he find? Will it be a suggestion from his Mom or Dad? Or will encouragement from friends make risky behaviors more likely?

Positive support is the major advantage parents have in competing against their teen's friends who encourage and criticize without much thought. Parents have to hold to limits that are not always popular, but also must inspire new tasks that build self-respect.

One fast way to alienate a member from a group (or family) is to deny him a chance to contribute when he's ready. Gripe as a son may about chore assignments and household jobs, recognition of his step forward now will help maintain his genuine satisfaction with himself later on when peers encourage dangerous habits.

Practical and active projects can inspire a teenager. Projects in home improvement, cooking, financial management, small business management, mortgages, stock markets, setting up a new cell phone and tracking diet and exercise all encourage boys as well as girls to be proud of their abilities right now. Even abstract subjects can include practical projects.

2. Who is Gifted?

Soccer and basketball coaches are not the only adults putting kids to the test and seeking the stars. The schools are forever testing our teens, looking for the "gifted." They do it because they have special programs for special kids. And some of us want "trophy children." But how would a parent recognize, and how should a parent react to, their teenager's "gifts?"

Who were the geniuses of the past? Einstein, for sure, even though his genius wasn't detected until he was nearly an adult. Many people would include Mozart who was writing operas at the age of three. But neither the musical genius of Mozart or Michael Jackson guaranteed a long and happy life.

We might include others in math and theoretical physics, as well as additional nominations from the list of classical composers. No doubt these people were born with something special. Einstein even left his brain to science so they could try to figure out what it was—they have offered no conclusions.

Schools usually limit definitions of "gifted" to areas they teach and evaluate—math, science, language-related talents such as those seen in spelling bee winners, and sometimes music.

Other gifts, such as social skills, artistic ability, and common sense, are not so easily evaluated. It may even seem silly and arbitrary to think of the "County Common Sense Champion" or the "Personality State Champion." But these other talents need to be recognized so that a parent's expectations can keep pace. Business professionals tell us that the strengths which lead to success are likely to be perseverance, hard work and social skills—not academic trophies.

I know a fifth grader who represented his county grade school at the national spelling bee in Washington D.C. We don't know if his spelling talents mean he could learn other languages at an astounding rate, but we know that multi-lingual applicants will be prized by businesses of the future. If we wait too long to teach languages to him, he will not be able to learn another language without an accent.

Is it enough to be proud of his accomplishment and continue his schooling with no foreign language training until high school? Should we take the wide view of "gifted" and let him at least sample challenging language training now? How many seeds of unrecognized genius wither because they did not fall on fertile ground?

Parents are often aggravated by their talented teenager's failure to carry through and use unusual blessings. Why would he come up short on effort when he has the gift? The answer, sometimes, may be that procrastination has set in because of fear of failure, particularly if failure is defined by himself or his parents as anything less than perfect.

One Mom told me her son brought home a poor report card. When she looked through his backpack she found completed history assignments, weeks after they were due. What's going on? Her son said his work was "not quite right." So he's a gifted perfectionist who is flunking history.

Keep a modest reaction if a coach or teacher says your teenager is gifted. If he turns into a perfectionist, he may avoid the risks of trying new activities and expressing new ideas. Don't be misled by society's narrow views of gifts and talent. Look for and encourage all your son's or daughter's gifts.

Concerning the lighter side of early development, take Alex, now 16. He spent his babyhood thumbing through magazines while his fellow one-year-olds played with simple toys. By the time he was three, he would correct his mother if she skipped reading a line in a story by placing her finger on the missed phrase.

Alex has hyperlexia, a condition opposite, in many ways, to the learning disorder, dyslexia. He has a very advanced ability to identify individual sounds while reading, and he also has an advanced ability to manipulate those sounds in his head. Nevertheless, he had trouble understanding what he read and he was delayed in learning to speak.

He now speaks in a normal fashion but uses the cadence of reading out loud, and he avoids interjections such as "like" that many youngsters his age use incessantly.

But Alex is running for his student council and he may win because he is a fearless public speaker. Alex seems about normal in any category outside of his language ability.

Helpful parents deserve daily credit for encouraging all competencies beyond what a scientific test might discover. They can help in all cases by watching for chances to bolster confidence and by avoiding the straight diet of advice, quick fixes, and focus on shortcomings that hit vulnerable spots.

"Practice what you want to become" is a good rule for teenagers. "Model what you want your children to practice" is a good rule for parents.

How can you know which kids will get into trouble? The nightly news might give you the impression that low income and poor family structure are the primary causes of dangerous and destructive paths.

But the long-term Adolescent Health Study shows that the kids most likely to get into self-destructive activities such as drinking, drugs, or crime are kids who do poorly in school.

The study has been following 12,000 students since 1994 when they were 12 to 17 years old. It found all the familiar problems you would expect. At first, one in ten reported weekly drinking, and the amount of sexual behavior was alarming. One in five seventh and eighth graders had explored sexual activities, and two out of three high school juniors and seniors were sexually experienced.

After problems with school, the second best predictor of these bad habits was the amount of unsupervised time each teenager ordinarily had. This influence showed up in drug use, violent behavior, and sex. "Among all the factors that can be associated with teenage sex, the big one was opportunity," Dr. Robert Blum, the director of the study, said.

We seem to have adjusted to a daily routine that says, "Get teens up before it's light; get them to school by 7:45 ready or not; and let them out by 2:00." To do what?

Even a large proportion of adults have trouble being bright morning people. This goes double for teenagers going through the growth and hormone years.

Since after-school time is such a factor in risky and violent behaviors, maybe we should reorganize high school schedules. When classes begin at 7:45, teens may go home by 2:30 to an empty house, and three hours of unsupervised time before parents get home from work.

Bus drivers and others who have built their schedules around dropping the kids off early would find schedule changes troublesome. Sports practices would be disrupted by a later schedule, and part-time jobs would be more difficult to arrange, but what is our priority? Six dollars an hour or fewer teenage pregnancies? What sense is there in going to math class at 7:45 a.m. in a sleepy haze and going to football practice at your afternoon peak? It should be math at your peak and sports when they can be worked in.

Other studies investigating the sources of school violence show that almost half of all students are concerned about pressure for school grades. The stress builds with the morning rush followed by the cascade of short classes.

If a good education for our kids is our goal, it's time to get started. Let's plan to change their daily schedule to give them the best chance to learn and to practice safe habits.

3. Bullies, Victims and Hiding Out in School.

Every school day, 160,000 students will stay home because of bullies, the U. S. Department of Justice estimates. Also, 100,000 students will bring guns to school, 6,500 teachers will be threatened and 250 teachers will be attacked.

Bullies often justify their aggression by saying they were provoked and the victims deserved mistreatment because they didn't comply with the bully's demands. Bullies like to dominate others and think they should always get their way.

Girl bullies may use more subtle tactics than their more violent brothers such as insults and ridicule, but the terror they inflict can still be intense and cruel. So victims avoid unsupervised areas, restrooms, recreation areas, the lunchroom or Face Book just to keep from being the repeated targets.

Victims of bullies can be passive or provocative. Passive victims are often alone, anxious, sometimes weaker, and may cry easily. Provocative victims can bring trouble on themselves because they tease and irritate others and don't know when to back off. When they get an unwanted reaction, they sometimes fight back, but usually ineffectually.

What can a parent or teacher do? The single most effective deterrent to bullying is an adult authority. We parents and teachers should intervene. We can do it with a no-nonsense style, as a problem solver and as a third person who smoothes things over.

In the cafeteria, Taylor, who is 14 and has been the subject of many bullying complaints, shakes his fist at Richard and says, *"You'd better hand over that quarter left over from your lunch."*

Ms. Anderson, the social studies teacher, overhears and says, *"Taylor, that doesn't go here. Come to my room for the rest of your lunch time—we need to talk."* (The no-nonsense and prompt action approach.)

Preventative school policies hold bullies responsible for their behavior. Staff may feel uncomfortable confronting bully behavior and they may ignore it. Or they may feel isolated and unsupported when it comes to intervening in the lunchroom, hallways, or outside of school. The power balance needs to shift—the pendulum needs to swing away from power for bullies and back to the school staff.

"No-Bullying Rules" and school policies that encourage students to speak out and get adult help when needed should be supported by parents. Our goal should be to protect the victims and to help the bully replace negative behaviors with skills that involve treating others kindly.

This problem requires a statement right from the top. School superintendents should assure principals, and principals should assure teachers that they will be vigorously supported in their efforts to stop bullying in the school and out of school.

One excellent source for help is *Bully-Proofing Your School: A Comprehensive Approach for Elementary Schools,* published by Sopris West, 4093 Specialty Place, Longmont, Colorado, 80504 or, sopriswest.com. This book describes effective long-range programs for schools and parents and it provides useful handouts, exercises, and needed strategies.

The West Middle School of Detroit, Michigan, began its anti-bullying program by displaying school posters with anti-bullying messages such as "Friends aren't friends if they put you down" and "Your silence means your approval." The school also has a "bully box" for students to anonymously report incidents. "No-Bullying Rules" and these school policies encourage students to speak out and to get adult help when needed, and they should be supported by parents of bullies as well as parents of victims. The Detroit program alerts parents to watch their students for telltale habits:

* Making excuses for not wanting to go to school.

* Increased fear of school situations such as riding the bus, going outside or using the rest room.

* Missing personal items or needing extra school supplies or money.

* Extra trips to the school nurse, unexplained bruises or torn clothing.

Until parents take up that awareness, kids will be hiding out in school and losing out on their education while they try to stay out of harm's way. "If I don't go to the bathroom (gym, school bus, outside areas, or lunchroom), I can avoid Billy (or Beth) Bully for another day."

Teachers and principals deserve your support. And many teenagers need special practice learning how to talk firm, walk tall, look a tormentor in the eye and say loudly, "Back off!" As city police often tell us, some people need to practice how to avoid looking and acting like a victim.

Also the bullies need help. They, too, are missing out on their education while their attention is on confronting, fighting, and abusing.

They will soon be out of school with minimal social skills and the mistaken notion that abusing others is acceptable. They need redirection.

Let's help them now while they are in school and teachers and staff have an influence.

The person who brings the problem to our attention is often denounced as a "tattletale." One reason tattletales annoy us is that the help requested is not easy or comfortable. In some cases, it's dangerous. The bully may retaliate or the bully's parents may object to our interference.

Our freedom and safety exist only because most people will not tolerate behavior that endangers others. If we saw thugs beating up someone, we'd yell for help or call the police. We wouldn't expect the police to say the victim should "solve his own problem." And we would not expect to be ridiculed as a "tattletale."

Bullies at school are a local example of a weakening of the majority's will to protect the individual. Tattletales are not admired and neither are bullies. School polices should encourage students to object when one of their own is bullied by another. And teachers should support reasonable requests for help. Tattletales are not always wrong.

The internet site, CharacterCounts.org, suggests this pledge for schools: "Anti-bully Pledge: We will not bully other students. We will help others who are being bullied by speaking out and getting adult help. We will use extra efforts to include students in activities in our school."

School psychologist Izzy Kalman offers direct help for the kids with a free online manual, *How to Stop Being Teased and Bullied Without Really Trying*. His website, www.bullies2buddies.com also has a free manual and advice for adults.

The rewards for teasing and bullying are in the reactions of the victim, says Kalman. He makes specific suggestions about how a teen should react or not react.

The bullies of today will be the community problems of tomorrow. From their ranks will come the next generation of child abuse, spousal abuse, road rage, and "life rage".

4. Magical Thinking and Mental Habits.

The signers of the Declaration of Independence knew the value of both education and hard work. It was clear to them that effort and learning in school would be rewarded in work and life.

Today, many students believe they might "make it" even to enormous financial success just by luck, or by skill in sports, or by knowing the right people in the entertainment business. It's a possibility promoted by TV, news and state lotteries.

So without incentives to focus attention on the learning at hand, many students become victims of magical thinking about success, and they develop unrealistic views of how "luck" will carry them through.

We adults also become victims of magical thinking. That's why we now approve of lotteries and other gambling, but our grandparents wisely, I think, did not.

We sometimes engage in magical thinking not only about a financial windfall, but also about our students: *"The ones with the 'right stuff' will always do well." "Kids will work harder at school if parents take a harder (more punitive) line or if the teachers enforce strict (more punitive) rules."*

Faced with a student's failure and rebellion, a parent is tempted to criticize and punish. But the solution is on the positive side—with incentives, praise and respect expressed in concrete ways that raise self-esteem and confidence.

Some may object that gushing with praise is the wrong solution, but the danger for most of us isn't in overdoing it, but in doing it at all. Encouragement and parental support involve a commitment of time and attention.

But schools are crowded, teachers are very busy and our culture is inclined to provide little compensation for the essential activities of attending school and learning.

Representatives in Congress with their large salaries and teachers on the line with their modest ones should pause before objecting to the notion of rewarding students. It may be the most important part of the teaching and the parenting job. Few of us work for nothing.

I know it seems like a lot of trouble and we wish all students would work just for the joy of it and learn just for the love of learning, but most will not. We are a goal-oriented species with ambitions that can go astray. We need daily course corrections through positive feedback.

If a student behaves badly in school, we often say it is his fault—he is rebellious, aggressive, too distracted, or not very smart. In a well-known study focused on how we explain children's' problems, school psychologists listed the following causes of school problems:

1. The material was not appropriate,

2. The teacher was not doing a good job of teaching,

3. The organization of the school was wrong,

4.. The parents of the student were not supportive,

5. Something about the student was amiss—lack of motivation,

low ability, or emotional disturbance.

When teachers were asked to think back about the students they had taught, they attributed 85 percent of the problems to No. 5, the students themselves. This is partly true, of course, but it attributes the problem to the factor that is most difficult to change.

Both parents and their teens can also engage in the faulty mental habit of blaming a person's basic personality. This can get in the way of resolving the problems. Attention to the daily frequent successes with encouragements and compliments produces the best long-term progress. Knowing the pitfalls of blaming the teen's personality can clear the way to a better attitude and a better solution. Here are a few versions of faulty blaming habits that sometimes afflict both parents and teenagers.

1.   Oversimplification.

We are all inclined to simplify to keep order in our mind. Some disorder is inherent, but the habit is destructive.

"All those teachers are mean."

"Well, if you would try a little harder, I'm sure things would get better."

You can see that oversimplification can be both a parent's and a teen's problem. A good step forward in this conversation would be to ask a specific question, *"What would show your teachers your good side?"* Of course, this question won't get a direct and constructive answer, but it will turn the topic toward more productive advice than "trying harder."

2.   Absolutes.

We prefer absolutes. Gray areas and contradictions are too hard to handle while an absolute demand seems more likely to get results. Faced with an absolute demand, *"I want all your homework done before supper, not a bit left or no TV later,"* a teenager may react with his own no-room-for-argument tactic, *"Either you love me or you don't. If you loved me, you would let me do it when I want to, so I guess you don't love me."*

Mom could make better progress here by setting a reachable goal, *"If you have the writing part done before supper, you can do the math after your program."* This suggestion won't stop the arguing, but it is more likely to reach a solution.

3. I'll Make Them Sorry.

"I just won't do her stupid project; that will fix her."Mark, giving up won't hurt your teacher; it will only prolong the problem and it will lower your grade." Mark dreams of his power over the teacher, but Mom has to help him be realistic.

4. Everyone Is Watching Me.

"My hair looks terrible. And everyone will notice this shirt is crummy and faded."

"Lamont, your hair is fine and your shirt is fine, too." Mom could do better here by giving Lamont a broader view: *"Lamont, what were Althea and Larry wearing last Tuesday?"*

"Mom, how would I know?"

"People don't pay much attention, do they? The same goes for Althea and Larry."

We all want the best for our children and that's why we are tempted to point out the shortfalls, but it's the example you put in front of them—even the mental habit you show—that has the most impact. A discussion of all sides of the problem will produce the most useful conclusion.

When my daughter, Pam, was 14, she asked if she could go to

an older friend's high school party after the next football game. Luckily, I was distracted with yard work at the time and said her mother and I would talk about it. I asked Pam a few questions and heard that most of the kids would be older, but she didn't know much more about it.

Later we found out that her friend's parents would be out of town, and on other occasions they had supplied beer for parties since the kids were too young to buy it themselves.

We said no. Pam complained, said we never let her do anything, promised she wouldn't drink any beer, but we still said no. She made quite a production out of calling her friend and complaining about her old-fashioned parents who said she couldn't go.

Years later she told me that many times she was afraid of some of those "friends" and had hoped we would say no. That way she didn't have to think of herself as a wuss and could blame us for having to back out.

When she later had a 14-year-old of her own who asked if he could have beer at his birthday party, of course she said no. He whined that his friends said they had beer on their birthday. She said that because the argument lasted only a few minutes, she wondered if the strategy from her own teenage years was being repeated by her son.

The struggles between teenagers and parents may not always have clear motives. Even in the mind of the teen, impulses and good intentions may conflict. Sometimes parents have to help by setting down a strict rule.

Whether you are on your own or in a partnership, other parents can create a sounding board for your concerns and provide the assurance that others have problems similar to yours.

A few calls or an announcement in a church newsletter will

produce other parents who are willing to take an evening a month for a parent coffee chat.

As their kids reach early teens, some parents are surprised at how much guidance and practice their young teens need. School and friends begin taking up the largest amount of a teen's time and attention and just a little coaching from parents can be a long-lasting help for a teen struggling to adjust to everything at once.

Adults looking back realize that school success was a critical ingredient of happiness in their childhood and teenage years. Comfort and success in school strengthens your teen's self-image and parents' satisfaction. If you can help your teen in this important part of his or her life, what a gift it is! And that success provides more than confidence in academic abilities, it influences feelings of competence and usefulness outside of school as well.

Looking back again, we all remember how we compared ourselves to schoolmates and reached an impression of them and a judgment of ourselves as well—possibly before we were 10, but certainly during our teen years. Parents who have attended their own school reunion after a few years know how the reunion seems to measure us against that old bench mark again. This common reaction to reunions demonstrates how important help in school is to a teenage student.

Greg: *"Mom, I don't want to go to school anymore."*

Mom: *"What? I thought you liked school."*

Greg: *"Well, it's boring and a lot of it doesn't make sense."*

Mom: *"Getting along in school is hard. What part do you do best?"*

(Mom shows good listening skills in order to hear the whole story.)

Greg: *"Best? Oh, Math, I guess, but what good is it anyway? And in Geography I just can't remember all that stuff and the kids in there don't like me anyway."*

School is such a large part of a teen's life, and if it isn't going well, it clouds almost all other activities. Greg pointed out several sources of trouble when he said he was bored because he didn't see the use of math, couldn't remember the geography, *and* "the kids don't like me." Let's start with Greg's boredom.

5. Providing Answers to "Why Should I Do That Stuff?"

Kids who say, *"It's boring"* could be sending a confusing message. They could mean that they have little interest in the subject and they don't see the need, or they could mean they are bored because they can't keep up or, the opposite, they are too far ahead. Parents need to sort out these different meanings before they react.

The poor student who finds school lessons of "no use" usually means he finds no importance *for him* in the tasks that are requested: *"Why should I do that? It's just busy work."* A parent could be misled at this point and start explaining why *she*, the parent, thinks the work is important.

Mom: *"Math is important, Greg, because one day you'll have to manage your own money and figure out shopping and many other things in life."*

Greg: *"Uh, yeah."*

Mom: *"Also, you need it for the higher math that will get you into college."*

Greg: *"Higher math? There's higher math??? I think I won't go to college."*

Mom: *"Don't talk like that. Of course, you want to go to college."*

The "someday-you'll-need-these-things" approach to this problem is not on target with Greg's original objection. His point was that the work is not important *for him*. Greg's value of the "you'll-need-it-for-college" argument is revealed when he suggests giving up college just to avoid math problems tonight!

Mom needs an approach to the meaningfulness and importance of a good education that is within Greg's short-term view of the world. It won't help to provide more arguments about, *"You can't get anywhere without a good education,"* or, *"Jobs will be harder to get, promotions will be harder to come by, and you'll end up with a hard life!"*

At the moment—in the short run—Greg doesn't want to, or can't, deal with those things. The *"getting anywhere"* idea is too far in the future and too abstract—anyway the people on TV seem to do all right, and some of them don't have much education. And how much education would a person need to earn the amount of money that *Greg* would think is plenty?

So why should Greg study decimals tonight? What use is it to know portions of Geography or American History? Why is spelling important? The answers need to be in the present activities of Greg's life. Remember he's a person with short-term priorities.

As he gains new skills from school each day, he should be encouraged to use them at home. Sometimes that requires real creativity by a parent. Could Greg use his math to keep track of the family checking account? Receive a fee for doing so? Could Greg handle the grocery list? Take the money and do the shopping? Will he make costly mistakes? Yes. Couldn't he just stay interested in this stuff until he needs it? Probably not.

One mother I worked with showed how such skills are useful by taking her 13-year-old son to the bank with her. She allowed him to go in alone and pay the bills. When he returned with the correct change and explained it all, she gave him a "tip." The "tip" is a parental judgment call and might not be necessary for many boys who would be happy with the importance of the task and trust they were given, but her son will never ask why he has to know decimals —he knows why.

He also bakes for his mother. And when recipes need to be halved or doubled she does not interfere in the calculations. From bitter (and sour) experience he knows the importance of these skills. And he feels a little better about his own worth. He's not *just* a kid, he's a kid with useful skills that his parents respect.

Many skills not covered in school are also important to learn. Cooking, washing clothes, caring for your room, and later on, car care. All tasks present opportunities for teens to learn and gain a feeling of self-esteem as they become competent. The chores may be domestic ones that adults shun or view as burdens, but they still have the potential of letting your teen be productive and helpful *now*.

Parents may need to show great tolerance as they allow practice with these important school-related tasks or tasks of everyday drudgery that parents could do faster. Calm your impatience with the knowledge that just mastering the task is rewarding and insures the further benefit of a little self-pride. Mistakes are easier to tolerate because the benefits of pride and competence form part of their teen's protection against later temptations of self-abuse— drugs and alcohol, for example.

When the task is closer to drudgery than to adventure, more enthusiastic praise will be needed. Ordinarily a person gains very little respect from others for drudgery. Drudgery has little in it to be proud of. So when a teen asks, *"Why should I do this?"* it may be the beginning of an argument, but it also signals his need for appreciation for doing the job. He's counting on your support for activities that are not very important, fun, or "adult." His question about drudgery is a signal to focus on encouraging him and praising him for a job well done. Also, you may need concrete rewards as in the family economies described later in Step 7.

Learning must be useful now. Parents should provide experiences that point out, here and now, the usefulness of things learned in school. Certainly even a ten- or twelve-year-old can handle a checking account for the family, or plan and carry out the family food shopping. For school subjects that do not easily apply to daily tasks, parents can influence their teen's respect for the subject by asking questions.

Mom: *"What was your work in science today?"*

Greg: *"We named the chambers of the heart and followed a drop of blood through the vessels."*

Mom: *"I always wanted to know more about that. How does it go through?"*

Show interest in school projects and point out, from news-of-the-day, where knowledge applies. Parent-teen conversations that bring in schoolwork show the usefulness of Greg's work and improve his respect for himself.

6. Homework Strategies that Work.

Greg's second complaint about school also showed up in Geography. This time it wasn't that he questioned the usefulness of the subject by saying it's "boring," but that he found it "boring" because he was not doing well. This requires parental help beyond showing the topic's usefulness—Greg needs study skills.

Homework that requires staring at materials and memorization can be boring and hard to stick with:

Greg: *"I just can't keep the states straight. We're supposed to know them by Friday!"*

Dad: *"What are they going to ask you about them?"*

Greg: *"We have to point to them on a blank map with no words or any names at all."*

Dad: *"Do you have a map?"*

Greg: *"I have the one in this book. I've been studying it a lot, but I don't remember much."*

Dad: *"How do you do the "studying" part?"*

Greg: *"Well, I look at the states and try to remember which ones go where."*

Dad: *"Greg, I think you need to go through a few drills in a situation like the one you're going to have on Friday. How about tracing that map so we can have one that's blank like the one you'll see on Friday. Then we'll make a few copies when we go shopping."*

Greg: *"OK. Then I could practice by filling in the names on the copies we make."*

Studying requires practice. Greg has been trying to practice in his mind *("I've been studying it a lot"),* but sitting and staring at a book or homework sheet is not real practice—performance—and Greg has not made much progress.

To make homework time successful, Dad first asks Greg what he is *doing.* Most students who are falling behind don't have a specific target for their effort. When they study, they stare at things—notes or books—they don't *DO* anything.

Most of us don't have the kind of memory that retains a great deal from just looking; it's the *doing* that will be remembered.

What do you remember from your high school days? Spelling? Math and vocabulary you still use (*do* things with)? But I'll bet you remember very little of social studies, geography, history, or math you never use.

We usually tell our teens to *"work hard"* in school. The "work hard" idea is good advice but by itself, it leaves out the specifics. Successful work shows up in grades if the student is shown how

the "work hard" idea is turned into overt practice; not just staring at pages, but reading aloud; not just "trying to remember,"
but talking to others about the work; drilling important concepts,
rewriting notes and important material, and drawing new diagrams
or tables that organize facts differently. That's how the idea of
"work hard" becomes successful learning.

If you are skeptical of this strategy, try the following experiment:

Pick out a favorite magazine in which there are two articles or
stories you have not yet read. Read the first story to yourself in
your usual way. Find someone to listen to your report of the story
or article and tell them all the detail you can remember —who
wrote it, who was in it, what was going on, conclusions reached
and so on.

Now go back to the magazine and read the second article or
story. This time, stand up and read out loud, with good emphasis
and inflection—to the wall if necessary.

Now find your listener again and report this story giving all the
details you can remember of who, what, and where. By the end of
the second report, I'm sure you will notice how much more you
remember of the second story. As one student put it to me, *"Well
of course I remember that one, I remember what I said!"*

For the purpose of learning and changing habits there is no
substitute for active practice. On your vacation, stare at pages in a
novel while lying on the beach if you enjoy it, but if it's for learning, "work hard."

Reading assignments often lead the student to this mistake of
leaving out the *doing* part of learning. Many of my students have
said, *"I can't believe I did poorly. I went through (stared at) all the material for the test!"*

If you only read it (not really practice) and never use it, it will be gone soon. If reading is the assignment, have your student take reading notes—preferably on cards—for each page. *"Never turn a page without writing something,"* should be the rule.

Give your student the advantage. The reading-note requirement helps in several ways.

1. Notes become a source of motivation because they are a concrete product which can give the student a feeling of accomplishment, right away.

2. Notes are a product that parents can encourage, review, and use as a basis for other rewards, if that's in the plan.

3. The third and most important advantage is that notes provide benchmarks of progress that allow the student to pick up at the right place after an interruption.

It's surprising how much studying is done in small sessions of only a few minutes between interruptions by phone calls, snacks, and chores. Without a note-taking habit, most of us start again at the same place we started before. With past notes, we have a record of where we are and can move on to new material.

4. At review time, the work is condensed as notes, maps, tables, and drill sheets guaranteeing the right material will be memorized. Your student can thereby avoid the misery of thrashing madly through unorganized papers.

A Harvard professor I know has several good guidelines for study time. He always distributes a slip of paper to each student before class. The top line on the slip reads, *"The main point of the day was . . ."* followed by a space for the student to complete the statement. The next line says, *"My question for today is..."* followed by more writing room.

The professor collects the slips each day to see how the main point has been understood and what confusion is in need of more attention during the next class. Students must think, summarize, and question, and the professor has excellent feedback. Many professors now use this procedure.

The most important advice on learning comes from early history when Sophocles said, *"The learning is in the doing of the thing."* When it comes to school work, it's easy for the student to forget how much *practice counts*.

The following guidelines summarize the important points for homework time.

GUIDELINE 1: Use Homework Time in an Active Way!

Action Example 1: Always have pencil and paper handy when reading. Note-taking is good practice, and good practice is good learning. Take notes on every page of reading. Authors and publishers of school books are always struggling to keep the size and expense of books down; nearly every page has something to say. What is it? Write it down.

It's a good idea to put many of these notes in question form. The student should use the headings in the book to make up the questions and use note cards if they are convenient. Note cards encourage review of specifics. As test-time approaches, students with the note-taking habit will already have their own review to study!

Action Example 2: Students should make new lists, drawings and summaries of class materials. Any new "doing" will help the student remember. Working with other students can produce the same kind of practice and drill. New lists, drawings and charts are more easily remembered by those who create them. I have never had a student fail a course when he produced study notes and other evidence of practice!

Action Example 3: Make up the test. If your students are still concerned about a test, they should construct their own version of the test trying to make it as similar as possible to the one expected. Students often report that more than half of their questions were the same as the ones on the teacher's test! With those questions answered in advance, the students easily remembered their answers and were quickly half way to a good test grade.

Action Example 4: Keep a calendar! The calendar should include plans for homework for each day and a record of successes. It should also include priorities for assignments to study so time is spent on the most important work of the moment.

GUIDELINE 2: Reinforce Practice

Many competing activities have built-in payoffs, but the benefits of studying are often a long way off. Students become more efficient as good study skills develop and the longer they practice good habits the more reliable and useful the skills become. This includes taking study notes, re-doing materials, and keeping a calendar. Future opportunities, grades and preparation for new subjects will have long-range benefits but may be weak motivators for present effort.

So what can a teacher or parent do to reinforce a student who needs to acquire new attitudes and skills to study effectively? While the calendar helps in planning time to study, parents need to help in planning a place to study.

1. Provide a place where active note-taking is convenient. This is just as important to the learning place as freedom from distraction.

2. Talk about subjects your students are taking and create examples of the usefulness of the material.

3. Reinforce knowledge about the subjects by asking questions—even questions that stump parents as well as the student. It might be necessary to look up the answer in the homework materials.

4. Reinforce and praise *daily and weekly grades* that reflect knowledge learned.

GUIDELINE 3: Use a Strategy for Tests

Even after students have acquired good study habits through the guidelines of their own practice and encouragement from parents and teachers, they often complain about having trouble with tests. These test strategies bring positive results in either essay or objective tests.

During objective tests:

Certainly every student intends to answer each question, but very often items go unanswered. Two reasons for this are: fear of guessing and failure to remember the question. The student should carefully read *and eliminate* options. Checking off poor choices allows the student to focus on the remaining options and improve chances that small differences will be discovered.

Once an answer is selected, the student should read the first part of the item one more time to be sure that the selection actually answers this particular question. Wrong options are often, in themselves, correct, but not the answer to the initial question.

For essay tests:

The important guideline here is to answer each question twice—once in outline form and then as an essay answer. A student having trouble with these tests should write a brief outline on another sheet before beginning essay answers. This first answer can be in the student's own words and shorthand. For example, in response to the question, *"What was important about the Gettysburg Address?"* the student might jot down, *"Lincoln; at graveyard; during Civil War; trying to unite the country; said country must try hard to finish the war; for equality and people to run government; give quote."*

Now, looking at the first answer, the student is likely to complete the second answer in good form. Also, as the student is writing the final answer, new points may come to mind to add to the final answer.

The teacher is more likely to give a high score when the major points are easy to find. And major points will be found more easily if your student's writing is as neat as possible. If this is a problem, buy an erasable ink pen before the next test!

7. How About a Computer Program to Help Learning?

Computer programs from school or at home can be helpful, especially if the drills are very similar to the other school work and to the tests that evaluate progress. Math and language programs often include useful drills because the content of the drills and the test that comes up later are almost the same.

But for programs in other areas where content can vary, you'll need advice from school about *what* spelling, history, government, or social studies the program should cover.

For most teens, adult encouragements and real life applications are needed to keep interest up. It's the same support from parents and teachers that homework and lessons have always required. Leaving a student on a chair, even one in front of a computer, may not produce learning that shows up on school tests unless parents provide encouragement for practice.

A second limitation of computer effectiveness is in the *action* the student is asked to perform. Remember, learning is in the *doing*. If a student learns to press the right buttons on a keyboard to answer math questions, his performance will be best there and not as good on paper and pencil tests and verbal drills.

It's amazing to us adults that learning 3 plus 5 or the usefulness of 3.1416 on a computer doesn't result in a correct answer on those points on every test paper after that. The student can improve with a computer program, but how the improvement shows up on tests depends partly on how similar the test is to the program, not only in content, but in the *way* the student is asked to provide answers.

Here's another place a parent can contribute: make up some tests. Arrange to collect information from your teen's school. You need to know the nature and general format of the evaluations they use in the computer subjects you have at home. Then, you can construct practice tests on the computer material, but in the format and style your student will encounter at school. Perhaps *your student* could make up these practice tests for himself and others. Quizzes and drills with pencil and paper will give your teen practice in expressing the answers as required later—when no keyboard is around.

8. An Additional Schoolroom Strategy.

Counselors often coach students to improve their *classroom* habits as well as study habits. Use incentives to encourage your teen to try them also, particularly in classes where your student is "having trouble with the teacher."

1. A student influences a teacher's attitude just as a teacher influences a student's.

When there is a choice, your student could sit in a seat as close to the front as possible and keep good eye contact with the teacher during presentations—just as you would practice good listening skills in a private situation.

2. Your student should be alert for a question to ask concerning the material.

A continual banter of questions that are unnecessary will do no good, but good questions help learning *and* teaching. Einstein's mother used to ask him when he came home from school, *"Did you ask any good questions today?"* If you try to ask good questions in class, you have reasons to follow the teacher's presentations more closely, and are more likely to learn.

3. Your student should occasionally talk to the teacher about the subject.

On at least a weekly basis, he should speak to the teacher about the class with a question or comparison to some aspect of other subjects or experiences.

Some people may object to the contrived nature of these suggestions, but many teens have the mistaken notion that the classroom is, or should be, a place where completely passive learning takes place.

The student needs to know that an active, assertive role is necessary. The fact is that a classroom is a social situation where exchanges are a part of the learning. The exchanges may not influence the teacher's grading, but your teen's relationship with his/her teacher will improve active learning and *that* will improve grades!

Look for, and
encourage,
all your son's or
daughter's
gifts.

Step 7: Talking About Loving, Liking and Sex

After *"How can I make good grades?"* another crucial growing-up question is, *"Mom, how can I get along with the other kids? or, How can I get the other kids to like me?"*

What heart-breaking questions! Remember Greg had this problem as part of his trouble with school. Of course there are no quick-fix answers, but a parent can pass along rules of conversation and a little advice about being interested in the other person.

Brian: *"So, Greg, how did your soccer game go?"*

Greg: *"What? Oh, it was OK."*

Brian: *"Must have been a mess with all that rain."*

Greg: *"Yeah, you should have seen the mud down at the goal; our goalie looked like a pig!"*

Brian: *"Our field still had some grass down there."*

Greg: *"Did you have to play that Kickers team?"*

Brian: *"Yes. Have you played them yet?"*

Brian has a good social habit of an occasional question. Most adults learn early that part of getting along is remembering to express some genuine unselfish interest in other people.

1. Being Loved and Being Liked.

When I am invited to give a talk at a local school's PTA or PTSA (Parents, Teachers and Students Association), I often begin with this question, "How many of you folks love your children?" My audience usually thinks this is a peculiar question but after some hesitation, most raise their hand. Then I ask, "Here's a similar question, how many of you like them?" Now the hesitations are longer but many finally raise their hands. Some may even volunteer, "I love them, but I just don't always like what they do."

With some discussion, we often agree that love is about our basic attitude toward someone, but liking is about individual behaviors.

Many parents tell their kids they love them almost every day, but they say "I like you" much less often. And most teens love their parents but they can be cynical and believe that being "likable" is different. They think it's an "inborn" characteristic and each of us must suffer with our inherited "personality." But most adults have seen a low responder like Greg "brighten up" or "turn around" with a compliment or question that shows interest in his life. How responsive and "attractive" Greg is can change. It depends on his companions and his own effort.

Brian's attractive habit is often imitated and Greg, who is not usually outgoing, picks up the topic and finally has a question of his own about "that Kickers team." Brian partly creates his own pleasant social world. Both Brian and Greg probably like each other because of the reactions they "draw out" of each other.

2. Being "Likable" is More
Than Asking Questions.

Some kids are likable for reasons way beyond appearance and "personality." We parents know that being "likable" is also made up of specific behaviors; it's a matter of *showing* some genuine unselfish *liking* of others—not by using those words, "I like you," but by approving, praising or agreeing with particular remarks or behaviors. People with this attractive habit are not only likable but also they are often imitated. Therefore, they create more attractive behavior in the people around them. Just asking a few questions, as Brian does, will not turn a person's social life around. He will need to make other efforts as well. And he may still believe that appearance is first on the *"Likable Characteristics List"* and that saying clever, cool, or funny remarks is second. But he has learned the liking principle. This characteristic is missing from the list, but usually shows up when our teen is asked who *he* likes. Usually, the answer is that he likes people who accept him, admire him, and want to spend time with *him*!

Sometimes the view from the other person's perspective leads to the discovery that: *"To be liked, I should watch out for being too critical and make an effort in my social habits."* This would include habits of asking about the other person but would also include showing concern, complimenting, expressing agreement instead of criticism, and paying attention to the listening tips of Step 1.

One mom described the difference between her daughters to me this way: *"Dianne and her sister Kelly are so different! Kelly can't stop talking and Dianne hardly says a word. It's hard to believe they were raised in the same family!*

"Last week, I picked them up from a neighborhood party and when I asked them how it went, Kelly said, 'It was great! They dropped all these

balloons on us and everyone screamed! Sally was there, Ann was there, Betty, Millie, and all the boys, Frank, Donald, David and Chris.'"

When Mom asked Dianne how it went she just said, *"It was OK. Everyone was just acting silly."* But Kelly said Dianne just stood around.

Being sociable is like many other activities: If you're good at it, you like it, and you tend to practice more of it. On the other hand, if you don't get started with others easily, you will have a little less practice and the cycle continues.

Kelly's focus is on others; she asks a lot of questions and remembers a lot of details about others that she is forever talking about. Dianne's concern is for her own security. She can't seem to think of anything safe to say.

Both girls have habits that perpetuate their attitudes. Kelly talks a great deal, she is loud, and she has learned about the other kids. Dianne doesn't talk much, she uses a soft voice, and her lack of experience with the others leaves her short on subjects to bring up.

Dianne doesn't have a "problem." She has a quiet style which sometimes makes her feel left out, but she shouldn't be given the extra burden of being told she has something wrong with her.

Her parents could give her extra social ammunition before she goes into a social situation. Adults help each other with this kind of priming quite often: *"Remember* (Mom says on the way to her office party with Dad) *my boss, Jane, has a boat out on the town lake, and she just got back from Florida. Tom bought a car like ours and Bob Teak's daughter recently made him a grandfather."*

These little bits of information will allow Dad to *"go more than half way"* in starting some conversation with Mom's co-workers— if he wants to.

Dianne needs some help with information too. She may complain that *"No one came over to me at the party,"* but the parental reflex of *"Did you go over to any of them?"* could be left off while providing whatever information might be helpful to Dianne in thinking up something to start a conversation.

Dad doesn't get a lecture on how to correct some defect in himself on the way to Mom's party, he's just provided with a better chance of doing what he wants to do with information about the others. And Dianne doesn't need more criticism either, just some long-term help as the situations come up so that if she is inclined to join in the talk, the detail of thinking of a topic will be easier.

A person who is good at socializing has many friends; they laugh at the same things and cooperate on the same tasks. They don't seem to try to please each other, they just do. The notion of being pleasing in order to get along with others may seem a little simple-minded and of little use until pleasing, agreeing, disagreeing, fighting and cooperating are seen as special cases of social rewards and mild punishments.

Most teens worry about how attractive or likable they are and certainly some primping before an outing can make a difference. However, like adults, *they* think their attractiveness is largely based on their physical appearance while their judgment of others largely depends on what the others *do!* So it follows that in order to be lik*able*, teens will have to do some lik*ing*.

Cool, moody, critical, sarcastic, angry, or bitter people make interesting characters in movies. But in real life, such characters are not well-liked because they rarely show genuine interest in others.

Without making an effort to like others, teens may have uneasy and insecure feelings. At the end of an evening with peers they probably feel they missed something. *Liking is a behavior that bears a message to the receiver*, a communication that must be sent in order to be received. Consider the following example.

Anne was nervous before John came by for her. When all her adjusting and posturing in front of the mirror was done, the best help would be to plan ways to show she liked John. Physical attractiveness is important, but the other part of being attractive is letting your friend or date know you like him or her. Anne adjusted her hair after the walk to the car and remembered not to slouch when they were riding along. She wondered if he would like her to talk about his football game.

Did Anne look at the date from John's side? If she did, she needed to show it by asking John some questions about his activities, family, job, and school work. She probably needs to do some planning of these topics before the next date. If she did like John, she didn't show it because she was too preoccupied with herself.

Did John think Anne liked him? He didn't know, so he fell into the same mistake Anne was trying to avoid in the first place—worrying about being lik*able* when a little lik*ing* would have been a better strategy. He wondered how he could impress Anne: Tell her about his football game? Drive in a daring way? Tell her about his latest success? Instead, he could have sent *his own liking messages—asking questions about Anne and complimenting her.*

Would Anne go out with him again? Maybe—if she liked him *and* if she thought she was liked! Will he call again? Anne probably thought that depended on whether he liked her or not, partly true, but it also depended on whether he thought he was liked.

3. Liking and Caring Behaviors are Attractive.

Do your family members use liking behaviors? If so, then preparing for an outing will not be a stressful time for your teen because he/she understands the basics that make a person likable.

The moments before a party can be planning time: *"At the party I want to spend time with . . . I want to talk to . . . I will show I like (fill in the blank) by . . ."*

Natural liking behaviors are consistent attention, questions, encouragement, and praise, instead of preoccupation with your own looks and interests. If you do more asking and listening than you do telling, then you're probably on the right track. Liking behaviors are habits that grow with practice and replace their opposites—silence or criticism, sarcasm, and negative comments.

Answers are impressive, but questions send the messages. A teen asks about her boyfriend's studying; he asks about her day. The messages show concern—they say, *"I'm interested in you."*

In marital counseling a common assignment for both members of the couple is to have "caring days"—days when he or she does a particular thing for his or her spouse—without being asked or expecting anything in return. What do you suppose is the request most often listed for the caring day by the wife? She says, *"I wish he would ask me about my day sometimes."* Out of all the things a husband could say, this simple wish is the most common request: personalized interest and attention.

Liking is not always returned, and two-way relationships will not balance exactly. One person will be required to go more than half-way to make it work. Socially successful and likable people put out more than their share of effort in relationships that are not ideally balanced in regard to effort.

Teens need to live with less than ideal situations at times, and discover when to accept and when to change a relationship, so as not to be unfairly used. Keeping too tight a score on how much you put yourself out for someone may keep things so even that the relationship is not appreciated. A little extra effort with persons at home or school can help smooth troubles as they come up.

When talking with your teen about why certain people are attractive, look at the behaviors of those people. Teens need to discover that Jonny Depp and Angelina Jolie are attractive in their films for a combination of reasons. Their physical characteristics are not easily copied, but look carefully at how Jonny Depp plays in his romantic scenes. He's concerned, involved, and ready to be a part of his leading lady's solution to problems.

Isn't this the fantasy, *"If he were here, he would be interested in me, too?"* When a film wishes to portray the disillusionment of the common fellow who pursues a beautiful and too-sophisticated woman, the script doesn't turn her ugly—just vain, uninterested and not capable of liking others.

4. The Media Can Help Communication About Social Skills.

Parents can use the popularity of the media with teenagers to trigger listening times. When teens and parents watch a TV show together or read the same magazine article, they can talk it over. Ask teens about the situations or characters' actions. Raise questions and then listen, instead of moralizing. Listening helps teens express their developing views; telling them what to think turns them off to the adult and the topic.

Teens and parents need variety from the daily routine and repetitious discussion topics: friends, school, and hobbies. When Mom and Dad make separate lists of topics they discuss with their teenager, TV programs often show up on the list. Parents may see TV as an intruder to parental influence, but it is also a rich source of neutral, lively subjects for conversation, especially when adults and teens watch together.

Dad: *"What did you think of that show?"*

Lisa: *"The babies stole the show! They were cute."*

Dad: *"Never cried or needed diaper changes."*

Lisa: *"Not very realistic, I guess, but I liked the way the grandpa talked to the twins."*

Dad: *"Babies need to hear a lot of talk to learn."*

TV situations are not threatening because they happen to someone else and your teen has as much information as his parent since both watched the same show. Help your teens react to and question TV shows, instead of simply letting them be passive viewers. You have your attitudes and answers to life's questions, and TV can help your teens form their views, especially when someone is there to listen and ask questions.

How the media portray sexuality is a good example. TV and magazines sell products by using material about sex to attract and keep their audience. They show sex in favorable ways, while omitting negatives. Casual and irresponsible sex seems like innocent fun with no consequences on TV, but we are not shown the realistic side with stress and need for understanding and intimacy on many levels. We are often spared any discussion of unwanted pregnancy, abortion, and the nine-month stresses of pregnancy without a husband's support—much less the anxiety of expectations and commitment. Television rarely shows the caring for a sick baby or close-ups of venereal disease.

In a short time span the media can't possibly cover the 18 years it takes to raise a person from baby to adult, or the lifetime commitment of being a parent. Parents who discuss media's omissions with their teens can raise questions about these issues occasionally and provide a means to help teens develop their own adjustment to sexuality.

5. Sexual Adjustment.

If sexual *behavior* doesn't seem to qualify for your list of priority concerns about your very young teenager, his or her *preoccupation* with the topic should earn it a place on the list. The body of a pre-teen may still be undergoing sexual development, but the mind is far ahead.

A parent-coach can help a teen with sexual adjustment by listening as he or she explores experiences, feelings, and issues. Total ignorance of sexual matters is not possible today because of peers and the media. Sex education at school can provide the objective facts, but your teen's anxieties and confusions are not likely to be trotted out for all to hear at school.

Of course, sex is an emotional issue, so a parent needs to examine his/her own feelings before trying to help a teen. Which topics are you ready to deal with? Dating? Differences between sex drives of girls and boys? Sex before marriage? Building a serious relationship? Contraception? Pregnancy? Disease? Decide what you think is important for your teen to understand first; then prepare to be a listener your teenager can count on.

Teens will decide their own sexual adjustments, but parents can influence them. Besides listening, how can you help? You could discuss a dating policy and a policy for going out with a group. The two situations usually overlap these days so you need to set your expectations of your teen in both group and one-on-one situations. What are the acceptable places to go and what places are off-limits? What days of the week are acceptable for dates and what curfews do you have?

It's always a surprise to me how few parents have straightforward answers to these questions, even after serious problems have come up. If they haven't faced up to making a few rules, how was their teen supposed to know what the rules were?

Coach your son or daughter about getting along with another person one-on-one for a whole evening. Explore relationship and sex topics with your teen and keep communication flowing.

One mother told me about a conversation with her daughter that seemed to start with her curiosity about how Mom and her husband decided to have children. But as you will see, the daughter was really looking for information about her own risks. It went like this:

Marie: *"Mom, you and Dad waited a long time to have me and Andy, didn't you?"*

Mom: *"Well, Marie, it was a long time, but we weren't waiting."*

Marie: *"You weren't waiting?"*

Mom: *"We wanted children, we just...didn't."*

Marie: *"So it took a long time?"*

Mom: *"Yes, sometimes it does."*

Marie: *"So you didn't have a baby right off, right?"*

Mom: *"No, not right off."*

Marie: *"Lauren said you could have a baby after... just one time—she's always spouting off."*

Mom: *"It could happen right off."*

Marie: *"But it wouldn't, if you are careful."*

Mom had a choice at this point. She could have said, *"Marie, I know what you're thinking and let me tell you you'd better stop thinking about anything like that! You could get pregnant easily, get a disease, and anyway it's wrong to think about getting into a relationship like that at your age."*

Another choice for Mom is to continue this "objective" conversation, talking about risks and their probabilities. Mom kept the conversation away from a confrontation, and Marie eventually asked for her mother's opinion as well as information. That's the best Mom could hope for in this talk. So it went like this:

Mom: *"It's hard to be careful in that situation."*

Marie: *"But if you use the right thing..."*

Mom: *"What's the right thing?"*

Marie: *"Well, you know, a condom."*

Mom: *"Still a chance of getting pregnant."*

Marie: *"Well, how about something else? The pill."*

Mom: *"That works pretty well, but it doesn't protect you from diseases."*

Marie: *"Both then. Why not both?"*

Mom: *"Both is good. Staying on the pill too long is not good."*

Marie: *"You could use timing."*

Mom: *"Not very reliable, that was our problem in having you kids in the first place."*

Marie: *"This is too complicated."*

Mom: *"Well, in a long-term relationship you can talk this all out and it's not embarrassing, but in dating, the practical part is too embarrassing to talk about and that's where the trouble starts."*

Marie: *"I guess."*

You may still be worried about Marie. The talk doesn't end with much assurance about what she's going to do next. But the talk never had a chance of guaranteeing Marie's future; the best Mom could hope for is to provide more guidance to keep Marie on the right path. This is not a place for an efficiency-oriented demand or proclamation and, a talk, too short on facts will only lead Marie to ask someone else.

One mother told me, *"I don't have time for all that dancing around. I just tell them."* I would advise making time for dancing around— take time away from something less important. Otherwise, you'll never learn what it was they wanted you to tell them.

"Mom, I think I have a problem." We all hope this problem turns out to be simple and not too serious—maybe a tough homework assignment or a fellow student with bad social skills. We hope it is not the forever life-changing announcement. But you might have a moment of fear if you have heard the statistics concerning teenage pregnancies.

How should a parent talk to his or her teen about this sensitive subject? Avoiding the topic and withholding information will not postpone the risks. "If I don't know how to do it safely, I won't do it," is not a popular teenage motto.

A conversation too short, too fast, or with too many family members chiming in is not likely to help. Pick a good time when you can go slowly with time to listen in a one-on-one situation.

Make sure your teen gets the facts straight. One teenage girl told me, "I want to be safe. If I have sex, I always sneak one of Mom's pills the next day."

In the United States, teenage daughters have a 1 in 20 chance of becoming pregnant, and both sons and daughters are at three times that risk for sexually transmitted diseases. This is not just a "girl problem."

Before you talk with your teen, a little self-inspection is in order. What do you want to say to your son about his responsibilities in a relationship? What message does he get in the non-serious moments about his (and his Dad's) attitude toward women and sex? What do you want to say about contraceptives? Abortion? At what age do you want to bring these topics up?

The fathers who cause high school teen pregnancies are usually long out of high school themselves, so caution your teenager daughter about these "older kids" and talk to your 17-and-something son about this temptation.

Alcohol is the most common excuse young women give for making the big mistake. What attitudes should a parent model on this subject?

When it's time to get serious, remember all those listening skills. Keep your pace of conversation slow. Reserve your answers and advice until your teen has a chance to express his/her opinion. Before you give all your guidance, you need to learn what they know, or think they know.

Remember that one session on this topic will not be enough, so conclusions with "You should...," "Don't ever...," and "Be careful not to..." don't have to be said in the first conversation. Take your time on this subject, it may be the most important part of your influence on your son's or daughter's future.

6. Create a Dating Policy.

Studies link early one-on-one dating, at ages 13-15, to early sexual experiences. Some parents encourage going out in groups as an alternative to the one-on-one situation. Talk with parents of other teens for suggestions and support.

If your teen belongs to a club or interest group, their activities provide opportunities for outings with the opposite sex, without one-on-one pairings.

Most teenagers and many adults feel the pressure when going it alone for a whole evening of four or five hours of one-on-one dating. Trying to keep the conversation and activity going well can be an uncomfortable experience.

Teens are usually more comfortable in a group situation where the social demands are neither intimate nor continuous. In a group, you are not always responsible for conversation or ideas of what to do. That kind of social sophistication comes later. But in a group, when things get slow with one person, you can always turn to another. On your own in a one-on-one situation and without social competence, it's easy to select a dangerous activity by default.

Coach about dating customs. Since Mom and Dad's courting days, customs have changed, but your teenager still needs your guidance to feel comfortable. We've already stressed attention and questions as listening skills between friends.

Your son needs to realize, as old-fashioned as it sounds, that he is still expected to take the lead to plan a successful evening. You may be able to help with this when you discuss transportation or car use. A son needs to plan something he enjoys and ask his date about her likes.

A teen can help make dates successful by being honest: *"You choose the show, and I'll choose the snack place for later, but I don't do horror movies!"* or *"I guess we could go to that movie, but I give it a 6. What do you think of the comedy at the other cinema instead?"* Ways to compromise will be learned.

Both persons are probably thinking *"I need to act right!"* and they need to see that the best plan is to let their dating partner know about their own feelings, likes and dislikes. Then with some high-priority choices handy, an agreement is likely. When your son or daughter leaves for a date, encourage some planning of what they are going to do. Then build confidence with praise for looks and wishes for a good time. Self-confidence is fragile, so no last-minute criticism, no parting shots.

Did you have someone to listen when your outing was good and you wanted to share the experience? Or when it was a disaster and you wondered why things went wrong? Your teen needs a reliable listener. Chances are when he/she comes home, it will be a bad time for you to bring up your concerns, so other things will have to wait while "teen-listening-time" goes ahead. Weave in some stories of your own best and worst dates to show that the two of you have common ground.

7. Set Priorities, Raise Questions and Listen.

Parents report success from initial talks with teens when they opened communication lines. The important part, and the hardest part, for your teen, is listening. Parents want to make their cases for postponing sex, but your teen can probably only tolerate one point before feeling frustrated at being the listener.

With Daughters. Mom brought up building ideal relationships with Caitlin while they were walking around the lake. Mom had thought about it and had even written down her ideas. She knew she wouldn't be able to say everything, but she had her ideas in mind: building a relationship of knowledge and trust with someone of the opposite sex takes a lot of time, time to learn the other person's interests, values, behaviors, goals, and dreams. Trust and commitment increase slowly from small bits of time spent together. The eventual bond of marriage is built on many times of trust and caring.

Mom: *"What do you want from an ideal relationship with a boy?"*

Caitlin: *"I don't know. Gee, I guess respect for me and my ideas. Someone who is there for me, someone who likes sports, and has a sense of humor."*

Mom: *"I think respect is real important too. And trust. I learned to trust your dad when I saw him every day and we talked, over snacks, between classes."*

Caitlin: *"You and Dad knew each other less than a year before you were married."*

Mom: *"Yes, but we spent time together every day talking about our pasts, present, and futures. We came to know the real persons under our college student shells."*

Caitlin: *"I'll never find a man like Dad. The guys I know don't begin to have it together.''*

Mom: *"Men take time to grow up."*

Caitlin: *"They have a long way to go!"*

And Caitlin does too. But she has Mom and Dad to listen and share her journey.

Dad should plan his listening session with Caitlin, too. He wants her to understand that when boys have sex, they don't always feel commitment, whereas girls often think having sex *means* commitment. Also, he wants her to realize that contraception before marriage is more likely to be used incorrectly, but teens don't like to hear that, because it implies they're not smart. So instead of trying to get across his whole agenda, Dad will try to do something much harder, be a neutral, encouraging listener most of the time.

Dad: *"In your family life class, did they discuss differences in the sex drive between girls and guys?"*

Caitlin: *"Gosh, we heard more about physical differences than drives. But our teacher said boys have stronger feelings about sex than girls. Do you think that's right?"*

Dad: *"Well, different anyway. Boys have sex on their minds a lot of the time!"*

Caitlin: *Yeah, the boys make so much of it when someone says something even a little bit sexy in class."*

Dad: *"Guys can be more inconsiderate and selfish than girls about sex. It's good to know that."*

If Caitlin continues to find a reliable listener in Dad, he may be able to help her understand her own sexual adjustment and the opposite sex.

With Sons. Parents need to keep the lines open with sons as well as daughters. Boys appreciate dads and moms taking time to listen and ask questions to help their sons' sexual adjustments too.

Before Todd had his first serious date alone, he and Dad spent a weekend camping together. Dad noted the important things he wanted Todd to know:

• If you postpone sex you get to know the other person without the stress, preoccupation and anxiety of sex with no real relationship.

• Waiting means you can both trust each other about sex, and you don't have to hide what you're doing from friends or parents.

• If you wait for sex, you have a better chance avoiding an unwanted pregnancy, abortion, or disease.

• The sex drive is a very strong want, but it's a short-run need; building a relationship of trust and caring is both a short and long-run need.

Dad: *"What does a girl want in going out?"*

Todd: *"A good time, I guess, and a lot of talking."*

Dad: *"Just to get to know you."*

Todd: *"I guess."*

Dad: *"You talk a lot on dates?"*

Todd: *"Yeah."*

Dad: *"Do you ask a lot about her?"*

Todd: *"Sometimes. Not much, I guess."*

Dad: *"People like someone who asks them about themselves—just as you like it."*

Dad's on his way to helping Todd learn about relationships by asking questions and letting Todd explore his problem. Todd may even discover that his need is not as simple as just sex, but includes companionship and intimacy at many levels.

Questions and stories help keep communication flowing.

Dad: *"How was your date?"*

Todd: *"OK, but Jennifer and I just don't get along so well anymore."*

Dad: *"You're having some rough spots now."*

Todd: *"Yeah, she likes those horror movies. We always seem to do her thing."*

Dad: *"What did she think of your new shirt?"*

Todd: *"OK, I guess. She didn't say. Sounds like she doesn't care, doesn't it?"*

Dad: *"A little."* Dad's listening helped and when Todd is ready, he'll find someone who cares more.

Mom: *"How was the movie last night, Susan?"*

Susan: *"Pretty good. Coming out we started talking to Jim and his friends."*

Mom: *"He's a senior, right?"*

Susan: *"Yeah, and he comes on strong. They gave us a ride back and he was all over me! He's nice though. I wish he'd ask me out, but he won't unless I, you know, do more."*

Mom: *"I had a boyfriend like that once."*

Susan: *"What did you do?"*

Mom: *"Well, not much. I told him where I stood and we got along, but it was always a running battle. He'd try something and I'd always put him off. It didn't last long."*

Susan: *"He stopped asking you out?"*

Mom: *"Yes, we were both tired of the struggle. I dated someone else and 'Come-On-Strong' looked for someone more... willing."*

Finding out that Mom went through similar experiences, Susan feels more confident.

Let's look at two more cases, Kendra and Derek.

Mom: *"How was your date last night?"*

Kendra: *"Oh, fine, I guess."*

Mom: *"Just 'fine'?"*

Kendra: *"Tom and I always end up in the same old argument."*

Mom *"Really? About what?"*

Kendra *"Well, you know, like about how far to go."*

Up to this point Mom has been pretty neutral and not argumentative. But conversations with teens can have a turning point if a parent signals her intention to be authoritarian, or sympathetic and helpful. Let's have Mom come up with a question that keeps the conversation in Kendra's control.

Mom: *"What kinds of arguments come up?"* (Mom interested, not angry or opinionated, yet.)

Kendra: *"Oh, he says it won't make any problems."*

Mom: *"No problems? Just like a man! There are lots of problems. For example . . ."*

Well, Mom has slipped into a lecture mode, and Kendra is probably moving toward the door, so let's take this one back and replace it with . . .

Mom: *"Well, I guess you think there would be some problems."* (Again the control of the conversation goes back to Kendra.)

Kendra: *"Tom thinks there's no problem. Right, for him, maybe!"*

Mom: *"Right."*

Kendra: *"Yeah, it's no risk for him!"*

Mom: *"Being pregnant, you mean."*

Kendra: *"Yes!"*

Mom: *"Good point."*

Kendra's position seems stronger now and straighter in her mind. No need for closing arguments. Let Mom and Kendra walk out in agreement. It's the most we could hope for and extracting a promise would not have as great an influence as Kendra's own conviction that she is right.

Talk of sex with an open channel for your teen to talk, discover, and state opinions will result in a less confused person who is more likely to make reasonable decisions.

Mom's talk with Kendra can expand to the general topic of relationships so that the role of sex for good and bad can be understood. How has it worked out for Kendra's other friends? Let's look at a father-son example.

Derek: *"Girls can be such a pain!"*

Dad: *"How so?"*

Derek: *"Well, they don't know what they want. They want to go out, but then they get, well, stand-offish."*

Dad: *They don't want to go far enough?"*

Derek: *"Well, yeah. It's not like we're doing, you know, everything!"*

Dad: *"You don't want to do that?"*

Derek: *"Well, I mean I don't expect it."*

Dad: *"Until later."*

Derek: *"Yeah."*

Dad: *"You know that you could get in a lot of trouble with sex."*

That's too argumentative. Let's give Dad the same chance we gave Mom. Dad seemed to get by the choice between authoritarian and helpful at first, but now he's getting ready to lecture. Dad's last remark starts with *"you"* and it is not hard to figure what's coming. So in Dad's second try let's give him some *"it"* rather than *"you"* statements. That should provide a little less confrontation and a little more learning.

Dad: *"It can be a lot of trouble."*

Derek: *"Well, you have to be careful."*

Dad: *"You're right. But I was thinking of the social trouble."*

Derek: *"I don't get it."*

Dad: *"Don't people think of sex as a kind of permanent commitment?"*

Derek: *"I guess. That was the problem with Tom and Kendra. They broke up in a big argument."*

Dad: *"I guess that's one of the problems. Sometimes sex makes a relationship much deeper for one person than the other. Especially if they barely know each other."*

Derek: *"Well, you should be sure of the relationship."*

Dad: *"It takes time."*

Derek *"Yeah."*

The "lot of trouble" Dad had in mind in the first reaction can now come up by discussing other people, not Derek. For example, how has it been for Derek's friends, Tom and Kendra? How does the media handle relationships, sex roles, and "trouble"? Exploring the one-sidedness of TV can appeal to a teen's occasional negative focus. You hardly ever get a close look at a diaper change on TV. Realistic decisions will come from realistic views provided by long, open conversations.

8. A Disposition Creates
Its Own Surroundings.

When kids imitate bad dispositions, they must use threats in a subtle way because they are less powerful than adults. Fighting back, a teen puts off her parents or teacher and may put off their requests for work. That reaction creates further negative reactions from adults who are viewed by many teenagers as confirmation of their cynical expectations of others.

Consider Lisa at age 14. She has developed a negative attitude and is often cynical and pessimistic at school. You can imagine that it is easy to feel uncomfortable or aggravated around her. At home with her family, Lisa receives a bit more attention, but the aggravation and frustration that others feel usually shows through:

Mom: *"How was school today, Lisa?"*

Lisa: *"OK."*

Mom: *"Well, tell me about it!"*

Lisa: *"Do you have to know everything?"*

Mom: *"I was just interested."*

Lisa: *"Just leave me alone."*

Lisa is a non-rewarder. She is self-centered, thinking little of others and asking little of them. She's no trouble, but somehow she's still troublesome. She brings out the worst in others and then reacts to that by getting worse herself. The cycle continues. To break the cycle, someone will have to be big enough to not play the game. That requires love, because it means performing good social behavior with no support from Lisa, possibly with punishment from her instead.

Lisa herself might grow up enough to be the "someone" who will break the cycle someday. However, in the short run, it's not likely that anyone will spontaneously change. The most likely adjustment Lisa will make is to *"give them back what they give me."* If they give you bad behavior, let them taste their own medicine! Punishment for punishment; silence for silence, or even, silence for punishment (*"They won't get anything out of me!"*).

Lisa may extend her use of punishment and later, learn to use warnings of punishments to coerce her teachers or parents. If demands are not met, she increases the intensity of the demand, and then she uses nastiness or possibly a tantrum. It's coercion.

Adults may learn to avoid all this punishment by giving in early. Giving in serves as reward to Lisa, but it also rewards the adults because they successfully avoid Lisa's escalating nastiness. It is a common parent-teen relationship where *the teen's bad behavior is rewarded* by getting undeserved privileges or avoiding work, and a parent's "giving in" is rewarded by successfully avoiding the threat of more bad behavior. It's a case of negative reinforcement for parents and positive reinforcement for Lisa.

In order to have an effect on Lisa, the adults around her will need to model and maintain a more positive disposition than Lisa does.

9. Teenagers and Parents Learn Each Other's Habits.

A teen's most common reaction to everyday problems will probably be to imitate people he or she lives with at home and in school. Children becoming teens imitate *styles* of adults more often than specific adult behaviors.

Attitudes toward others, conversational style and temperament are the durable characteristics of teachers and parents that are copied. The result is a general disposition made up of habits and styles of encouragement and punishment from others. A teen can easily acquire a disposition almost entirely from the family air!

The disposition to punish and correct others can be learned just as easily as the disposition to encourage others. But to learn to police your disposition is a difficult task. There are no planned consequences for *you* as an adult, and adults change by practice with encouragements just as children do. So whether or not anything can be done about the dispositions in your home depends on the answer to the question *"Can these parents control themselves through conscientious effort and through feedback from their partner?"*

The positive approach emphasizes reward—not necessarily material ones, but approval, praise, smiling, etc. The job becomes more pleasant for you as a parent and leaves you with a teen who is still informative, friendly, responsive, and not always wanting to go somewhere else!

A positive reaction is much more efficient because it says that out of all the things he could have done, this is one of the right ones. A rewarding reaction is more difficult for parents, however, because they must take time to decide what they want to reward and what comment or material thing to use as reward. We're more likely to already know what we want to punish and how we would do it.

If you are a single parent, it may be all the more difficult to say to yourself, as a spouse might: *"Don't let me pick on the kids; stop me and point out my good reactions."*

The family's disposition can also be influenced by making plans about the small everyday social behaviors of kids. Many parents have developed a poor disposition in their teen by not planning the limits of *their* demands as carefully as they plan the kids' limits. A teen makes so many mistakes, we want him to do so many things right, and he can do so many things wrong. Without a plan, parents may not be sure what is right and what is wrong or where the limits are, so they are constantly after the kids for this behavior or that one.

10. Amazing Copies!

"Isn't it amazing how mother and daughter are alike!" said Ms. Jones. *"That woman reading at the end of the back row just <u>has</u> to be Regina's mother. Regina even reads at lunch time!"*

"Yes, it's unbelievable," whispered Ms. Miller. *"And I would recognize Bobby Comic's father anywhere. His attempt at a little joke. And Lisa Sour's father sulking while he waits for the meeting to start. You wouldn't believe such details could be inherited!"*

Ms. Jones and Ms. Miller are 7th and 8th grade teachers at PTA

back-to-school night. They told me that when they were waiting for the first-of-the-year meeting to start, they often played a
"Match the Parents Game." It's been their favorite for years and
they find their guesses to be very accurate. Their success with
matching parents and students comes, in part, from physical similarities that are inherited, but the way the students act is partly a
copy of their parents' styles. It's a hint the teachers find very useful
in their game. How talkative, pleasant, sarcastic, or happy each parent and student is, helps the teachers make their matches and they
are very successful.

Everyone contributes to the family atmosphere. Each con-
tributor also follows the lead of the others at times—modeling,
imitating, and reacting in a manner appropriate to past experience.
Respectful, loving parental reactions are copied by their teenagers
in their responses back to their parents and to others. The social
habits of the kids and their parents recycle through the family,
creating the general atmosphere as these habits are repeated.

"If I don't know
how to do it safely, I
won't do it," is not
a popular teenage
motto.

Step 8: Encourage Their Contributions to the Family

The school skills, social skills, and domestic skills your teen learns need to be put to use right away. The more they know, the more likely they are to take up the activities of a full life, and the self-esteem they experience from being useful will provide some of the protection they'll need when they encounter dangerous temptations.

1. Coach Teens to Find Life's Variety.

Everyone seeks variety in life, but teens seem to require heavy doses just to feel good about themselves and to keep from falling into a funk. *"Do they have to do something every night? Why is continual entertainment necessary? Can't teens just sit down and relax for a while?"* parents may ask.

The internet, TV and movies give teen's romantic notions of all the adventure and excitement that might be passing them by. They have already developed many adult capabilities and have an amazing amount of energy available. They also have a lot of ideas about the opportunities out there. Instead of satisfaction from everyday events, they seek dramatic happenings to fulfill their need for action.

Adults have discovered the satisfaction of doing everyday activities: job accomplishments, house and yard work, bills and taxes to pay, shopping for a new computer, book, or gadget. These chores are not the adventurous activities a teenager has in mind, but they do provide a need we all have for worthwhile actions.

Your teen's need to "do something" is usually not specific and needs some adult direction. Having several things you want to do helps you get through a slow day or week. Activities don't need to be tennis, skiing, movies, or going out with the gang; they can be puttering, shopping, or fixing things. These alternatives usually don't start out as fun, but they do get rid of the blues. Obsessions with music, video games, or TV may become the substitute for the adventure your teen misses in a world with limited opportunities for him or her. They may also be symptoms of needs for expanded personal responsibilities that provide personal pride.

Fourteen-year-old Maya had a big day coming up: she would turn in the social studies project she had worked on for a week and give a short talk about her science project. The band was meeting, and she would play her trumpet. After school she had to shop for shoes and help make supper. Later, she and Dad were going to change the oil on the car. Nothing very adventurous, but a schedule of activities that helped her feel good.

Thirteen-year-old Brent was thinking about his upcoming day at school: he expected flack for his late reading report, and math was confusing because he had skipped the homework for two nights. Even when he was not in trouble at school he had a hard time focusing on his work. After school, his friends were practicing football but he was ineligible until he raised his grades. His hobbies, biking and music, were on hold until he fixed his bike and cell phone. At a peak of energy in his life, Brent needs adult encouragement to do his schoolwork and chores.

2. The Most Dangerous Thing on Earth is a Human Being with Nothing to Do.

All kings, army officers, college presidents, and teachers learn this principle early or suffer the consequences. So again, planning incentives for productive activity is needed because if some structuring is not provided for a teen at loose ends, over the undirected years he or she will come up with some undesirable habits. Teens may entertain themselves in very bothersome ways if they have no responsibilities to fulfill, no opportunities for useful activity, and no reason to expect any benefit from their choices.

The constant watching here is for a teen's opportunities. It's not necessary to see that she always has something to do. Everyone needs a break and has their own pace of living. But ongoing responsibilities provide something to do when the urge hits them—something to be proud of and something that is a source of self-esteem.

A teen needs help beginning adult chores and focus on important activities such as schoolwork and fulfilling hobbies. Without some direction, you can expect complaining and escape to less worthwhile time fillers, such as TV, lap tops, and mobile devices. Possibly your companionship in the chore would help: do the dishes with me, not for me; work in the yard with me, and shop for groceries with me.

We adults have learned the activities we like, and we enjoy the therapeutic effects. How can Brent's mother pass along these insights? Brent's reaction to her suggestions is not likely to be encouraging, and Mom will have to continue to help with little appreciation from him. Frequent positive feedback for small successes here and now will help Brent try alternatives and practice important skills.

"Brent, if you show me your completed math and science work, you can go to the ice rink with Roger." Mom had experienced so much trouble with Brent and his schoolwork before that now she insists he *earn* privileges. After her complaints, he always argued, *"When I leave middle school I will do a lot better!"* Not satisfied with promises in the far-off future, Mom insisted that his incentives come as a result of his efforts now.

Mom checks frequently with Brent's teachers to ensure that his work is up-to-date. Brent responded to the incentives, and they helped him focus on important behaviors and earn a feeling of pride for his efforts.

3. Practice, Man, Practice.

Many jokesters know the old one about the visitor who stopped a native New Yorker and asked how to get to Carnegie Hall. The New Yorker answered, *"Practice, man, practice!"*

When practice has been lacking, painful experiences are ahead for a teen about to leave the nest. Life has disadvantages awaiting a girl with little experience deciding what to eat, when to eat, what to wear and when to wear it, what to say when making a dental appointment, and how to distinguish between "free" and "on credit"—a distinction lost on many college credit card holders now in trouble.

Without practice in all of these skills in her teenage years she will feel a little inadequate, dependent, and may question her own worth. As she leaves the family's protection, she will need to learn fast in a situation that is not as loving as her family, and she will bring little confidence to the task.

As girls and boys who are unpracticed leave for college or work or both, their parents may blurt out a last-minute barrage of instructions. Practicing to be an adult, requires a lot of parent-planned practice. Whether practice was left out because it seemed to risk too many mistakes, take too much time in the frantic family activities, or was withheld to protect a teen from life's drudgeries, in the end, parents realize there are consequences to reap and now they rush to get in all those cautions: *"Be sure you brush your teeth, get your rest, open a checking account, and choose friends wisely!"*

The first experience of being away from home can be all the more difficult and lonely if our offspring-now-sprung has little confidence in deciding when to study and when to rest, because parents always settled those questions before.

Many of my college students go to our campus counselor with the complaint that no one seems to care about them at the big university. A great deal of the "care" the student misses should have been gradually withdrawn years ago to make room for practice and pride in one's self. The only place there is love enough for all that practice is in the family.

One boy came to me to sign out of college. *"Sorry you're leaving,"* I said.

"I just can't handle all the problems."

"What problems?"

"Little things. For example, I can't get my laundry done."

"Why not?"

"Well, I went down to our laundry room and there were all these cycles and settings. Even my underwear came out pink."

"You could throw the laundry away and buy all new stuff," I joked, but then I added, *"I was just joking,"* when I saw his tears of frustration

welling up and he turned to leave..

"*I know, but I couldn't. I don't know my size!*"

For 19 years, the little number rode on the back elastic of his underwear and followed him around with other little notes about washing instructions, but he had no need for them as long as Mom was there. But now she wasn't.

Many of my students managed to survive the passage from home to campus despite painful evenings learning their size and how to use a washing machine. So lack of this practice doesn't always cause a great deal of permanent damage.

But in many cases, a critical period of the teenage years that could have nurtured a feeling of self-worth and comfort with life was missed. Later, *complete* development of self-confidence may be difficult to secure.

4. Practice Makes Almost Perfect.

All of us can remember the idea of practice in school work and we understand the necessity for practice when teaching something new. But when we are not teaching such things as tying shoelaces, playing the piano, or learning to drive a car, we often forget the importance of practice. It applies just as well to bed-making, washing clothes or dishes, time management and how to get along with others.

If Mom and Dad do these jobs for their son, he gets no practice. It is easy to be overprotective and slow down learning: "*I'll take your library book back,*" "*I'll get your running shoes repaired,*" "*I'll call for your dental appointment—you wait.*" and "*I'll be your time manager, you just do what I say.*" Some parents will protest that if they let their teen do these things, mistakes will happen. he'll be fined for late library books, never get the shoes fixed, say the wrong thing on the phone and waste time until deadlines pass. All true. And each parent will have to make the judgment—is he ready? Not, *"Is she ready to be perfect?"* But, *"Is he ready to gain something from practice?"* We shouldn't wait until a teen is ready to do it *without a flaw*. That may take forever.

Another advantage to early practice is that your student-teen can gain much to be proud of *now*. It's true you can't rely on a 13-year-old to choose a perfect diet, yet even 35-year-olds don't have perfect diets. But you do need to give over responsibilities so that you can guarantee your opportunities to encourage your teen's progress. A wise parent creates practice, not just for learning, but to improve a teen's *self-respect* and confidence. As one young teen told me, *"I'm not just a kid. I can do a lot around the house."*

5. Practice and Reward.

Perhaps you found that, in learning to play a musical instrument, even practice was not enough. And yet practice was enough to perfect your handwriting. What are the differences between your brief piano experience and your "learned forever" handwriting?

When learning to improve your handwriting, you were rewarded not only for the hours of practice but also for the first little successes. You wrote your own name, a friend's name, then a note to a friend and a letter to grandpa. The improvements were useful, shared with others, they had value and practice continued.

But too often the first improvements in playing the scales on the piano produce little or no admiration, they seem of little use, even to the one doing the practice, and scales are a long way from the performance dreamed of. Sometimes piano lessons are successful because learning a favorite piece or popular song was part of the early training. If that consideration was a part of your music lessons, practice probably continued. If not, you may have quit, but I bet you still remember the pieces you liked and the ones that attracted some attention.

If rewards come early for the first little successes, then a person will want to practice more small steps. If only big successes attract encouragement and little improvements are ignored, one can become discouraged along the way, *"I'll never be really good."* It is not the pot at the end of the rainbow that keeps the practice going, it's the next pat on the back or penny in the bank—and for some tasks, parents need to be frequent and generous with back-pats and pennies.

The most common error when beginning to teach something new is to demand too much for too little. The first steps need big rewards—not necessarily money or tangible goodies, but plenty of encouragement.

"This sounds like bribery," you might say. *"Shouldn't they do most of these things without contrived rewards? Can't they do it just for the love of learning? Some kids are good and do what is expected without 'rewards,' don't they?"*

To answer these questions we need to realize that those good kids *were* rewarded—socially and with parental respect and praise. Some start early and well, with plenty of encouragement. They perform so well that they receive a great deal of praise and a snowballing effect begins that is an advantage for years to come. If a teen starts off with good encouragement and is well "rewarded," he keeps going; if he keeps going, he is further rewarded and so on.

Snowballing can work the other way also. Some don't receive rewards or attention for the first steps to good performance and learning. They don't expect praise because little was given in the past. If their parents threaten them, they might do just the minimum out of fear, but even the minimum will disappear when the threat is gone.

So without someone providing positive feedback, a teen misses out on encouragement and slows up or stops practicing altogether. Without practice, more opportunities for encouragement will be missed, and even less practice will result. As he falls further behind his parents' expectations, any performance that should have been encouraged earlier will be ignored because *"He should have done that long ago."* Now even meager attempts at catching up are discouraged. If his success is viewed as "too late," the "pay" may be nothing. Without some "pay" he will fall further back.

Stanley: *"These math problems are really hard."*

Mom: *"You're really getting into some hard stuff now."*

Stanley: *"Yeah, they take too long."*

Mom: *"You got the first one, you should show your brother."*

Stanley: *"Hey, Larry, look at this!"*

Larry: *"We did those last year."*

Mom: *"And they were hard, but Stanley got the first one."*

Stanley: *"I'll try one more."*

Mom's intention here is to show respect for what Stanley has done so far, and a little encouragement to show it off. Larry doesn't help much, but Mom remains on the positive side and Stanley puts in a little more effort.

Does this mean that all successful parents are secret bribers? No. First, these words are unfair because they imply a situation in which a person is trying to corrupt another person so that he or she will do something wrong and usually illegal. Second, we are not involved in "bribery" just because we expect some return for our effort. No one works for nothing. Volunteers don't work for money, but for the satisfaction that is rooted in the reactions of others. The reward may be as subtle as another person saying we are doing well or as obvious as salaries for Congress and fees for doctors and lawyers.

On one occasion a father rejected my suggestion for encouraging his son's homework by saying, *"He should be grown up enough to want to do the right thing without some payoff."* When it came out that Dad was on strike for more money *and* was getting support from a union strike fund, his defense was that *he was an adult*. With his experience and knowledge he felt he deserved a tangible reward (as well as admiration and respect). His son, without experience or success, was to take his responsibilities for the love of it.

So in addition to practice, we need recognition, respect, encouragement and rewards. With all these right ingredients, success will come and, along with it, the self-respect.

Taylor told funny stories from his school experiences many evenings at dinner. Family laughter and comments made him feel good, and during supper he trusted his family not to raise embarrassing questions about his school performance. Ellen got a lot of recognition during suppertime too, but it took the form of arguments with Dad. Disagreements were a habit because she received little notice for her accomplishments, and she had learned to start arguments and settle for the unpleasant attention.

Taylor: *"So, John was looking the other way as he went around the corner at the end of the hall, and he ran right into Ms. Letty pushing a lab cart with crickets in a box. Boom! The crickets escaped when the cart was bumped and he said, 'Oh! I'm sorry. I didn't mean to dump your crickets. I hope it doesn't bug you!'"*

Dad: *"What a story! What happened?"*

Taylor: *"John and Ms. Letty were jumping around chasing the crickets and some other kids helped too, but some were yelling 'Oh! Get them away! Don't touch them!' Everyone started laughing."*

Ellen: *"I don't think that's so funny. Ms. Letty could have been hurt and so could the crickets."*

Dad: *"Don't be a grump. It's just one of those harmless accidents that adds humor to the day."*

Ellen: *"Big joke!"*

Dad: *"You ought to lighten up!"*

Since we understand that payoffs have a big influence on a teenager's behaviors, we can ask, *"How can I support the actions I want from my teenager?"* and *"How can I get rid of behavior I don't want by removing support?"*

In Ellen's case, her father could listen and ask neutral questions, instead of challenging Ellen at the supper table. Instead of arguing, he needs to *go more than halfway* to encourage her appropriate contributions. The effort is essential to change.

When Ellen said, *"I don't think it's so funny. Ms. Letty could have been hurt . . ."* she signaled the start of her arguing behavior. Dad could have decided to control his reaction to Ellen's negative behavior. Perhaps his next comment could have focused on the neutral part of Ellen's remark. Dad could have said, *"Yes, Ms. Letty could have been hurt and the crickets squished."*

Ellen: *"Yes, and John was lucky everyone was so busy catching crickets he didn't get into big trouble. Next time maybe he'll look where he's going."*

Taylor: *"That's not funny."*

Dad: *"Not funny, but a good idea for John."*

This strategy requires close attention from Dad and that means some planning and singling out of goals. The adult thoughtfulness of Dad and Mom can lead to the cure for poor teen behaviors.

Let's look at another example of specific behaviors and incentives that are related to school achievement.

Dan carried home a great report card. He put it between the pages of his social studies book to keep it clean on the way; it had to be neat when he showed it to Mom.

"How was school today?"

"Pretty good—we got our report cards. Want to see?"

"You bet I want to see!"

Dan brought out the improved card with a smile, and Mom looked over the contents. *"Up in math. Up in English. You didn't go down in anything! Really good! I bet our sessions after supper have helped. You try so hard."*

Mom's support of good behavior was important. She was as encouraging as she could be of Dan's success, and her compliments must have been a motivation for him. Additional credit probably goes to the encouragement in the sessions after supper.

There were two behaviors in this story: bringing home the report card *and* doing homework. The behavior that benefited from support was the **present** behavior. When Dan came in with his card, he was encouraged, he certainly looked forward to it, and everyone enjoyed it. After supper, a homework session will begin, and Mom will continue her positive attention and focus on the other crucial behavior—doing homework. Dan was getting help in **both** places right where he needed it.

Poor report cards and poor homework make up a pair of behaviors. The temptation in this case is to give punishment for poor report cards, with only a hope that the punishment will "spill over" to more homework effort. Another tactic is to try punishment for both report cards and poor homework. This unhappy solution seems to be a trap for bad things getting worse.

The situation requires an upbeat, positive side. We will need specifics about homework and Mom has a collection of responses that help Dan along with the task.

6. Teen Contributions to the Family.

Parents should gradually expand their teen's responsibility in helping with family decisions, entertainments, and chores. A continuing emphasis on membership in the family confirms your teen's roots and value as a family member.

Sharing decision-making with a teen provides practice with a skill that will be useful for a lifetime. Teens have already gained experience in creating family norms, rules, and consequences. It is rewarding to them to share in planning family purchases, trips, and chores.

How can family members spend time together and yet let everyone do something he/she enjoys? A family meeting in advance of the event can help. It can build excitement about family outings and allow each person to have a say in some aspect of the plans. For example, a trip to a different city might include a side trip selected by each member: visits to a museum, a landmark, a cemetery, a famous store, and a show. A lot of conversation about the choices will add to the anticipation, so instead of a passive, backseat passenger, we might have an excited learner. Afterwards, everyone will still be talking about each other's choices.

Now, after we get back, how can we split up the family work so everyone shares? Input from everyone makes the plan for sharing work a winner. Try assignments, then evaluate and make changes. Enthusiastic cheering and payoffs keep family members motivated. Responsibilities for teens might include shopping, putting away groceries, preparing meals and cleaning up, cleaning house, and caring for the yard and car.

It's an exciting, challenging time when teens reach for adult privileges and responsibilities. Parents improve their teen's chances for happiness and success as adults by gradually allowing them to master self-care and survival skills through contributions to the family.

7. Making Rules Together.

Making rules together means getting household members together to talk over their needs, feelings, and actions and then to turn them into livable agreements.

When poor teen behavior occurs, such as not doing homework, try out one of the alternatives to punishment discussed in Step 4. But if the wanted behavior doesn't come and you give it high priority, then it's time to discuss the situation at a family meeting and make a rule together.

Teenagers and younger children are very capable of understanding and discussing situations important to their lives and families. Everyone in the household old enough to participate should be at the family meeting.

Mom and Dad were upset about a call from Greg's math teacher. She said Greg had not done homework for a week, so Greg's parents focused on planning for a change in the long term. Dad brought up the problem at lunch.

Dad: *"Greg, your math teacher called to say you need to do your homework. You're getting a deficiency because you haven't done homework for a week."*

Greg: *"That math homework isn't important. I already know how to figure it. My other assignments are the ones I need to do. I can't spend any more time on busy work!"*

Dad: *"Greg, we will have to discuss this more, but tonight I want to see your assignment when it's done, before you spend time on other things."*

8. Preparing for the Family Meeting.

While Greg did his assignment, Mom and Dad discussed the math homework situation. Before a family meeting, an adults' session is important to air views and feelings and to explore possible solutions to suggest in the event that their teen doesn't come up with realistic proposals.

During the pre-meeting, adults need to emphasize specific actions and realistic levels of behavior and practice communication skills they want everyone to use during the meeting.

Greg's reaction to the call from school gave his parents ideas about ways to support his math work. He needed to be persuaded about the value of math homework.

Both Mom and Dad would share with Greg their belief in the teacher's assignment; she was the expert. They decided that one-half hour of math problems a night was a crucial part of learning to work hard and accurately and applying skills to problem-solving. They would tell Greg that part of earning a living is doing work you don't want to do. Practice at self-discipline enables you to do it. You can imagine what Greg's cynical reaction to such a philosophy will be, but it may still ring true and have an influence. They also examined what they were already doing to encourage Greg's homework behavior, and what needed to be done. They focused on providing more concrete rewards for doing math homework. They discussed different options and decided to give points for every assignment completed. Greg could then use those points toward a movie or other treat. They also decided to share math and logic puzzles and to ask math-related questions, *"Greg, what did you learn?"* and *"Give us a problem to solve."*

They would tell of ways *they* applied what they learned to their
life situations, to show the value of his skills. For instance, Mom
would tell her story of not wanting to do math homework as a
teen, but she finally overcame the math problems one by one.
From practice she found quicker ways to do the work and it became easier. Because she finally succeeded in math, she went on to
courses using higher calculations, and eventually, a science career.

After Greg showed them an improved report card, they would
celebrate his effort with a special meal.

When they discuss all this with Greg later at the family meeting, he might have better suggestions, but at least Mom and Dad
now have a positive plan to offer.

9. The Family Meeting.

Young people at a meeting will respect the outcome to the
extent they see it taking their needs into account. It takes time
to listen to every person so allow an ample period. When family
members start repeating what others have said instead of providing new input, you have probably covered the situation.

A regular weekly meeting can be helpful for airing concerns
before they reach the problem stage. The rules and consequences
the group agrees on may need reworking later, but be encouraged
that practice will improve everyone's skills and productivity.

Communication skills need plenty of application at these meetings. Also, parents should not push or expect solutions at every
meeting.

When Greg has an opportunity to set policy and abide by it,
like most teens and younger children, he is likely to take responsibility seriously. Parents need to make clear the importance of the

situation in the short and long run and follow up with a discussion of adjustments at future meetings.

Reasons need to be clearly stated. For example, if parents don't want Greg's older brother, John, to go out with friends more than one night a weekend for several reasons, they need to say so:

"We don't want to have to worry about your safety more than one night a weekend."

"We think studying one weekend night is important."

"And we want you to spend time with the family doing something special on some weekends."

All family members need to communicate their views of an event or problem, exploring alternative solutions to a situation and suggesting rules and consequences that are reasonable. If parents listen well, the keys to a workable solution can be discovered. Teens have a strong sense of fairness, but if teens do not participate appropriately, parents may need to postpone the agreement or set a temporary solution, to be adapted as needed. An ideal discussion raises issues, explores ways to handle them, and then postpones decisions until everyone has had time to mull over the whole matter. During the interval between sessions, reservations and shortcomings may surface. When a final agreement comes, it will be more realistic because of the added consideration of solutions.

10. Fat Cats.

Cats seem to be one of the best animals at taking human care for granted. Give them food, housing and a warm pillow and they can ignore you for days. Teens sometimes take a similar attitude. During a moment of rebellion, a teen can act on the false idea that she is perfectly capable of making it on her own.

Like the cat, she has been misled by a family situation that provides most of the essentials of life free and with no fanfare. You too could make it on very little if room, board, clothing, medical, and educational needs were free! The fat cat problem develops from too few demands for your teen to care for herself or himself and too few requests to contribute to the family. It's time for more realistic responsibility. But when you give more responsibility you will need to add more incentive also.

11. Matching Funds and Graduated Allowances.

Positive feedback for correct behavior is especially important for teens because they need the message as well as the encouragement. They are not yet sure of the right way to act. Should they try not to be messy or lazy, or is that "uncool?" They lack information as well as motivation.

We all need support and incentives for our actions: pleasant reactions, paychecks, awards, and of course, our own good feelings when we do things we value. Teens are still learning about what good behavior is so they crave a lot of encouragement and payoffs.

A graduated allowance pays off a variable amount depending upon the behavior of your teen. It uses the traditional allowance which is guaranteed and usually unrelated to performance, but guarantees only a minimum.

Responsibilities are listed for the teen and additional amounts can be earned during the week. Each time your teen finishes a task, it is recorded on a chart. Each task has a value and the accumulated amount is paid off at the end of the week.

The possible increase in allowance need not be more expensive for the family budget. As money accumulates, it doesn't all have to be spent on amusements. Consider a matching funds program for clothes, for example, where parents provide most of the funds, but for some items they require their teen to contribute from his or her earnings.

12. A Teen's Role in the Family Economy.

A system of payoffs can compensate teens for contributing to domestic necessities of the family. An exchange system could be set up where an activity receives some kind of compensation. Psychologists call this kind of exchange a token economy because in many early programs tokens were used to represent the payoff. The traditional allowance is one kind of token economy.

Since an allowance system is an inevitable part of family practice, parents and teens alike should benefit from an allowance based on the effort a teen puts toward self and family care each week. You and your teen could agree about chores which need to be done and how much each chore pays off. That agreement prevents a teen from timing requests for allowance according to his parents' moods.

Now you are ready to discuss chores and payoffs with your teenager. Your teen can record work done on a chart or checklist, using an honor system. This is a chance to show trust.

As the weeks progress, tallies on the weekly allowance chart will become more numerous, and your teen will start saving for shopping. The chart and a payoff time prevent the need for nagging and coercion. When chores are not done by the agreed time, instead of using fines, which undermine confidence in the economy, have your teen make amends, as suggested in Step 4. In this case, "allowance time" should occur with time left in the day for chores to be done if your teen is disappointed in the week's yield.

13. Planning the Token Economy

1. List the chores you think should be done each week by your teen. Consider your teen's starting level, need to grow, available time, and family work.

2. List your teen's weekly/monthly/long-range expenses. Some teens pay for their own school supplies, movies, tapes, and gifts to friends. Others save for big items such as a radio, clothes, a bike, or car.

3. Decide a tentative amount of payoff next to each chore, considering the minimum wage, amount of time your teen takes to do the work, your teen's expenses, and your own generous nature. This is a chance to be encouraging and fair to your teen and your budget.

Points can be used instead of money. When a teen accumulates enough points, they can be cashed in for a special treat, a small party for friends, a favorite meal, or an outing. However, teens need practice spending and saving money to learn those skills.

We hear complaints that the token economy uses bribery and over-emphasizes money. The concern for explicit rules about money and how your teenagers get their share might seem too detailed and too mechanical. But we all need some compensation for our work, and you are paying your teens for work, not bribing them to get things done. The label, bribe, takes away respect and the positive emphasis on earning rewards by honest effort that we all enjoy.

Always emphasize sincere social rewards as well: *"Well done! Your work helps our family!"* so your teen will value his/her accomplishments in addition to the money gained.

Teens will be given their share of family income by some means or other and, as adults, they will have to earn their own and they might as well learn gradually to earn their own way.

Once the token economy is firmly established, other incentives can be added. The most important of these are promotions based on good performance. This allows for duties on the chart to be changed, improved, and modified as your teen grows up. If your teen performs well on some of the more simple and tedious chores, she/he might be promoted to a better set of duties.

Promotions represent higher expectations and emphasize a parent's respect for improved capabilities. If no promotions occur in the token economy, then the system has failed because your teens are not growing up to new responsibilities.

For example, one mother developed a token-economy program to provide an incentive for her son's chores. After the system was applied for several weeks, the son complained that some of the things he was required to do were "kid stuff." Taking out wastebaskets and garbage bags were particularly unpleasant tasks for him. Mom then added a new procedure providing that if he successfully performed the task for 15 straight days without reminders from his mother, he would be promoted to a new task, washing the car. The chart would be changed, and the job of removing wastebaskets given to his younger brother.

The older son eagerly looked forward to this possible change of events because he liked doing anything with the car; the younger son welcomed an additional task, because he wanted more opportunities to perform duties within the system.

You learn
what
you do.

Step 9: Treat Compulsions and Fidgeting with Tolerance

1. Why Do Teens Behave the Way They Do?

Unchangeable physical characteristics and early experiences play important roles. People also adjust their behavior to achieve certain payoffs, such as self-satisfaction and enjoyment, attention from others, encouragement, and rewards. Although physical limitations and early experiences are unchangeable, we can change some of the "payoffs" teens receive for their behaviors.

The *"why"* of behavior is easy to see when we describe specific behaviors and their consequences. Instead of leading us to speculate about inherited traits and early traumas, the *"why"* question becomes *"What happens next, after the behavior?"* or *"What are the consequences?"*

Kim is irresponsible or Shanna is self-centered. Then what happens? Someone else irons Kim's wrinkled clothes. Shanna's parents help her even though she seldom returns the favor.

Those supports may be reasons *for* the poor behaviors.

2. Where Do the Kids Come Up with These Impulses?

Parents are often amazed at the variety of behaviors—both good and bad—their teenager shows. If you find it difficult to sort out what good behaviors you want, then you can see how difficult it will be *for them* to find out how they should behave. Of all the possibilities, what will they try first in a new situation? Most of the time they will try what worked best for them last time or in a similar situation. If nothing comes to mind, they may try out what you do. If it works for you, maybe it will work for them.

Just as you provide consequences for them, you are also the one they will imitate. Kids may deny it, adults often do, saying we won't do this or that the way our parents did. But then we are surprised to find ourselves acting very much like our parents: *"I can't believe I said that, I sound just like my father!"*

Your parents found the best adjustment for their problems, so you probably went with their choice, and your teen will follow you. When your teenager agrees, you can support him. That will be a reward, and another habit, good or bad, will have been passed along to another generation of the family tree!

So it's not always genetics, sometimes it's just plain imitation.

Mom: *"Carolyn really tries hard to be pleasant when any member of the expanded family comes over to visit. She asked Grandma Mildred if she wanted a refill on her coffee and later Carolyn asked her if she was tired!"*

Her husband said, *"I think she takes her cue from you; you always try to make sure everyone is comfortable when company comes. It just rubs off."*

3. What are Compulsions and Fidget Behaviors?

Carolyn's thoughtfulness may not seem to fit with the usual examples of compulsions such as nail-biting, hair-twirling, and lip-biting but they are similar because they are usually maintained partly by parental attention, the model a parent sets, and by the absence of something else to do. They are behaviors that fill up time and may be occasionally rewarded by parents.

Sometimes the smaller habits may be more annoying. Then we call it fidgeting. It happens in the slow, somewhat boring moments of life and almost everyone does it. At first it can be just the random squirming and wiggling of a teen. We may say, *"Stop that fidgeting!"* Later on, the little habits develop into hair-twirling, scratching, or ballpoint pen-clicking. Even eating and drinking can develop into fidget (fill-up-the-dull-time) behaviors.

A well-known psychology experiment concerning fidget behavior has been repeated many times. A laboratory white rat is trained to press a lever for a bit of food. He soon learns that the food is only given for a press after a long interval—about two minutes. In the meantime there is little to do but wait. What to do, what to do? A water bottle is available, but the rat has water all the time in his home cage so he is not thirsty. But, faced with nothing to do, he drinks (sound familiar?).

It's not in the rat's nature, nor ours, to do absolutely nothing. For humans, doing nothing is often embarrassing. So we pretend to read (or something) in waiting rooms, in restaurants, and at bus stops. Many of us wouldn't think of going to a restaurant alone without something to read or at least a cell phone to play with.

So the rat drinks. But he doesn't just sip. He may drink up to two times his body weight in water in a one hour session while waiting for each 2 minutes to pass! Since no rat has a bladder that big, you can see that the experiment requires regular cleaning chores.

All that was needed to stop our furry waterholic was to shorten the waiting time for food—down from 2 minutes to 30 seconds. With the shorter interval the excessive water drinking was gone. The food pellet pay-offs came more often, there was work to be done, and our "compulsive" rat had no time for fooling around!

So now we have *two* possible explanations for frequent, repeated, annoying behaviors—one, they could be attention-getting and two, they could be fidget behaviors to pass the boring time--they are called adjunctive behaviors. The difference is important.

For attention-getting behaviors, we need a strategy that reduces the attention for that behavior, but for fidget behaviors we need to also reduce the boredom of dull moments. Take a little extra time for reflection when you first see the beginnings of a "nervous" habit or a "compulsive" behavior.

Rewarding other behavior that is desirable will be a good strategy in either case, but the reaction to the annoying behavior itself should be a careful one. For attention-getting activities you certainly want to reduce attention, but if it's a fidget behavior, there is all the more reason to see that support and opportunity for more acceptable behaviors occur more often.

Sometimes compulsive behaviors like nail-biting happen because the family situation is too stressful for that person. Sometimes assessing the family atmosphere and making necessary changes so everyone feels more comfortable at home is a good step forward.

A teen's fidget behavior is due to down time—the lack of anything to do. At least your teen's view is that there is nothing to do. You wouldn't want to get into a *"I'll-bet-you-can't-make-me-happy"* game, but clearly some increase in action is called for.

Fidget behaviors can quickly develop into attention-getting or other reward-getting behaviors. Now that boredom has brought on the behavior, what reaction will it attract? "Jumping on" fidgeting behavior can be a dangerous parental habit. If the behavior is not important let's not make it so. Instead let's look to the situation for a way of enriching the moments. Any smoker or heavy drinker will recognize the fidgeting aspect of their habit and tell you that the worst time of temptation is during the low moments—not just the depressing ones, but the empty ones, also.

Your first question about a compulsive behavior then, should be, *"Is the behavior a problem serious enough to warrant any strategy at all?"* Your second question should be, *"Is there anything about the current reactions that could alleviate the tension and add some enrichment to the situation to "squeeze out" moments of temptation for fidgeting behavior?"* Along this line, you might consider what activities you want in the situation and what opportunities there are for those activities.

Another strategy used frequently is to reward the lack of compulsive behavior. For example, one mother told me she promised a dollar to her daughter if she could refrain from nail-biting long enough so that her nails would need cutting. Because this demand seemed a bit too large for a first step, her daughter was also given a quarter for *each one* of her fingernails that needed trimming because it had been allowed to grow.

Such a direct contingency upon a compulsive behavior must be used carefully. There is always a tendency to do more than state the rule, and nagging ensures that some attention will be connected to mistakes. As with any attention-getting behavior, in the teen's view, he or she is not getting enough attention and has now found a behavior that seems to alleviate the deprivation. If you now come along with a new strategy that sees to it that your teen's usual solution (nail-biting for attention) will not work, then you need to look for a newly designated, desirable behavior to trigger your special attention. The new way to appropriate attention should be one your teen can easily accomplish.

4. Rhythmic Habits.

Although rhythmic habits are sometimes symptoms of severe disorders, normal children and adults have rhythmic habits, too. Tapping a pencil, swinging a foot, and rocking to music may annoy parents but are probably too trivial to merit any strategy beyond ignoring it.

When a habit grows and becomes troublesome, most parents can remember it beginning as a less frequent event. This can be a case of parents trying to fix a non-problem and now they have a problem.

A behavior that started as just fidgeting became a gimmick for attention, and then a way to express exasperation at his parents. "Getting through to" his parents now produces a reprimand, a new kind of attention in a situation where positive attention seems unlikely but negative attention is good enough.

An occasional correction or request to stop the annoying habit is not likely to do much harm if his parent's emotional reaction can be kept in check.

Mom: (Aaron has been banging his foot on the chair leg at dinner for three minutes.) *"Aaron, stop kicking the chair—it's a bother when we're eating."*

Aaron: *"I can't help it."*

Mom: (Still in a very quiet tone.) *"Did you finish your science homework?"*

Aaron: (Still kicking the chair.) *"Yes, it's about DNA."*

Mom: *"DNA. I'd like to hear about that. Please don't kick."*

Aaron: *"I told you I can't help it."*

Mom is right to provide another direction for Aaron's focus. These other topics will have to become a regular part of Mom's habits *before* the chair kicking or other problem starts. She will have to be very steady in her conversation. If Mom only comes up with these interests when Aaron acts up, you can see where that will lead.

5. Taking All that "Flak."

One obvious characteristic of a teen's bad behavior is that it generally reduces the demands from his parents. Parents can silence a teen or keep him from acting up by taking a threatening pose that implies punishment. And, of course, *a teenager* learns and uses the same idea, but since he is a less powerful figure he must use it in a more subtle way.

A teen's threats and lack of compliance make up his version of "flak." Some parents will give in rather than "take all that flak."

Cindy uses flak to put her mother off and to avoid requests for work. But Cindy's behavior is also a result of the fact that the request, in Cindy's view, is *just* work. There's no payoff for her.

By this time you may be getting tired of the idea that everything has to pay off, but remember that what we mean by "pay off" in many cases is just the honest adult expression of appreciation, admiration, or support for something good or helpful.

Material rewards are frequently not necessary. In your job you probably do many things because you have come to believe that it is the right way to do it or that it will please someone. You don't necessarily do it just for the money.

Why don't you try flak with your boss? Because it won't work, I would bet. And also with a good boss, it never occurred to you to give her any flak because there is consistent support for doing the job—satisfaction and appreciation as well as pay.

Cindy's parents try to bring about some effort from Cindy by coercion and Cindy avoids that effort, if she can, because it is straight coercion without a significant parental reaction.

When Cindy is using flak, she often exposes the situation quite well by saying, *"Oh, why should I do that anyway?"* The statement is pure flak intended to stop a request from Mom or Dad, but, incidentally, it asks a very good question: *"What does Cindy get out of it?"*

Although coercing behavior is easy to attempt, planning and providing support is usually better and more permanent. Plan reasonable, positive consequences and opportunities for more social approval to open the way for more willing help next time.

6. Watch Out for Labels That Mean Too Much!

For many years psychologists have searched for solutions to the problems of parenthood. Their searches have usually focused on the reasons children and teens behave—in reacting to parents, siblings, friends, and at school. If the reasons could be known, the solutions could be found. The solutions would make life easier and parenting more enjoyable.

But solutions have been difficult to find because they seem buried in a maze of complicated answers concerning the genes children and teens inherit, the importance of early experiences, and the recent treatment they have encountered from parents and others.

Explanations and theories may vividly describe a possible reason for a teen's behavior and may help you understand the situation. That will be helpful in *thinking about* the problem in a calm and loving way. However, you will still need practical strategies for action at the moment when the problem come up.

Parents cannot afford the common craziness of doing the same thing over and over but expecting a magical new result. Instead, we could try a *new* reaction based on the events that produce a certain behavior and the reactions our teen gets for it. That is, what happens next? The search for solutions should always return to a concern for the question, *"What happens next?"*

Concentrating on behaviors and their consequences allows us to discover how to use *our* behaviors to change the behavior of the kids. The more recognizable the activity is, the more consistent the reactions to it can be. Therefore a teen's experience and learning will be more consistent. For example, the broad labels we use for teens, *"She is messy, he is rowdy,"* or *"He is hyperactive, she is lazy,"* seem to describe characteristics that are inside the person, beyond our reach. In fact, any mom or dad can influence even these characteristics once they identify the specific behaviors. Instead of shy, a little thought may focus on, *"Bill doesn't talk much or look at people when he does."* *"Rowdy"* could mean he speaks in a loud voice and pokes people. *"Hyperactive"* might become, *"Rog interrupts his homework by walking around the room every few minutes."* In specific terms, *"lazy"* breaks down to, *"Julie listens to music and naps instead of doing her chores or homework."*

The task of being *specific* about *complaints* is not difficult. Often both parents and teachers have rules about specific mistakes. The challenging part is in listing specifics on the *good* side. Most parents know what to reprimand but fumble with praise on only infrequent occasions. Lists of specific teen behaviors will help you plan specific parent reactions—negative when necessary, positive when deserved.

One objective is to influence the specifics and increase the good behavior. A second objective is to send a strong message to your beloved teens that there are many things you *like* about them. Be on the lookout for sending proper messages. Opportunities shouldn't be skipped.

7. Short-Term Benefits and Long-Term Goals.

While sorting out what happens next, both immediate and delayed reactions need to be considered.

Mom: *"Why does she go running out of the house without a jacket? She knows she gets a cold every time!"* (Yes, but that's <u>later</u>!)

Dad: *"My friend, George, is just like that at work. He snacks all the time, he's overweight, and he can barely climb a few stairs without panting. Someday he'll be a death-due-to-donuts! Can't he see what he's doing to himself in the long run?"* (That's later, also, and George gives in to the *"right now.")*

Teacher: *"I run two miles every morning. Sometimes it's hard to get started on it, but I feel better afterwards."* (Somehow this teacher resists the effects of inconvenience right now for a better feeling later. How does she do that?)

Brian: *"It's a good TV night, but if I attend every Scout meeting, I'll get a merit patch!"* (Here's a hint about how long-term benefits come to work: there's a *short-term* benefit as well!)

Behaviors tend to follow the short-term benefits at the expense of long-term goals. But with a few positive experiences, long-term benefits can overpower temporary temptations especially if someone supports the effort. How can a parent help this process of considering the long-term benefits of good behaviors and the long-term problems of bad ones?

The one common parental strategy is to try to talk a teen into considering the long-term. Talk by itself is often not enough as most of us dieters know. We need some symbol of the long-range goal *right now*—a reminder that we are making some progress: a daily chart with marks for successes, a record book, or diary. Teens may need something more concrete such as stickers, buttons, Scout badges or treats. If those little encouragements are given some respect, they can have an effect on the present behavior. Isn't that what compliments from the boss, new titles or privileges at work, promotions, and military medals are all about?

Many ideas for reactions in the here and now are not contrived tokens, medals, or promotions. They are simply people looking for an opportunity to compliment and praise the small steps of good habits. Being so observant and responsive is not easy, but those who do it have good results.

We all know how our morale is elevated by bosses who are positive and supporting and deflated by ones who only react to mistakes. When work and chores are only for the long-term benefit, a "boss" needs to put in some short-term encouragements that promote the good effort.

8. Cures and Changes.

The idea of a cure implies that some general change has taken place in the individual. Mom and Dad should focus instead on one or two problems, review and correct their reactions for these and then carry them out. For everything else going on, they have to rely on their reflex reactions and the reactions of others. The general cure will have to come from an accumulation of small changes.

When we visit the doctor, we all hope for a quick and effortless cure, a magic bottle with pills that are easy to take. Changes in teen-rearing rarely happen in that quick and easy way. Bold strokes that suddenly "get through to" a teen are seldom accomplished.

What your teen comes to expect as a result of consistent experiences will make up the long-lasting behavior patterns. There are no magic bullets. There's only you and your teen and what your teen does, what you do and, later, what the rest of the world does in return.

The changes in behavior brought about by these strategies may be relatively permanent, and that permanence can be somewhat ensured by supporting behaviors that you know are likely to be supported by others. For that, you must observe what consequences follow the individual activities that are important to you. Your effort should focus on single behaviors, blaming conditions inside a teen blames the person and lets us off the hook of finding an appropriate reaction.

Practice implies repetition and, in the context of this book, this means the repetition of consequences as well as the behavior.

9. Can Plans for Non-Behaviors Work?

Be careful when trying to arrange plans and consequences for non-behaviors. Rules that say, *"If you don't do such and such (watch too much TV, act too shy, walk on the flowers, sit on your sister) I'll reward you"* are difficult—even if the reward is a social reaction. The time of the promised reaction may be too arbitrary. When does *not* watching too much TV happen?

Better to build your rule around the *alternative* to TV—something that happens at a particular time and gives you a signal and opportunity to support your son or daughter at a particular moment, *"So you're working on your art, it's looking very professional!"*

The words we use for good behavior are usually not specific: "be nice" and "act right." Not having an exact idea of what good behaviors should be, we have trouble finding them.

The search is more difficult if "good" is described by what we *don't* want: *"don't make trouble, don't yell at your sister, don't sulk and slam doors just because you're annoyed."*

When should you react to *"not* fighting" or *"not* sulking?" And when these rules are finally learned, what is a teen *to do?* What should a parent look *for* in his or her teen's behavior? Better to think of specifics—help with setting the table, saying something complimentary to her sister, helping his kid brother practice his soccer.

Vague expectations about good behavior and specific descriptions of bad, can lead to a common situation of unbalanced parental reactions with bad behavior attracting most of the attention. This emphasis on the negative can lead parents to think of themselves more as police officers than as moms and dads.

Without specific positives to look for, some parents send fewer positive messages. Even the vague supports that occasionally surface, *"You're a good kid!"* and *"You're doing all right!,"* have such unclear targets that they don't influence anything in particular. *"Don't talk like that!" "Straighten up!"* and *"Clean up your mess!"* can be frequent and specific, but so frequent that the general message is *"you're bad."* We need to select specific positive targets to avoid too-frequent criticism.

I asked one dad to give me some specifics about his complaint that his daughter, Kim, was "messy." I thought he could be more helpful by deciding the specific actions he wanted her to perform. After some thought, he said, *"I want her to make her bed, put dirty clothes in the laundry hamper, pile her belongings on wall shelves, and dust and vacuum her room."*

Instead of accusing her of being "messy," a comment on the

whole person of his daughter, he used the list to direct attention toward one of these specific actions. By focusing, he could take one step toward specific changes in the behaviors he felt were important. Also, Dad could begin to plan when he could praise instead of bringing up the old complaints like, *"you're messy"* that may be interpreted as, *"(I don't like you), you're messy."*

He chose the best time to talk with Kim about the work, decided on the level to expect from her at first, and was ready with his approval and other rewards for her effort. Then he began to look for ways to encourage improvement in her performance.

My experience with Ryan is a good example of sour messages. Ryan came into our office waiting area and first sat on a convenient chair; Mom chose to sit on the opposite side of the seating area. *"Sit over here,"* she said. He moved to the seat next to her. *"Don't swing your foot like that!"* Ryan picked up a magazine from the table. *"Be careful with that,"* she said. He turned a page noisily. *"Shh, I told you to be careful!"*

As it turned out, one of the complaints from both teachers and Mom was that *Ryan* (!) was bossy and constantly critical of others! Mom had developed low expectations and low tolerance, and it was contagious. In turn, Ryan developed his own habit of being critical of others.

The problem illustrated by Ryan's mother is almost always the result of a lack of planning. The critical part of planning that is left out is determining which behaviors are important and which are trivial. Had Mom ever thought about whether Ryan should always sit next to her? She said she had not. Why had she told him to do so? She said she was afraid he "might do something wrong over there." She said she had no *specific* fear he would do anything wrong, she just didn't trust him. Some boys might deserve such

distrust, but for Ryan it was just Mom's habit with a little reprimand thrown in. A psychological leash had been put on, and it was
jerked regularly.

When Ryan's mom tried the *"catch 'em being good"* suggestion,
she told Ryan how well he was doing on a part of his homework
and, another time, how well he had cleaned up his room. His reaction was, *"What's the matter with you?"*

In the second week, after a few more compliments, Ryan's re-
action could melt your heart. *"Do you like me?"* he asked. Mom said,
"Ryan, I love you. Of course, I like you." And Ryan said, *"Wow."* At 12,
Ryan is just finding out his mother likes him.

The psychological leash is worth breaking for additional reasons. Corrections that are intended as reprimands may become
rewards over a long time. The leash replaces a teen's responsibility
for his own behavior. He just does what he wants while he depends on his parent to make all the corrections. So while striving
for perfection, total dependence is achieved.

The corrections with the psychological leash may come to be
learned by teens as a nagging strategy they can use on others. All
parents know this drill very well. It's the nagging that never dies!

Rachel: *"But Mom, why can't I ride to school with Nathan?"* (Rachel
is 13.)

Mom: *"I already told you why, Rachel."*

Rachel: *"I know, but pleeease! Nathan's a good driver."*

Mom: *"No. He just got his license and driving to school is just asking for
trouble."*

The next day it starts all over again:

Rachel: *"Mom, Nathan wants me to ride with him to the mall, can I go?
We're not going near school."*

What events maintain Rachel's nagging? It's a topic that brings disagreement and punishment, but she brings it up anyway. The first and most likely reason for this running battle is that Mom and Dad have never held a brief planning session about the problem. Without this planning session, the reasons given to Rachel change from time to time; her parents disagree from time to time; and they lose confidence in these decisions from time to time as details (mall or school) change.

The inconsistency encourages Rachel to keep trying because one day she thinks she might hit the right combination of details and get to go. She probably will.

The planning session would nail down the reasons, pinpoint the agreement between Rachel's parents and give them confidence. It would help by stating the honest reasons for the decisions in detail.

Mom: *"Your father and I have decided you may not ride with boys to school or on errands without an adult. We think other students will get in on it and make trouble whether it's school or anywhere else. When you are 15, it might be all right. Right, David?"*

Dad: *"Right."*

Now will Rachel stop nagging? Probably not, but the amount of nagging will decrease, and Rachel will be a little happier because the situation is now clear, honest, and fair—at least Rachel's parents think so, and it gives them confidence. For Rachel, the structure makes the situation more comfortable than the continual argument, although it's still not what she wants. Rachel's argumentative behavior will mellow because the statement of the rule is concrete and detailed—not much room for loopholes.

Rachel's parents should not be discouraged because there is no dramatic change in the argument. The planning session is to make them feel more in control and less vulnerable to the nagging.

Rachel is not going to be satisfied on this topic until she gets what she wants, probably when she's 15 or older. But her parents can be a bit more comfortable knowing they have an agreed-on policy.

As the air clears, Rachel's parents need to stay alert and make a special effort to engage her in more positive conversation. They don't want this vacuum to fill up with other nagging.

Good parental strategies, such as the consistent rules of Rachel's parents and the focus on positive behavior that Ryan's mother needed are habits with important benefits. Parents sometimes develop different habits when dealing with their kids than when dealing with adults. They come to expect something different from their kids and worry about any deviation from their expectations. But often the expectations themselves have never been worked out.

What at first appears to be a high standard of behavior by Ryan's mother turns out to be actually *no specific* standard at all. So a parent in such a situation punishes (in mild ways) nearly everything and finds no opportunity to reward good behavior.

One teacher I talked to was surprised that Ryan was having problems, *"I know he can be difficult, but I have decided to catch him doing well. I focus on finding his good moments and when I find one, I let him know it. I think he knows I'm giving him a chance and that I like him."*

Adults expect the same of us, more tolerance, more chances to make amends for mistakes, and we show them a better disposition. What is expected of us, and what we expect, create the social atmosphere we live in. The adult rule is, *"Don't correct or reprimand until a mistake has been made. Certainly withhold punishment, it creates bad feelings."* Here's one reason the atmosphere is better in the teachers' coffee room than in the hallway.

Another high school teacher I know said that as she went

down the school hallway, she noticed classes reacting to teachers in ways that were "typical" of each teacher's classes. She was
surprised that students could make such quick adjustments as they
went from Math to Art to Gym, creating a recognizable atmosphere in each place.

From a selfish point of view, if you were a parent or teacher of
these kids, how would you like to spend your day? With teens who
are modeling positive behavior, or with teens who are modeling
punishment?

The most effective reward we use is praise and encouragement.
When praise is consistently used in an obvious way for a particular
behavior, results are gratifying. An additional improvement comes
when the attitude is imitated. Some parents and teachers may de-
value the effect of their positive attention because they only briefly
observe an immediate target activity. In the longer view however,
a teen's disposition will become a close copy of the surrounding
adult attitudes.

The non-behavior rule not only fails the specific time test, it
also fails to tell your teen exactly what to do. *"Karen watches too much
TV"* needs to explore what Karen *should* do. Karen's parents would
be at a loss to keep her busy every moment but it's a situation
where the *extent* of TV is the problem. Karen's parents could plan
some encouragement for a few alternatives to the chatter from the
screen.

Does this mean that Karen's parents should load up on toys,
food, and money to lure Karen away from TV? Probably not.
Most parents have found these rewards to have temporary effects—except in the case of money which will become a bigger
part of Karen's life soon enough without using it frequently here.

For problems such as Karen's we need to look around for

something useful that we might encourage her to do. Also, we hope to find something that would have the additional advantage of making Karen feel a little more important. She might be proud of doing some of the drudgery of life. How about setting the table, cooking, sweeping, cleaning, or painting. Painting? *"But she won't do it right!"* you might say. *"She'll mess it up. Cooking? That must be a joke."*

Of course it's true that you could do any of these tasks better than a 12-year-old. To get it done right, do it yourself. But the purpose here is not to get the job done right, it's the self-esteem, the learning, and the alternative to TV. How well the job is done is not a top priority.

What happens
next, after
The behavior?

Step 10: The Bad Habits of Alcohol, Drugs, and Cars

When the dangerous subjects come up, what's the best way to handle it? No one can tell you exactly what to say, but first, Mom and Dad might do some intense soul-searching of their own attitudes. Some facts presented here may help with your preparation.

1. Is Alcohol the Most Dangerous Substance?

The most dramatic teen-drug stories in the media involve illegal drugs, but statistics tell us that your teen is more likely to abuse alcohol than any of those other dangerous substances. Drugs often produce the most dramatic problems, but in number of abusers, alcohol still wins. Drug symptoms are listed in the next section, but the first attention goes to alcohol because it's more available and its interaction with other substances can be so lethal.

Alcohol abusers are defined as persons whose drinking habits produce excessive absenteeism from work or school and complaints from friends and family. By this definition one quarter of our teens are classified as alcohol abusers by the time they reach college age. And alcohol-related accidents will still be the biggest killer of our teens until they pass college age. Your teen is picking up messages everyday about alcohol use and abuse.

In earlier generations the risks of alcohol and drugs were most frequently restricted to older teenagers. Yet in these tough times stories of the sad behaviors and sad consequences reach down to eight-year-olds, and the accident and death rates are now peaking earlier in each generation.

2. Don't Send the Wrong Messages.

The way you listen and teach, and the role-model you present, all influence risks in the dangerous business of growing up. The smothering wave of media hype and information will present all the possibilities of the abusive behaviors. Your listening can help straighten out the information; your observations and your model can highlight the successes in following the right direction.

It is hard for parents to keep up their effort because their influence shows itself gradually, usually without a teen's dramatic announcement or abrupt change.

"Dad, do you drink?"

"I have had a beer on a hot day and wine sometimes."

"How does it make you feel?"

"I don't drink enough to feel anything. I've learned it just makes me sleepy right away and sick later. Why do you ask?"

"I was just wondering. John's father was drinking a beer the other day."

"It's not a good habit, and it's been shown to be hard on young brains."

"Can I try it?"

"Maybe when you are older."

I think most of us parents would feel uncomfortable in this conversation. We are in the dangerous area of hypocrisy and not much progress is being made. As far as extracting a guarantee of abstinence from a teen, we may feel impatient with Dad. But in building an attitude, a little progress on the big job may have been accomplished.

The topic is so dangerous that the necessary long talks themselves seem dangerous. When our own shortcomings are dragged out for review, the temptation is to fall back on lecturing. The lecture will be an attempt to extract a promise of abstinence, but the only guarantee of safe behavior is in the long term of establishing values. I would give this Dad high marks for keeping his eye on that goal.

Listening is critical in the discussions of dangerous behaviors. A feeling of confidence and self-esteem, as overworked as those terms are in teen-rearing, are the best protection parents have to offer a teen today.

Don't send the message that alcohol is a problem solver. Your model is one of the best predictors of later drinking habits. Yet families that approve of moderate alcohol use, for example, Jewish families where wine is a part of religious services, do not show a greater risk of teenage alcohol abuse. The important factor seems to be the message concerning the role of alcohol consumption. "I've had a tough day; I need a drink!" is a message that alcohol can solve lots of problems.

Don't send the message that alcohol is necessary for social situations. The message that stress or social inhibitions are eased by alcohol is part of the foundation of alcohol dependence. Using alcohol for its temporary relaxing effect only postpones learning better social skills. The habit also becomes entrenched long before the person becomes addicted in other ways. So, for example, many people not yet addicted can't enjoy a party until alcohol has had its effect.

TV and other media glamorize alcohol and imply that alcohol is essential to having a good time. "Things go better with Bud" is not necessarily true, as many of us adults have learned.

Don't send the message that behavior under the influence of alcohol is somehow more sincere, natural or free. Teens often think less thoughtful behavior is somehow more genuine. The notion that because behavior under the influence is less filtered by inhibitions and thoughtfulness shouldn't lead to the conclusion that the actions are better. Inhibitions have been learned from experience, and thoughtfulness is a precious human quality.

Parents need to set a healthy model of problem-solving based on skills and strategies. When teens depend on alcohol to break down social inhibitions, the breakdown of sexual inhibitions will quickly become the next bad habit. Intoxication is the most common reason given for unsafe sex in surveys of teenagers.

Spending time with your teen sends the message that your teen is a valuable person. A teen who feels valued and capable is less likely to start using alcohol than teens who feel they have "nothing to lose." Recognize your teen as an increasingly capable, valued family member.

3. Drugs and Self-Esteem.

I'm not going to have a drink for lunch today, nor drugs this afternoon. The statistics would say you will probably avoid the same things. Why? Because we both feel we have too much to lose! We have family and work responsibilities and goals we have set for ourselves. We hope to make a contribution to our community and family and have some success in our jobs. Too much to lose— that's how we see ourselves.

Who will point out what wonderful talents and potentials a

teen has to lose? My conversation with a drug-experimenting pre-teen is tragically typical:

"So let me get this all straight. You took some white powder your friend had in his garage, put it on a piece of glass in a little row. Then you took a straw and sucked it up your nose?"

"Well, yeah."

"What about the dirt, let alone the stuff itself. How could you be sure it was clean or even made of what your friend said it was?"

"Well, I didn't know, but I figure, you know, what have I got to lose?"

(My parent outrage almost pops out.) "What have you got to lose!? You've got your whole life ahead of you..."

I know what I have to lose, why doesn't this kid know what he has to lose? All those lectures in school—about health, brain damage, infection, addiction, and the violence of the people involved in these trades—and he still can ask, "What do I have to lose?" The lectures are to groups, of course, and they leave out the personal abilities, individual prospects and talents of the individuals. Who will tell our sons and daughters what they, personally, have to lose?

How does a teen learn to value himself, learn what he has to lose? That self-respect will come from developing competencies—even everyday ones like cooking, keeping track of money, and doing domestic chores. One of the best protections against dangerous behaviors is the parental habit of providing satisfying tasks that build confidence.

One 12-year-old boy said to me that he told his friends he couldn't cruise the mall that day because, "I make dinner on Tuesdays and I already bought the stuff." There's a small step in the direction of self-confidence.

4. Medications: "I didn't get
my pill today, can I help it?"

What's the answer to those annoying outbursts from the kids—
the crying fits and the hyperactivity? Even when medications are
necessary both parents and physicians are worried about long-term
effects and hope to add natural long-term remedies that will provide a more fundamental adjustment.

Parents may view the problem as a product of unfortunate
circumstances. For example, a parent will say, "He has a hard time
behaving because he was upset when his father and I divorced."
Or, "He was upset when I remarried." Other parents suspect that
bipolar symptoms exist in one or both sides of the family tree.
Others complain their child-teen rejects discipline because his or
her father won't cooperate with his wife or both parents agree with
his teacher who said, "He might have ADHD (attention deficit
and hyperactivity disorder)."

Of course any of these speculations could be true, or partly
true, but regardless of underlying causes, changing a child-teen's
behavior using careful parental reactions may hold the only hope
for long-term improvement.

Studies by the U.S. Department of Agriculture show children
and teens guzzle 64 gallons of soft drinks a year with an average
of 38 milligrams of caffeine in every ounce. For adults, it's coffee
and, if it's fancy coffee, the caffeine may be as high as 200 milligrams per cup.

After the temporary boost in energy, there's the inevitable drop
in energy and disposition that follows. A re-supply of caffeine will
produce another burst of energy, but an addiction is beginning to
form just to avoid the downturn-aftereffect. Addiction is funda-

mentally a negative reinforcement effect (see part 2 of Step 4).

Hofstra University Professor Jennifer Schare studied 400 preschoolers for a year and found that the heavy users of caffeine had more "uncontrollable energy," which could be, and occasionally was, diagnosed as ADHD. If caffeine is occasional, provided at school but not at home, for example, a "bipolar disorder" might be suspected. At school he is wired and always in trouble, but at home he calms down, but is grumpy. Caffeine effects and the additional sleep disturbance that comes with them, provide pharmaceutical companies with a host of prescriptions for "disturbed" children.

Physicians often recommend less than 100 milligrams of caffeine per day—two ounces of most colas—for the whole day. Why they recommend any at all is hard to understand.

In addition to a diet that contains caffeine and sugar in large quantities, food allergies can add to the problem. In the United States, processed foods contain nearly 7,000 new additives all approved for use in our food, and most were not heard of a century ago. By contrast, Northern Europeans have approved only about 70 of the 7,000 food additives that are legal over here. That may explain some of our expanding allergies.

The National Institutes of Health reports that 50 million Americans suffer from allergic diseases and 54 percent test positive for one or more allergens. The most common disruptive culprits in children's diet besides caffeine and sugar are milk products, citrus fruits, nuts, tomatoes, bananas and certain food additives.

"Food intolerances" occur when the digestive process rejects a certain kind of food. Other problems are food allergies in which certain (usually stomach) tissues are irritated by the food. In either case, keeping careful records of what your teenager eats and when he acts up can identify foods that produce behavioral side effects.

A teenager who is sensitive to particular foods is likely to be more frequently irritated by parents, teachers and siblings. He or she is not likely to understand that disrupted sleep and the result-ing unhappiness may be an additional allergy symptom along with his/her runny nose, stuffiness, wheezing, stomach ache, itchy eyes or muscle ache. Even his or her parents may not recognize the connection.

Parents should be cautious in focusing on one solution for a troublesome child. Here's a true example.

When Jeff was six, he was a model child. He was easy-going and seldom any trouble at school, but when he started second grade, he became agitated and impatient and fought with other students. Tantrums became a daily burden at home and in school. At home the tantrums usually built up around bedtime or later at night when he woke up restless and irritated.

Had he been assigned to a bad teacher? Did something happen at home?

I knew Jeff's mother well. She was a steady, dedicated and loving mom. Because of the surprising change in Jeff's charac-ter, I asked her to keep a record of everything Jeff ate and when disruptions happened. Although Jeff was already on some medi-cation for his disruptive behavior, Mom took it as a challenge to note every scrap and snack that he had. In six weeks her records showed a peculiar but common event: Every time Jeff had pizza, his behavior got worse.

So we started the pizza experiment. No pizza for two weeks and the frequency of his tantrums went down a little, but his troubles at school and home continued.

There was no dramatic result until Jeff's mom (remember, she's the dedicated type) declared all tomato products off limits for the family. That's not an easy task when you think about all the sources – ketchup, salads, pizzas, salad dressings, spaghetti sauce, casseroles and the list goes on. But it turned out Jeff had an allergy.

Without tomatoes, Jeff's old self started coming back, but every time he slipped up (one time we discovered tomato was in the salad dressing), the irritations returned. To protect Jeff (and everyone else), the whole family stayed off tomatoes.

Where do such allergies come from? It's a mystery how we get these sensitivities, but our expanding diet in the U.S. certainly helps us find them. Oranges from Florida are not just a holiday treat any more, and milk no longer comes from a farm in your county. You can't even be sure your food comes from this hemisphere. The greater the variety of food sources you sample, the more likely you are to take in something that disagrees with you.

Jeff, by the way, grew up to be an emergency room physician. He is still his easy-going self, and he's still off tomatoes.

Certainly diet, allergies and parental habits play a role in these problems. Even if medications are already a part of the answer, a record of bad behavior as well as allergic reactions, variations in parental habits and diet may show other sources of the problem.

Nevertheless, 350 million doses of Ritalin, Adderall, and Dexedrine will be given this year in the United States to control bad behavior in children—triple the doses given in all other countries put together. In many cases these medications are helpful, but allergy testing and careful recording of everything a child-teen eats and the time he eats it can show aggravating sensitivities that cause family problems.

Even a teenager diagnosed with Autism or ADHD is not merely afflicted with one wrong process. Diet and what happens

next still influence bad habits. The thoughtful use of reactions
and consequences, watching for good behaviors to highlight and
encouraging self-esteem through useful tasks, all of these remain a
part of the answer to bad social habits.

Seasonal Affective Syndrome turned out to be eight-year-old
Carl's problem discovered when his Mom kept records over the
weeks of a fall semester. As the days grew shorter, Carl's temper
grew shorter. When a set of bright fluorescent lights were added
to his dark morning hours, Carl's behavior improved.

Carl also had problems with psychoactive substances—sugar
and caffeine. Removing these sources will nearly always be part of
the answer.

Prescriptions can be a convenient answer to common rowdi-
ness, sleeplessness and school problems, but medications can
cover up other causes.

Start with a record of the most likely culprits: caffeine, sugar,
chocolate, eggs, and milk products. Draw up a chart with the days
marked down the side and hours across the top. Tape it on the
refrigerator.

Try to record the time and date of every bit of these foods
that your adolescent eats. Very small amounts can trigger reactions.
Many adults complain of sleep problems or headaches after one
cup of tea, even in the early morning, while others have problems
only if they drink tea or coffee before bed.

Also, record any other factors that might be relevant. The kids
will not see these connections in themselves. One teen who had
violent tantrums over the slightest problem turned out to be allergic
to chocolate. Even a small brownie after school extracted a price in
the family evening. The source wasn't discovered until Mom brought
in three weeks of recordings of his snacks, meals and tantrums.

Another Mom complained that after her always-pleasant son turned four, "he became mean and angry and yelled a lot." She agreed to record her rating of his behavior every hour they were together – 1 for very nice, 2 for just a slight problem, 5 for getting mad about something trivial, 10 for a full, losing-it tantrum—usually more than one a day. She also recorded everything he ate at all snacks and meals. Eggs turned out to be a big part of the problem. No hives, no itchy eyes or stomach aches, just irritation and prickliness.

Since behaviors are partly controlled by what happens before and after, I also ask parents to include a record of the events just before and after the problem behavior surfaces. Two hours of TV right before the melt-down or an entertaining argument with Mom can indicate an answer that would help as much as any pill.

The solution will also have to include what is good about our problem-teenager's behavior. What do we want to encourage and how can we encourage it? If he does his homework, then what happens? Do we look it over and admire the work or go on to getting dinner ready because, for the moment, the problem is solved?

Medications can be life savers for parents suffering with a severely disturbed child. Drug companies have a right to be proud of the help they provide. But it is not right to belittle environmental effects just because medications can reduce the symptoms.

Every parent has been amazed by a healthy teen finding 200 ways to sit on a chair, 10 ways to lose his hat, and 30 ways to tangle shoelaces. Activity, even hyperactivity, seems to be just part of growing up.

But one child in ten suffers from behavioral disorders such as attention deficit/hyperactivity disorder (ADHD), separation anxiety, or social phobia. And about 3.4 million U.S. children under

18 are said to be seriously depressed. Ritalin and similar medications are life-savers and family-savers for those situations in which a child or teenager is extremely agitated for long periods every day.

5. Drugs and Other Troubles After School.

The prime time for juvenile crime is from 2 to 6 p.m. You might think it would be at night, but for this young age group, a survey found violent juvenile crime peaked between 3 and 4 p.m. "Fight Crime: Invest in Kids of California," a nonprofit organization, conducted the survey of their state's law enforcement agencies in 1999.

Even in the rest of the nation, after-school hours are the most dangerous hours for serious car accidents involving teenagers as well as juvenile crime. Vandalism, theft and violent crimes are reduced when kids attend after-school programs. Without continued support from parents and schools for a variety of after-school programs, troubles multiply.

Some parent groups meet regularly to talk over their teens' situation at school and plans for sharing of after-school supervision. Parent groups can have healthy effects and relieve the loneliness a parent can feel if things start to go wrong. Parents also gain strength from these talks and from agreements to enforce standards for TV, for computer time and cell phone time.

After-school programs are not the whole answer to the drug problem, but an understanding of the many circumstances that sometimes influence drug taking can help.

We were all shocked in the 60's and 70's to find drugs becoming common in affluent schools. We should have known that these would be the most obvious targets. Addicts need money, lots of money, and they hope to get it from your kids. A pusher isn't interested in a kid who doesn't have much money. Your teen should not carry any more money than necessary to school or afternoon outings.

Parents should also stay informed about the money their teens have. How much does she make from her job? Where does her money go? Better spent on clothes and fun than available for trouble. Just some conversations about weekly activities ought to keep parents up to date without prying. If things don't add up, parents should get nosy and pry. Changes in your teen's appetite, hours of sleep, and symptoms that seem like an allergy or cold but linger too long, should be explored.

Some parents want to show their children that Mom and Dad are "cool" about drugs. Parents who approve of their own drug use or misuse of medications and alcohol encourage an irresponsible attitude in their kids and set the stage for trouble.

Remember, however, that talk about drugs and other adventurous and dangerous activities are favorite topics for all healthy teenagers. They need this free conversation as a way of exploring these topics easily. Parents and other adults around the teen should not react too impulsively to just talk and save dramatic reactions for a time when the concrete evidence of drug or alcohol use is in.

Volunteering for after-school programs is helpful and allows parents another opportunity to learn what's going on with their kids. Contact your school about its programs. Even an afternoon each week can be a worthwhile contribution.

As a treatment for Attention Deficit Hyperactivity Disorder, Ritalin increases nervous system alertness and thereby increases focus and ability to concentrate. Millions of prescriptions for Ritalin are written each year to treat ADHD. The use of Adderall and Dexedrine is not far behind Ritalin in the totals for ADHD treatment, up 2,000 percent in the last two decades.

Yet a study by Drs. Adrian Angold and Jane Costello found that the majority of children and adolescents who receive these medications do not fully meet the criteria for ADHD—even with the expanded criteria for ADHD approved by the American Psychiatric Association.

Many parents have made medications their first solution to behavior problems. Dr. Lawrence H. Diller, a pediatrician, is the author of *Running on Ritalin: A Physician Reflects on Children, Society and Performance in a Pill*. He concludes: "How we deal with our kids' problems reflects our thinking and a much larger problem in our culture." An editorial in the Journal of the American Medical Association reported that drugs have tripled for children under five, increased 170 percent for five- to 14-year-olds and again up 300 percent for the 15- to 19-year-olds.

Many parents want a solution that requires no more work or attention beyond making sure the troublesome youngster gets his medication. Physicians also hope prescriptions will do the job. The business world hopes to sell caffeine, sugar and additives, regardless of the behavioral effects. Limiting these in your teen's diet may be more effective than medications that have no proven track record with very young persons. For ADHD children who are temporarily so hot-wired they cannot be reached and cannot be taught, Ritalin can be a godsend. And a day in school can go much better for a student who would otherwise wreck a school day for the other students as well.

When absolutely necessary parental time is added, a teenager in need of medication may develop and adjust to life and soon leave the medications behind. However, you will have to defend a distinction between "drugs" and medications in family discussions later on.

Parents need to keep a close eye on the possible sources of problems to be sure medications continue only when and as long as, needed.

The concern about alcohol and drugs also requires strategies focusing on learning what is going on. The effects of experimental drug-taking, for example, are the same symptoms parents see everyday, cold-like symptoms, changes in sleeping and eating patterns, new friends, new attitudes, new demands about money, longer hours at the mall, and hanging out. All are very normal unless they all happen at once.

It's the clustering that should ring an alarm. When the hangout, the mall or corner, suddenly takes much more time, the sniffles become an annoyance to the whole family, demands for new curfew hours increase, and there is money suddenly missing, or suddenly acquired and cannot be explained, it's time to be suspicious.

"Tune in" to your teen's life, habits, and problems. Notice general changes in eating, sleeping, health, and friends.

6. Checklists for Changes in Habits and Behavior

Checklist Number One: Changes in Habits

1. Does your teenager need more money than usual, or is money missing from the house?

2. Is your teen spending more time in his/her room with the door closed or locked?

3. Have sleeping or eating habits changed or has irritability increased?

4. Has your teenager changed friends or become secretive about friends?

One mom told me she liked to eat dinner slowly so she and her teenage son could talk. It allowed her to learn about his activities with school and friends. When she saw an unexplained change in his appetite, she asked him about it and found out that he had started stopping off with friends at a fast food restaurant after school. She was put at ease about a possible danger sign.

Watch the Money. The drug business is about money. Where can an unemployed addict get $90 or more a day to support his habit? Recruiting new users is one of the best sources for money. Drug pushers look for teen buyers with extra money, so your teen should carry only the needed amount to school or stores. Listen for information about the amount of money your teen has. Encourage putting money away in savings or shift responsibilities such as buying clothes and personal items to your teen.

A bank account for a teen may not seem related to the drug problem, but it is, since a teen with extra money is a tempting target for a frantic user.

Talk with other parents. One dad told me he made a point of calling parents of the friends of his daughter, Angie. As a single parent he liked to compare his teen's experiences with what others were going through. He liked to keep up on the latest news but was careful not to tell Angie's secrets because he respected her right to privacy. He knew it was an important part of the trust they shared.

Set an example for your teen to follow in the use of tobacco, alcohol, and drugs. Teens copy you much more than you think. Review your habits for the sake of your teen.

As much as you think your teen will never abuse alcohol or take drugs, you need to know the signs of use. Checklist Number Two contains characteristics that all teens have at one time or another. Abrupt changes in these characteristics should, however, increase your curiosity, and if you're not satisfied, you should be suspicious. This is especially true when these changes occur along with the habits listed in Check List Number One.

Checklist Number Two: Watch for Changes in Physical Symptoms

1. Lack of concentration; extreme agitation

2. Red eyes, watery eyes, droopy eyelids

3. Runny nose, increased infections and colds

4. Change in sleeping habits—sleeping all day, up all night

5. Slurred or garbled speech, forgetting thoughts or ideas

6. Change in appetite, either increased or decreased; cravings for certain foods

7. Change in activity level; fatigue or hyperactivity

8. Change in appearance, becoming sloppy

9. Lack of coordination, clumsiness, stumbling, sluggishness

10. Shortness of breath, coughing, peculiar odor to breath and clothes

All teens show some variety of these characteristics from time to time so these characteristics do not necessarily indicate drug abuse. The difference that deserves attention is a cluster of abrupt changes.

"John started going with those older kids last summer and suddenly he didn't care how he looked; he was sloppy, always sniffing, getting up later and later, and he lost interest in everything!"

This mother found drug paraphernalia in her son's room the first time she looked! The cluster of changes in social habits, attitude, and self-care were enough for her to investigate.

7. Depression

The behavior disorder of clinical depression occurs in 4 percent of preschoolers and in about 15 to 20 percent of teenagers.

The numbers for teens can be higher than 20 percent because we often brush off their complaints saying they "always talk like that."

The statistics vary partly because the definition of depression varies. Preschoolers don't know the word and, with teenagers, the perception of the word depends on when you talk to them and what they say.

Yet 19 million people in the U.S. complain of depression enough to make it into the clinical medical records. In 2005, 118 million prescriptions for antidepressants were written, twice as many as in 1995, says the Center for Disease Control.

Preschoolers are the fastest growing market for antidepressants. Yet the British Journal of Medicine reported no scientific evidence that antidepressants work for these young children. For children under 18, Britain has banned all but Prozac which is used for complicated emotional problems.

Of course we all get the "blues" and "feel down in the dumps" from time to time. The solution is usually an increase in physical activity—sports or exercise class—or just a change of scene.

For many of us, and especially for teenagers, diet can be a part of the problem. An 11-year-old boy half the weight of his Dad can get far too much sugar from a candy bar or an overdose of fat or caffeine from a portion that would have no effect on his father.

Mental habits can also influence clinical depression. While adults can take encouragement from looking ahead to summer activities or vacations, teenagers are shortsighted. If homework is due tomorrow morning, depression can develop because the prospect of friends coming over tomorrow afternoon is too far in the future as is any upcoming weekend fun.

A teenager's active imagination concerning the magical powers of Harry Potter or the dreams of becoming a soccer star may serve an important antidepressant purpose for a person who has not yet developed the necessary foresight to form realistic goals beyond next week.

In cases where dreams of future success are not enough to pull a grumpy teenager out of depression, a review of activities, diet and mental habits may help parents understand the cause of their teen's depression. Jennifer Conner, psychologist with the Oregon Counseling Organization, lists symptoms of depression such as fatigue, lack of energy, and bad temper. Also, irritability, fear, tension and anxiety are common symptoms as well as a drop in school performance and repeated physical complaints without medical cause (headaches, stomach aches, aching arm or legs).

Of course all of these behaviors occur in all children, but excessive and continuing amounts of these symptoms deserve attention.

Conner suggests seeking immediate professional advice for serious symptoms, but most depression is usually temporary. Allow your teen space and time. Keep caffeine at absolute zero. Alcohol use by children is never appropriate. Learn more about any medications your teenager is taking. Discourage meal skipping. Regular meals, regular sleep, and regular routines are a crucial part of your teen's ability to cope.

Take time to be a part of your adolescent's physical activity. It will help you as well as them, and it will be an opportunity to listen and understand. Activities such as tennis, swimming, bicycling can last a lifetime. Team sports (soccer, football and baseball) may fade away in the adult years.

Every parent needs to save time for giving attention, communication, and companionship. Consistent supportive attention for a teenager having a low day can make the difference between a habit of depression and a habit of bouncing back.

Communication can be just what the doctor (should have) ordered when a teen needs to tell someone how scary the world sometimes seems. And companionship helps in moments when TV heroes and stars are unattainable and a teenager needs a friend. Love, attention and support from Mom and Dad will help protect a vulnerable teenager from the promises that understanding predators seem to offer. The best thing to spend on your kids is time.

8. Smoking.

I haven't seen any plans for tobacco companies to go out of business, so I guess they are counting on somebody's children to fill in for smokers who die off. During the first decade of our new century, nearly 3,000 American teenagers under 18 began daily smoking each day. In 2014, there was evidence of a growing preference for E-cigarettes among the new teenage smokers. However, this choice still includes nicotine which may lead to addiction to regular cigarettes. If your child delays joining the ranks, there are good consequences.

For example, two teeth. Yes, smokers lose, on the average, two more teeth each decade than nonsmokers. So just delaying smoking from eight until 18 saves two teeth! Of course another 10 teeth are goners in the decades between 18 and 68.

If your children delay smoking until 20, then, in addition to saving two teeth, they are likely to delay turning prematurely gray as well, since smokers are four times more likely to turn gray prematurely. Also delaying smoking will put off balding since men who smoke are twice as likely to be bald or balding as non-smoking men.

In the long term, smokers have thinner, less elastic skin which means more wrinkles than nonsmokers. So children who wait until 25 to start smoking may look ten years younger at age 50 than classmates who started smoking at 15. I guess that's an advantage.

But starting young has other consequences. For example, young smokers have twice the likelihood of colds, flu, and respiratory disorders each year. Young smokers are also much more likely to try marijuana, and teens who have tried marijuana are twice as likely to try other drugs.

If your child delays smoking until 30, other statistics kick in. First, he or she is likely to forget to start smoking at all (more than 80 percent of starters begin in high school, 90 percent before 21).

So when should your child start smoking? The later the better, but never is better than later.

Actually, the percentage of young people starting to smoke hasn't changed much over the decades. But the increasing number of quitters has gone up resulting in an overall decrease in adult smokers in the U.S. from almost 80 percent in 1948 to 44 percent in 1964, to 29 percent in 1987, and 10 to 15 percent today depending on the state.

For all those ex-smokers, the health and longevity benefits start coming right away.

After 20 minutes without smoking, blood pressure decreases, pulse rate drops, body temperature of hands and feet increase.

Eight hours after quitting, carbon monoxide levels in the blood drop to normal and the oxygen level increases to normal. After 24 hours the chance of a heart attack decreases. After two weeks circulation improves and walking is easier.

At one year, the excess risk of heart disease is decreased to half that of a smoker. Five years and stroke risk is down to that of a non-smoker. Ten years and lung cancer risk is down by half. Fifteen years and risk of heart disease and death rate are reduced to almost that of non-smokers.

Mom's and Dad's smoking habits are the biggest factor in children delaying smoking or never starting at all. Over 60 percent of smokers under age 19 are children of parents who smoke (70 percent for girls and 54 percent of boys). Only 35 percent of the smokers under 19 are children of nonsmokers.

So after all the arguing about smoking statistics, what's the best thing a smoking parent can do to steer the kids in the right direction?

Quit.

9. The Battle of the Bulge.

Obesity is an unpleasant word reserved for body fat that's out of control. For children, obesity is reached when total body weight is more than 25 percent fat for boys, 32 percent for girls. Normally, two out of ten children are in this category, but the number can reach eight out of ten children when both of their parents are obese.

In 1970 we Americans fed ourselves on 3,300 calories each day. That was the production from food companies consumed in the USA in those days. Now we are up to 3,800 calories a day according to Marion Nestlé's book, *Food Politics: How the Food Industry Influences Nutrition and Health.*

The extra 500 daily calories (equivalent to an extra banana split every day) has added 10 pounds to the average weight of a teenager compared with kids of the 90s, says the Pediatricians

Research Group of Woodlands, TX. It's not surprising when you consider we tempt ourselves with over 10,000 new food products each year—mostly candy, snacks, soft drinks, baked goods, and ice creams.

Of course exercise enters in. Teenagers who report more than five hours of sedentary TV per day are five times more likely to be overweight than kids watching less than two hours each day. Snacks during TV, say, a small bag of potato chips each day, will add a half pound each week. Not much you might think, but it totals up to a 26-pound weight-gain each year.

The weight problem of our children is bulging about as fast as their parents' poundage. Back in 1991, when we were each consuming not much more than 3,300 calories per day, only Mississippi, Alabama, and West Virginia had more than 15 percent obese adults. Now more than 20 percent of adults are obese in over half the states.

No doubt the food pushers both at home and in the food business deserve some of the blame for the increases. TV with too many commercials about food and computer time with too much junk food next to the keyboard are bad routines.

Parents can set a slow pace at family meals, even when eating out as much as Americans do. Serving sizes in restaurants are ever larger and parents should keep limits in place even there. The kids could take a doggy bag home, also.

At home, serving water at every meal and having everyone serve their plates, then putting the extra away before sitting down, are healthy habits.

Everything we do requires some effort and inconvenience. All behaviors, even getting out the donuts or hot snack, have an inconvenience. You have to get a plate, find a fork, warm it up, get a drink to go with it.

So keep the healthy food handy and ready—fruit, instead of chips, on the table, ice water instead of soft drinks in the fridge. Let the fat, salt and sugar be the ones that are the most trouble to get from the store and the most troublesome to get out at home. The kids will buy other snacks, but at least at home your diet and their diet will be better.

10. Cars and the Driving Threat

The biggest danger to teenagers, bigger than all the other diseases and accidents of childhood put together, comes when they are almost grown. In the late teenage years, emergency room visits jump from 30 to 60 per million per day and the death rate skyrockets from one per million per day to 10!

The big change is, of course, driving.

A survey by the Liberty Mutual Insurance Company and Students Against Destructive Decisions asked high school students to interview over 1300 teen drivers with accidents or recent near misses. All parents should know the survey results these dedicated students reported after interviewing their fellow drivers.

Over 68 percent of these teens who have had traffic incidents said they were distracted at the crucial moment (47 percent had more than two passengers with them). Sixty-one percent were changing songs on their radio, or CD player. And 36 percent said they were texting when the accident or near miss occurred and the same proportion said they were on their cell phone. Forty-six percent admitted they were speeding.

The number of teenage drivers involved in fatal crashes has decreased almost 55 percent since the highs in years prior to 2005.

Nevertheless, 2500 lives are lost every year according to the Centers for Disease Control and Prevention. Graduated licenses that limit night driving and the restriction on the number of passengers for younger teen drivers can take much of the credit for the reduced numbers.

The driving hours of these multi-taskers increases in the summer.

In July and August teens in the Liberty Mutual study averaged 28.6 driving hours per week. In the school year they averaged 16.4 hours. Still only seven percent said summer driving was more dangerous.

Parents insist on using car seats and seat belts with young children, but when the kids turn 16, all parental efforts are overwhelmed and swept aside by the shocking statistics of driving and riding with reckless friends.

Girls are now almost as much at risk as boys. In 1990, 160 of every 1000 under-18 girls wrecked their cars that year and by 2000 the number was 175. The boys are steady at 210 per 1000 per year.

Alcohol abuse plays a large role. The National Center on Addiction and Substance Abuse reports that girls drink just as much as boys—48 percent of girls drink; 52 percent of boys. In 2000, among high school freshmen, girls nudged out the boys for first place in reports of regular drinking—41 percent of girls and 40 percent of boys.

This summer will bring another round of deaths from drunk driving and risky driving. You don't want to wake up in the middle of the night to that terrible phone call, "This is Officer Smith of the State Police, Your daughter (son) has been . . ."

Parents who get that call will pray, in that first heart-stopping moment, that it only involves an arrest or accident and not an injury or death.

The statistics would say Mom and Dad probably gave permission for the driving plan after extracting a few promises—no deviations from the plan, no craziness, and, they might have said, no drinking—but all were likely violated at the fatal moment.

Saying, "Be careful" is not enough. Limitations and restrictions need to be enforced. Better yet, join a parent team that will check on your teen's friends and their evening plans in exchange for your promise to check on yours.

Nothing about safety you have ever done to protect them during all their growing up years is as important as your riding and driving rules.

Mastering use of a car follows the same principles as learning other skills, but your teen places extra value on it. A driving school will help your teen master driving, but you will influence the early practice and a great deal of the long-term habits.

At the first driving session with your teenager he/she can simulate driving. Have him/her sit in the car and pretend starting, braking, and turning the car, to become comfortable with the controls. Talk through a drive around the neighborhood, pretend you accelerate up the hill, pull out around a parked car, and look both ways at the stop sign.

After one or two pretend sessions on the controls and learning permit in hand, have your teen practice driving in an empty parking lot to gain real experience with controls and maneuvering the car. Repeat this several times before moving to the next step. Plan your route each time before starting the car. Most traumatic moments start with a misunderstanding of what was to be done:

Dad: *"Turn here!"*

Teen: *"What? Which way?"*

Dad: *"Right here!"*

Teen: *"Right?"*

Dad: *"No, no, left, right here!"*

Teen: *"Left, right, make up your mind!"*

The next sound you hear in this situation may be the sound of collapsing metal and plastic. Review plans before taking off. Also review the rules of the road as they apply to parking lots. The most likely minor accident of teens is one in a parking lot where right-of-way is not obvious, and a lot of backing up is required.

Now, before our new driver gets the idea all of this is for free, set up a matching funds program for gasoline, car servicing, driver's license, and insurance fees. And for self-esteem, use your new driver's help with errands and family transportation.

A teen's use of the car is an effective incentive for schoolwork or chores. Work out a plan everyone has a stake in and understands. Earned time can be recorded on the refrigerator door and used as your teen needs it. Instead of taking away earned driving time for poor behavior, use alternatives to punishment.

When Jeff didn't do his big English project, Mom and Dad heard about it and postponed his car use that week. When he completed the report and was up-to-date in his work, he was able to use his accumulated driving time.

Oversee driving practice. When Tom's family traveled to visit relatives in the next state, he did part of the driving, and when Mom or Dad did local errands, Tom was the chauffeur. Before he had too much time out on his own, Tom had gained valuable experience and he was encouraged for his good driving habits.

Using appropriate speed is especially important to practice. Excessive speed is the most common cause of fatal car accidents. After Barb drove Dad to the mall and back, he praised her. *"I felt safe with you driving because you kept to the speed limit. Also, when we stopped at an intersection, I noticed you looked both ways before starting again. So many people run the yellow lights now, a green light doesn't always mean the road will be clear for you."*

Mom let Tom know when she felt uneasy riding with him. *"Leave more room between yourself and the next car. What if he had to stop suddenly? We'd crash into him!"* Over-balance corrections with praise for your teen's desirable habits to keep a positive feeling about sharing car rides with you.

In spite of your driving model and encouragement of safety, your teen may have poor driving habits. Talk over options to encourage the behavior or limit car use, if that is necessary. Emphasize the desired behavior, but take steps to limit the driving privilege until your teen commits him or herself to the safe driving goal.

**Most people
will not treat
your kids any better
than you do.**

Step 11: Encourage Your Almost-Adult

At the beginning, listening was the most critical parent skill. Now as our near-adult faces dangerous temptations, listening with respect becomes an even more critical parent skill. Begin treating them like adults now.

1. Beware the "You're-just-not-perfect" game.

"You're the son I hoped you would be!" That's the most important compliment most young men want to hear from their dad.

I think daughters live for the same acceptance, and I'm sure sons and daughters both hope for their mother's approval just as intensely as Dad's.

One father told about how he successfully changed his expectations of his son this way: *"I always felt I just didn't know where to start with Frank. He always did so many things wrong!"*

"So what did you work on first?" I asked.

"Everything, I guess—all his mistakes. Whenever I had the chance I went after something. But this shotgun approach just made him more and more angry. He thought I hated him!

"When he said he wanted to be treated like an adult, I thought he meant he wanted unreasonable adult freedoms. I guess he did mean that, but when I started treating him like an adult in the sense of leaving out little criticisms, judgments, and petty punishments, our relationship started to change. I sharpened my focus and gave up my expectations for perfect. I took your advice of "Catch him being good," doing right on little things. When I got realistic about what Frank might do well, he began to improve and we got along better, too."

Mealtimes can often give a representative picture of how family relationships are going. You might think that if the family counselor came to visit, everyone would only show their best side, but I have found that most people fall back to regular habits before we're done with the soup.

On one family visit, Dad showed me his new super computer. His old one had been passed down to his two sons, and they were busy playing games on it. After the tour of the information highway, we were ready for lunch, but the boys wanted to show me their computer also. They had done some clever work with Dad's drafting program on the old computer. Dad said it was amazing how fast they had picked up the use of the program. The boys immediately switched to showing Dad the latest accomplishments instead of explaining it to me. They zeroed right in on Dad's admiration. Since he was usually generous with it, they always wanted to tell Dad the latest about the computer.

Dad later told me that when his father was fatally ill, he had stayed with his mother who would otherwise have been alone at that terrible time. Near the end his father said, *"You're a wonderful son."*

"It was a great moment, but it was also an awful moment, I only wish he had mentioned it 30 years sooner."

2. Start at a Level You Can Encourage.

The key here is to start at a level where you can guarantee yourself an opportunity to encourage your teen's behavior. Let's say you want your teen to help around the house and to talk pleasantly to his younger sister. Watch for the rare incident when your teen helps or talks nicely with his sibling. Praise the behavior in a sincere way: *"I noticed how you helped Lisa with her baseball mitt, thanks."*

Recognize the aid even if it was not a big deal. It is a beginning and the social support for it will have a powerful effect. If you don't notice any help or pleasant talk between siblings, you need to suggest a small way in which it can happen. Tell him to help his younger brother (or sister) pump up a tire so the bicycle can be used. Be sure to show honest praise. Until such help or pleasant talk is a habit, you will need to notice or initiate it often and support it with appreciation.

Choose a behavior you want your teen to use. If you decide that spending a longer time working on schoolwork is a desired behavior, give recognition for even the first small improvement in studying. This is a starting level and encouragement should come right away. As the behavior increases you can expand your expectations, as we do with adults in the work place.

3. What Are Realistic Expectations?

"Mom, can you help me sew this patch on my jeans?"
"Sure, why don't you let me do it? It'll be faster."
Oops, this is a missed opportunity for learning by practice. How about replacing this first reaction with a more productive one?

"Sure, you go ahead and I'll let you know when you go wrong." That's

better. Now there will be practice—he will not *learn* if he doesn't *do*. But the negative emphasis on the possibility of being wrong certainly makes it hard for a teen to feel comfortable. Let's try to improve the chances for a positive outcome.

"Sure, let me baste it into place; then I'm sure you can handle it." Here's a good start; it sets up a situation where the son will practice with a better chance for success, and Mom has a good chance to be encouraging. We need to carefully match a teen's capabilities, needs, and interests to the tasks parents can encourage that will produce the best progress and the happiest experiences.

Psychologists worry about our modern society forcing adult concerns on a child-teen too soon. And yes, we shouldn't be tempted to force financial, social, or career concerns on teens too soon as a means of "growing them up." But we can gradually allow our teen's real practice by increasing responsibilities to help them increase their abilities and self-esteem as they get older.

Tolerate a teen's mistakes because it is an essential part of learning new skills. Errors are a part of learning but they may be hard to tolerate. Parents might be tempted to do the job because they are more efficient, but learning is in the doing. In giving over new responsibilities, a little early is better than a little late.

Take a thoughtful look at a list of responsibilities you can gradually give over to your teen. Of course, they can make their own bed, lunch, and phone calls, but they can also arrange rides to activities, make dental appointments, keep a bank account and choose a summer camp.

Ask yourself, *"How many other responsibilities are important for my teen to master?"* Make a list and decide which one can come next.

Fill in the ages you think are appropriate for children and teens to begin taking these responsibilities. At the start of each new responsibility there will be mistakes, but through practice, behaviors will be mastered before the young adult leaves home. Consider the following list and the suggested ages. What age would you choose?

Responsibility	Suggested Age
Clean-up room	4?
Make bed	6?
Select clothes to wear	7?
Bathe frequently	8?
Cook meals (with help)	9?
Use allowance without advice	9?
Decide hobbies and sports	9?
Choose his own diet from what is served	10?
Do homework (no nagging)	10?
Choose bedtime	11?
Show good manners at meals	11?
Save and spend money	11?
Plan and cook meals	12?
Buy clothes	12?
Do own laundry	12?
Choose summer camp	13?
Decide evening schedule	13?
TV and homework scheduling	14?
Plan some hours on weekends	15?
Choose weekend hours	17?

Mom tolerated a half-hour of mistakes and spills before hearing Keith say, *"OK, Mom, I'm putting my cake in the oven."*

Mom: *"Great. What temperature?"*

Keith: *"350 degrees, I'm setting it now."*

Mom: *"Keith, why don't you wait on putting in the cake for a few minutes so the oven can warm up. Then the cake won't be crusty from having the heat on so long at the beginning."*

Keith: *"Oh. That's what 'preheat' means in the recipe?"*

Mom: *"Right. What a treat this will be with supper!"*

A parent can learn to tolerate the inconvenience of allowing a teen to make mistakes and improve with practice when trying is viewed as a sign of growing to adulthood. Give responsibility now, gradually, not abruptly on the steps of a college dormitory or in the back of a church just before a ceremony. And always keep the praise and incentives handy.

4. Avoid Rules That Only Work Once.

Some parental reactions may not be easily repeated. "If you don't stop picking fights with your sister, we will not sign you up for dance this year!"

Signing up for dance is a single future event not likely to be repeated for some time. It is tempting to repeat the threat as the consequence many times since dance class registration itself will only happen once. It's negative reinforcement using repeated threats, but the dance sign-up is a single event. This consequence is so far off that verbal decorations seem required because any outcome, way down the road, will seem weak at a distance.

Then after all the argument, you either give in and sign the kid up for dance or you hold to your threat, don't sign her up, and admit you are giving no credit for the better behaviors. This says that, overall, she has been a bad kid. It's a one-shot consequence with no winners and little chance of a satisfactory outcome.

With a one-time consequence, parents are tempted to do a lot of talking in order to "milk" all the influence they can from the upcoming big event. The temptation is to hold out the possibility of punishment over your teenager for days or weeks.

A better strategy is to allow yourself and your family the enjoyment of individual events without trying to use them to limit bad behavior or produce good behavior. Instead, choose a smaller event that can come up more frequently, something that's not so severe and has a positive side to emphasize. For example, instead of threatening to ground you teen every time he delays doing as you requested for too long, could you put fifty cents on his desk when he does as requested in a reasonable time? Now we would have a repeatable consequence that requires no verbal decorations. Change the numbers to fit your situation.

This procedure can work well when breaking curfew is the problem. After she is ten minutes late every minute costs a point. Ten points subtracts one weekend evening out. This is kind of punishment but it is mild. Possibly you could exclude certain important events from the grounding and allow your daughter to select the weekend evening to stay in.

This procedure has the advantage of being consistent, repeatable and not so severe as to make parents feel guilty and inconsistent. It is logically related to the problem of staying out too late.

A very repeatable consequence makes it much easier to refrain from nagging. The repetition does the reminding. Nagging can stop and that will open the airways for more pleasant family talk.

5. "When are You Going to Start Treating Me Like an Adult?"

Kids changing into adults can be so demanding! They are horses at the starting gate, anxious, often aggravated, pushing at the restraints that keep them back. When can we give in to their demands and which restraints should go first?

Fortunately, the analogy to the horse at the starting gate ends when you consider how many different starting gates we have for teens and that we can close and re-open many of them. We don't have just one moment to start the challenge of adulthood, but we do need to start opening some doors for the sake of practice and to give our teens some running room to build feelings of importance and accomplishment.

As teens grow they are expected to take added responsibility and to learn skills needed to survive as happy, independent adults. They are also expected to contribute to the family. For a person still clinging too much to childhood, these expectations add up to a lot of worry and confusion. If the responsibilities are begun early so they can be added slowly, a teen struggling to be an adult can be proud of new capabilities instead of anxious about new demands. Capabilities lead to usefulness which leads to contentment with one's self as a person who carries some of his own load.

At any age after the toddler years, a person's feeling of self-worth can be improved by practicing self-reliance and helping others. Skills learned now will be a source of pride. The self-esteem gained from new competence and appreciation from others is important to happiness.

Mastering survival skills also brings rewards in the short and long terms: school skills benefit life-long learning; skill and understanding in dealing with friends now benefit later relationships, and responsibilities now benefit later career plans, success at part-time jobs, and time and money management.

As their skills develop, teens' concerns become more similar to ours every day.

6. Parents Become Coaches.

Teens still need a lot of help from their parents, but they need a different delivery system from when they were children. Parents should adjust their parenting styles to their teenagers' growing sensitivities about taking increasing control over their lives and discovering their own solutions to life's demands and problems. Parents represent a decreasing portion of their teen's experience but have more advice to give. The parent's role is changing from leader and provider of consequences to companion and coach.

An effective coach provides practice and also advice from the sidelines while the consequences come (more and more) from the other players. A coach is a good observer, listener, planner, enabler, storyteller, and model. Observing and listening can reveal a teen's needs, and a parent-coach can provide more help to his or her teen's understanding of what's going on. Without careful listening, coaching teens is difficult. It's like running a practice without knowing what happened in last week's game.

Good coaching also uses storytelling and companionship as pleasant ways to pass along experiences. Stories are less threatening than straightforward advice. They set out alternatives and work well with other activities.

Practice can have its ups and downs. At times teens will be optimistic, ready to enjoy moments of life and set aside responsibilities (Bumper Sticker: *Let's Party!*). Paradoxically, at other times they are pessimistic, less confident in their abilities, and negative about nearly everything (Bumper Sticker, same car: *There is No Gravity, the Earth Sucks!*).

The same cycles are common in adults. Parents who recognize the temporary nature of both extremes can remain calm, providing a steady influence for realistic attitudes and opportunities for lessons to learn. The main role of a parent-coach here is to hold a reasonable view of life while the younger members of the family swing from side to side.

7. Self-Esteem is Learned from Your Parents.

How well does your teenager like himself or herself? A person's value of self is always a concern, but in teens it's nearly a preoccupation. High self-esteem builds confidence, productivity, and a resistance to risky temptations. A teen who can say, *"I'm a valuable person,"* will resist self-abuses such as alcohol, drug abuse, depression, and self-degrading sex.

So another role for parents is to enable your teen to learn by doing, to provide practice so that your teen's value of him or herself is increased. For example, Elsa's dad noticed that Elsa spent a lot of time tapping on the table and listening to rock music. She moved around the house a lot, but didn't focus on any satisfying activity. When she mentioned the school band and drums, Dad encouraged her to look into it, talk to the teacher, and learn about what was required.

Elsa and Dad went out to buy the instrument together. The project involved some parental coaching, some doing on the part of Elsa, and some direct parental help from Dad.

When Brian's school backpack was beyond repair, Mom didn't run out and buy one. She said he should check around on his own to compare values and prices for a new pack on his computer.

Then they went together to make a selection.

As teens experience success or failure at coping with the world's demands and their own ambitions, their self-esteem follows the roller coaster. Having less experience with the ups and downs than we do, they can reach extreme opinions about themselves, inflated or depressed. Their mood changes can be deeper than those of thicker-skinned adults.

Parents can help teens learn to improve and maintain high self-esteem. Our most helpful influence is the model we set of feeling good about ourselves. Share your highs concerning your own accomplishments and in some small way compliment your teen everyday for his/her strengths and achievements. Encourage your teen to praise his/her *own* accomplishments and concentrate on the strengths of others.

Often your example of just being active will be imitated and helpful. *"Whenever I feel down, I shoot some baskets."* Activity is therapeutic—if we can get it started. Teens gain satisfaction from an activity that interests them: a hobby, school assignment, or spending time with others who have common interests. Special experiences such as a part-time job can also increase satisfaction.

Using these guidelines can help your teenager gain and maintain high self-esteem.

8. Mastering Self-Care.

Confidence and independence increase when teens assume responsibility for their diet, hygiene, grooming, room care, and language. Teens may not like making their own school lunches, but they will feel more capable and grown up when they do.

Eating. The best place to influence a teen's diet is at the market. Teens will choose from what you serve, even if they can choose other items when they are out. If parents have not already allowed food choices from balanced offerings at mealtimes, without comment and coercion, the teenage years are not too late to start. In the short term, teens may make unbalanced selections, and, of course, will eat carry-out food, but presented with consistently healthy choices at home and parent-coaches as models, their diet will be on the whole adequate and healthy.

Grooming. Peer pressure usually makes a teen adopt acceptable grooming habits. Choosing unusual hairstyles and clothing may be calls for attention and help, or they may indicate concern for fashion. Within reason, it is probably best not to create a confrontation over fashion and style. Consider how you would react to an adult visitor, with respect to your grooming choices. When teens assert themselves through unusual clothes and hairdos, parents need to see it as growth toward adulthood and not a reflection of their own values.

A teen needs to make clothing purchases. This is an opportunity to make and follow a budget. Along with clothes selection comes care of clothing. Show your teen how to use the washer and dryer, if needed. Make a check list together to specify what clothes are washed how and when. The checklist can also reduce the nagging.

Room Care. Sometimes teens love to fix up their rooms to their own tastes and the variety (some would have a less complimentary name for it) is remarkable! Be tolerant. Encourage your teen to select his/her own furnishings, as much as possible, with your help on shopping.

If a young person has gradually learned to pick up clothes, make the bed, dust, and vacuum, it's time for him/her to take over the total job of room care. How well they keep their own private space should be viewed with your best tolerance.

Before a positive incentive is worked out, parents will have to make an important judgment. How important is a minimum clean-up and how often do you want it done? An answer to these "value" questions will lead to an easier decision about how to do the encouragement part and avoid unpredictable blowups when Mom or Dad visit their teen's private space. If the request is to be small and infrequent, then just a little support and encouragement might be enough. A major cleaning every week may require something more concrete.

A clean-up check list spells out the little things, chips away resistance to an all-or-nothing effort, and pays off at an agreed time. What is clean enough for a compliment? The one who has to live with the room the way it is should have the most say.

Language use is modeled, but extremes picked up from peers or the media can become a habit. Coach Dad told a story from work about losing respect for his boss when she used foul words, and Coach Mom told of her soccer teammate who was high on her scale until she used a lot of profanity arguing at a game. Family members were fond of repeating the remark of a favorite short teacher who stood up to a tall student when he used bad language. She said, *"Profanity is a sign of a limited mind."*

9. Learning Adult Survival Skills.

Beyond self-care, teens are expected to master life skills essential to their happiness and independence during their teen and early adult years: schoolwork, social relationships, recreational activities, career plans, part-time jobs, and money management.

Parents often complain to their teens, *"If you can't go out and spend or eat, you think there's nothing to do!"*

With many adult physical capabilities and a great deal of information about all the opportunities out there, teens are ready for action and adventure. Chores can fill in some boring moments in a teen's life, but where are the little successes that come from hobbies and recreations?

Teens need help developing satisfaction from their activities. A mom who enjoys tinkering with her car is a model for her teenager as surely as the father who loves knitting sweaters. Encourage a teen to choose two school or community activities, clubs, or pastimes that follow his/her interests. This is a time for your teenager to take control and make choices. You can share the cost for fees and supplies and provide transportation to events. Generosity will pay double dividends when helping a teen learn new interests. Recognize effort and achievement as your teen pursues his/her interests.

TV is popular with many teens who look forward to their favorite shows as recreation or an escape from problems or boredom. Teens can learn much that is worthwhile from TV.

But teens have a tremendous need to develop skills by doing, by interacting with people or things, not through the passive activity of staring. So work with your teen to agree on limits for TV viewing; be available as a companion to listen and do alternative activities together that you both enjoy, and help your teenager find active interests to replace TV.

One family controlled TV time by keeping it off on school afternoons and evenings, unless a parent OK'd turning it on. Teens in that family pursued swim team, soccer, piano, ballet, and raised a seeing-eye dog. The swim team experience led to summertime pool jobs. A lot of parent encouragement and transportation helped these teens start and continue their skill-building hobbies.

10. A Part-Time Job.

Just as hobbies can be therapeutic to a teen, an outside job can fill spare time in a worthwhile way. A job can help a teenager apply learning from home and school, such as ways to get along with a boss and co-workers, organize time and materials, communicate with the public, and be dependable.

Seven out of ten jobs filled every day come from grapevine leads, so a teen needs to let people know he/she is seeking a position. Encourage a teen to be selective. Since a teen learns what he/she does, the tasks of a part-time job should be worthwhile and not take too many hours at the wrong times so schoolwork suffers.

An outside job can mean less help with home chores, so plan to lift some of those requirements when your teen starts his or her first job. There is bound to be increased independence, so discuss hours and chores expected, and be extra encouraging for behaviors you agree on. Consider, *"What would be fair if I had an adult boarder?"*

Of course an adult boarder would take care of his/her own chores, and would also have other activities, friends, and a job. Your teen is reaching for adult responsibility and independence, but unlike an adult boarder, your teen still needs your support, coaching, and limits.

11. Managing Money.

As a teen's allowance and job earnings grow, provide new ways to spend it besides for your teen's own amusement and stomach. Teens can contribute to expenses for birthday gifts, the family car and a savings account for a long-range purchase. A matching funds program for buying clothes lets parents and teens share costs, giving a sense of responsibility in selecting clothes and caring for them.

An Exercise About Career Interests and Strengths. This activity can help your teen think about jobs they could be part of now and ones for which they can plan. Psychologists tell us that teens who have a career goal are more likely to complete their education and stay clear of drugs, crime and teen pregnancy than those who have no long-range plan. The goal may extend your teen's present interests and abilities even though they may change along the way.

1. Have your teen list his/her ten strongest interests.

Examples: nature, health, music, soccer, computers, work with wood, cooking, helping people, business, and politics.

2. Now have your teen list his/her ten strongest abilities.

Examples: organization, grooming, art, math, reading, understanding others, working quickly, persuading others, working alone, and mechanics.

3. Have your teen list five places in the nearby area that have jobs related to each area of interest and strength.

Some jobs may be long-term goals, others may be in reach now, and they could ask to volunteer or assist others.

An example for music would be: library—audio-visual librarian; record store—clerk; piano store—salesperson; music pavilion—booking agent; school—music teacher.

4. If your teen is interested in a particular career, you might find a friend in that career who will talk about it to your teen.

I know one mother who, when her daughter said she wanted to own her own business some day, invited friends who had their own businesses to a dinner party and a discussion about owning their own business. One business owner couldn't make it because of a business crisis. That was a lesson in itself.

These exercises increase your teen's understanding of him or herself and a parent's understanding of when to listen up. Help your teen make a resume and consider part-time jobs related to his or her areas of interests and strengths.

Extra money should create opportunities for teens to expand control and responsibilities for their own lives. They can begin to cover their day-to-day expenses, not just acquire money they spend for special things. It is cruel training to allow a teen to reap family benefits in the household while paying nothing in return.

A teen with too much money is a dangerous problem! Your teen may have worked for, and have a right to spend the money, but some things should no longer be free for the newly rich. A teen can begin to pay for transportation, extra clothes, and entertainment. For a young teen, however, food and room are part of family sharing and security. They should not be paid for by a teen until he/she completes school and has a full-time, self-supporting job.

In a more perfect world, everyone would do the right things for the right reasons. We wouldn't need special incentives such as paychecks, bonuses, benefits, or parents using the right reaction. The work would be done because we all know it needs to be done. In the real world, all dieters, regular working folks, and exercisers know that free-floating motivation is hard to maintain. We either keep going in order to avoid the negative reinforcement, or some positive reinforcement better be in the offing.

Concrete rewards may also be needed when laziness becomes habitual and resistance to change so strong that we need contrived rewards to make even small steps in progress. For example, to improve the homework study habit, you might adjust the weekly allowance according to the amount of homework done. The teen should be able to rely on a minimum allowance, but there is important school work to be done, so the real world might as well start right here—the work and the pay go together.

Set the limits, both minimums and maximums, so that you can't be cornered into an unreasonable position such as allowing *no* money if no homework gets done or having to pay too much if all the homework is done. You will want to keep it simple, but without stated limits you'll be tempted to give out undeserved money or have to refuse to pay up for a sudden burst of activity.

It will be better to set limits at the beginning—say a $6.00 minimum and a $15 maximum each week. The practice is the most important thing going on in your teen's life, so let's give practice some importance. We guarantee the minimum by saying, *"The $6.00 is for every week, but I'll add two dollars for each night your homework is all done, and two extra for a whole week of successful homework nights."* You could tie the definition of "homework done" to pages of workbooks or the teacher assignments or time spent on homework each night.

With this amount of structure, you'll avoid being an ogre who won't give any allowance, and you'll avoid extravagant payoffs for bursts of activity. After a few weeks, you may want to add special incentives for some subjects or change the definition of homework done, or add an extra pay increase for special efforts. All rules are subject to change.

One of the keys to success in using incentives is to make very reasonable requests, especially at first. These requests should not be based on what *should* be done but on what *has been the usual.* An incentive for doing a half-hour or hour of homework for a teen who has not been able to stick with it for 10 minutes in the last three months is doomed to failure. Start at the current level of your teen now, add a very small extra for the first allowance increment, then the requests can be increased.

On day one, you want to guarantee that you will have an opportunity to use your incentive! Plan an incentive for a performance not only within your teen's ability but within his/her inclination as well. For example, you might ask that only one page of a workbook assignment be completed before a whole half-hour of TV is approved. The pay-off is so attractive, and the price tag so small that a success is likely.

With small successes "in the bank," we can start a progression toward the amount of homework required before the reward is available. The increments should be small enough to allow a smooth and easy increase in effort.

You must be careful when selecting "less logical or materialistic" rewards because they are usually not a natural benefit of the behavior, and the time will come when your teens will be on their own to be motivated by other less generous people. This means that your encouragement, admiration, and praise need to remain a major part of the rules even when concrete rewards are used. Your reactions send the message of the importance and usefulness of the activities you support. You hope that your target objectives are likely to be supported outside the family in a way that is at least enough to keep your teen on the right path.

The activities that other people support and believe important are probably the same as yours. Chores such as washing the car, mowing the lawn, painting, cooking, and shopping are some of the easy ones. A young person usually values the same activities even though it may not be "in" to say so.

Your teen's habitual attitude toward chores should not mislead you. Even teenagers who moan and complain when asked to pitch in, still grow a little when they *do* pitch in. Everyone wants to feel competent and able. So when you ask your teen to do chores, take heart in the fact that the advantage goes far beyond getting the chores done. As a matter of fact, the boost in your teen's self-respect may be the most important outcome!

Now as you allow your offspring to take part in adult activities, remember to include the fun parts of the job and not just the less desirable ones. When washing the car, she should get to use the hose as well as scrub the wheels. When shopping for food, he should be allowed to pick out a goody as well as get the soap.

One last caution concerning the first efforts to support good behavior: the proof of a little success is in the daily and weekly changes, *not* the immediate reactions of the kids. Remember kids can be very pessimistic about your power. This pessimism may stem partly from their own feelings of powerlessness and partly from a desire to discourage you from trying to influence them. Don't buy it. The proof of change is in the longer term reactions and adjustment.

A second related tactic of teens may be to belittle the *consequence* as too weak to do any good. The power of consequences is in their accumulated numbers. Small compliments and encouragements, such as *"You're running the laundry through by yourself? You really are growing up!"* or *"Gerry, why don't you call in the pizza order, you're getting so good on the phone."*

Every penny in the bank adds up—don't be talked out of it, just say (or think), *"Let's see how it goes."*

Self-esteem
Is learned From
Your parents.

Step 12: Protect Yourself During the Parenting Job

Most parents are willing to give whatever effort is needed to produce good results. But usually they give very little consideration to their own comfort and welfare in the child/teen rearing process. This is a serious oversight. Raising a teen is a long process, and parents need to be as comfortable with it as possible.

Also, whatever parents are willing to take will become a tolerance level that their teen is likely to acquire through imitation. Many mothers hope their daughters and sons will stick up for themselves in their occupation, marriage, and the sexist world they live in. And many regret some moments of over-reaction and hope for more thoughtful reactions from their own children. So now, for the benefit of both you *and* your teen, let's consider how raising an adult should come out *for you!*

1. Who Is Responsible?

Teenage cries for help often include accusations that parents are to blame for whatever their teen is or does. Of course, parents do carry some responsibility, but their offspring will have to take responsibility for *themselves* if they are to grow up.

Even on the trivial side, these accusations should not go unchallenged because they prolong the childhood that now must be left behind: *"Mom, the car won't start!" "Dad, where are my shoes? I'm late!"* In trying to help with car trouble and lost shoes and then face the demands of their own work, Mom and Dad often overlook their own feelings and rights.

A parent who continually accepts responsibility and blame and feels accountable for whatever goes wrong, sacrifices his/her own self-esteem. Although it is contradictory to do so, a teen may model a parent's sacrificial and self-deprecating disposition and at the same time be disappointed in his parent. Teens want to copy someone and the parent, right or wrong, is the most likely person. So teenagers may crave people who provide unreasonable sacrifices for them, and yet need parents to set an example that's better than that—an example where parents protect their own feelings and rights while balancing family and work loyalties.

When parents take care of their own needs, they help their teens as well as themselves.

2. Nine Parent Rights.

Parents have the right to react when they are not treated with respect, and to say *"no"* when their rights and values are threatened. At times when efforts are not appreciated and interactions have soured, moms and dads have the right to express their feelings, to think over choices, and change their minds. Parents have the right to make mistakes and still feel good about themselves.

These statements may seem too basic to be emphasized, but many parents need to remind themselves of their right to being less than perfect. It is unfair to hold a person to a standard of perfection—parent *or* teen. With the standard of perfection excluded, one feels a greater freedom to go ahead and try new solutions. Mistakes become evidence of trying some solution, not evidence of failure. *Both* parent and teen will find more solutions if their right to make mistakes is respected.

Many of the rights discussed here were first described in *The Assertive Option: Your Rights and Responsibilities* by Patricia Jakubowski and Arthur J. Lange, plus one or two variations I have added. Using these rights will provide a feeling of satisfaction with yourself and your family and preserve your spirit through your teen's growing-up years.

1. You Have the Right to Your Own Values.

How much time do you want to put toward cleaning your car? Car care may have low priority on your list, and you may have to take some heat from family members who want a cleaner vehicle, less filled with "junk."

Parents have the right to spend time in ways that promote their own values, their own view of the important things in life, as long as others' rights are not hurt. So complaints about the poor condition of the car can trigger a plan for a future family activity but need not make you feel guilty.

We cannot let others, even unintentionally, deny the important things in our lives. If your teenager wants to use the car tonight, you may want to make time for a *shared* session of car care or suggest that your teen be the one to wash and vacuum it.

This may help us understand a teenager's resistance to cleaning his/her room. Parents do well to use caution in criticizing a teen's tolerance for clutter and disarray.

Tolerance for the habits of good health can be the goal to help a teen achieve room cleanliness.

2. You Have the Right to Speak Out and Take Action If You Are Not Treated Respectfully.

One father told me he met his son, Bill, talking with a group of school friends at the mall. But after Bill said, *"Hi!"* he continued his conversation with one friend instead of introducing his father. So Dad introduced himself, shaking hands with each student and talking to the nearest one.

Bill probably realized his mistake when his father took the initiative to make introductions. Later Dad can tell Bill how he felt, so next time his son might remember his responsibility. By taking action Dad showed respect for himself and set an example of how the situation could be better.

After Bill loaned his team shirt to his sister, she left it in a heap on the floor of her room. Bill was mad. *"If you want to borrow my shirt, show some respect for it. Hang it up and return it when you're done so I'll feel like loaning you other things."* Jane knows she was wrong and is more likely to take Bill's comments seriously, because he told her what he expected instead of just demanding the shirt back.

For an exercise about respect, each person in your family could write about a situation in which he/she was not respected—not necessarily within the family. Pass the situations to the left several times. Each person can read an example and tell what action he/ she would do. How would other family members react? How can we call attention to the need for respect for that person?

3. You Have the Right to Say "No" When Your Rights Are Not Respected.

One mother told me about a caller who asked her to canvass

the neighborhood for a charity drive. She quickly evaluated her energy limits and answered, *"No."* Time was short, and she realized she couldn't meet commitments to family and work if she took on yet another charity role. In the past, Mom had felt worn out from trying to do everything whenever anyone asked for her help. Later she focused on only the highest priorities and guarded against giving away family time.

Saying *"no"* is often so difficult we have to regularly remind ourselves of priorities and rehearse our *"no"* for that next request that may come today. Family priorities are continuous and can easily slip to a lower place on the list. Parents need to guard against that temptation.

A teen has a right to say *"no,"* also. Laurie knew she would feel sick from the long drive to see an elderly relative; she was able to stay behind by making an alternate plan: visiting a friend's house and taking an afternoon bike ride. If the activity was *required,* Mom and Dad could still respect her feelings about the car ride by playing *her* radio station and breaking up the trip with meals. If she had been old enough, she could have driven part of the distance each way.

Priorities could be reviewed in an exercise where each family member makes a weekly time page: 7 A.M. at the top left side of a sheet of paper, and the hours down the page to 10 P.M. Across the top, list the days. Fill in daily activities and free half-hours.

Now think of one new activity you would say *"yes"* to, and one you would answer with *"no."* Share your schedules and activity choices. While some parents resent driving teens to friends' houses or tagging along on shopping trips, some do not. One father enjoyed the chance to have time alone with his teenager, confiding feelings, sharing special stories, and building a closer relationship.

4. You Have the Right to Feel the Way You Do and to Express Your Feelings.

Dad felt down when he came home from work. He'd had a run-in with an associate and other things had not gone well. Instead of trying to turn his feelings around while they ate supper, Mom and his daughters listened to his story without saying he should feel differently. They sat longer than usual around the table as each person pictured the way it was for Dad, and then told about their own day's events. Sharing the way he felt, instead of trying to cover up, helped Dad accept what had happened and look ahead.

Fourteen-year-old Chris complained, *"There's nothing to do around here!"* Mom felt he was trying to get her to play *"I-bet-you-can't-make-me-happy,"* but instead of making suggestions, she just let him know she heard him, *"You sound bored."*

"Yes, everyone's sick, and there's nothing I feel like doing."

"With everybody sick, it's hard to find something." Mom saw her teenager as growing up but still looking to her for help with the universal problem of managing time. If Chris were an adult he might have the same complaint. He had hobbies and chores that could be done, but it would take a while for him to work out an answer of his own choosing. Numerous suggestions from Mom would probably only continue an unsatisfying game of suggestions, objections, and more suggestions by Mom.

To get a better "feel for feelings," the family exercise could ask each person to share a memory, a time when he/she felt happy, angry, excited, disappointed, or some other emotion, and was accepted for having that feeling. Then they could share an incident when they were told their feelings were wrong. How did it make a difference?

5. You Have the Right to Take Time to Think About Choices.

If parents don't take time to consider their reactions, a teen may disrupt the family with disturbing announcements: *"I'm flunking math!"* *"I'm quitting band!"* *"I have to work in Ocean City this summer!"*

Parents need to ask themselves, *"Is the dramatic announcement a way to get into a conversation or a way to draw attention to a legitimate problem?"*

Waiting for more information may help a parent decide what is really intended. A reaction is not necessary since these are just words, not actions.

A calm approach helps your teen think over the problem. Use listening skills to get the whole story while helping your teen examine details. When both parents are there, they should hold out for a private parent-to-parent strategy session to find a compromise, instead of allowing teens to play each parent against the other right there on the spot. If other relatives live with you, enlist their agreement too, without teens present.

Teenagers also benefit from having time to think over consequences before making choices. *"Which friend do you want to invite on the camping trip?"* *"What kind of birthday celebration do you want to have next month?"* *"What courses will you take next year?"* Given choices and time, teens can learn to take charge of their lives.

Making choices could be part of a family exercise by having each member list a decision you had to make this past week, and recall how much time you spent considering choices. Did you need more time to make a good decision? How did your choice work out?

6. You Have the Right to Change Your Mind.

To coach a growing teenager requires flexibility as your teen's capabilities increase and circumstances change. One family I know didn't allow sleep-over friends for a long time because their teen, Eric, became sick and impossibly grumpy following those occasions. But as the years matured their teen, an occasional try seemed only fair.

The right to change your mind includes the right to hold to your present position, too. When teens argue for a change in rules, parents can remind them that parental limits are not the only obstacle to independence and good times. Teens are more limited by lack of education and restricted job opportunities than by parental rules. But restrictions need to be reduced as a teen demonstrates increasing responsibility and self-reliance. When Eric's sleepover problems had eased, he presented a reasonable plan to get chores and homework done so he could go on a weekend trip. He convinced his parents to change their initial negative reaction.

Teens also have a right to change their minds. Teens are learning to plan ahead and often find they make more commitments than they can keep. Danny signed up for several clubs and then had to drop out of two activities. When he didn't help with supper because of a club meeting, Dad filled in instead, and Danny made it up the next night.

A practice exercise in changing your mind could encourage family members to share stories. When did they make an agreement and then change it? Have each person tell what happened and how he/she felt about it.

7. You Have the Right to Ask for What You Need or Want.

As all working folk know, you *won't* get what you *don't* ask for. Some parents sacrifice for their teenagers instead of requesting help. Mom wanted assistance unloading and storing groceries, but instead of asking for it, she thought, *"My teenagers are tired, and I can do this for them.*" After she finished the work she felt worn out, and her sacrificial attitude had turned to resentment. She might be teaching her teens to take advantage of her (by acting tired), and she *and they* are likely to pay a price for that.

As a practice exercise here, have each person think of a time they asked or did not ask for help to meet a need or want. How did the experience work out, and how did they feel about it?

8. You Have the Right to Make Mistakes.

Dad forgot to pick up Bryan after a team practice at school. Bryan felt let down and disappointed with his father. When it happened a second time, Dad evaluated his efforts. Lately, work and community activities had been too demanding to allow him to give his son the time he needed. *"Everybody makes mistakes, including me,"* Dad said, *"but I'm going to ask for a replacement on the townhouse committee and leave work at 4:30 regularly."*

Mistakes are part of living, but feeling guilty doesn't help. When we do slip up, we can plan a change to make amends.

When her teen acted in ways Mom disliked, Mom started using the adage, *"I like you, but not your behavior."* Then she realized she needed to request certain actions and praise specific behaviors. *"I made a mistake by not adding the positive expectation. Now I'm going to try a better way."*

For an exercise about mistakes, ask each family member to share something new he/she is able to do this year that was not possible last year. Let everyone describe what made the learning possible, including mistakes.

9. You Have the Right to Feel Good About Yourself.

Parents can set a good example for their teenager by adopting the habit of accepting credit and blame only for their own actions.

A teen will learn to accept responsibility for problems as well as successes if his parent does not accept blame where there is no control. Guide your teen to connect outcomes with his/her own behaviors and not use past parent behaviors as a scapegoat.

Parents know that teens need to take the consequences for their actions, but parents' feelings of embarrassment, blame, and guilt can be strong, even if others don't blame Mom or Dad. Those feelings need to be recognized, and they can be put to a useful purpose: to analyze problems and plan for changes.

For the happiness of both parent and family, it can be a time for positive steps, to remind everyone of personal and family strengths. Put negative things in perspective by making lists of things you like about yourself and things you feel proud of. Here are a few examples.

1. I like myself because:

I work hard, I exercise to stay healthy, I am honest, I listen to others, have activities I like to do, am faithful.

2. Things I have done that make me feel proud are:

I helped my husband and kids, helped people at work saved money for trips

3. Ways I have helped my family members are:

I set an example, explored alternatives, listened, provided transportation, and helped plan ahead.

4. I feel proud of my family members because they are:

caring, intelligent, honest and hard-working.

3. An Exercise About Values.

Have each person in your family list five values they hold and two ways they carry them out every day. Collect and shuffle these lists. Pass them out and have each person read the list he or she has, letting others guess who made it.

Some Suggestions for Values on the list:

achievements, good looks, marriage

recreation, animals, hobbies

mental health, religion, beauty

honesty, money, sexuality

social acceptance, independence

parenting, sports, ethics

learning, peace, work (job)

friendship, loyalty, possessions

power

In the conversation, each person can give examples of their own list of items

For example, I value:

1. My family, so I spend time during activities with them that are fun, and I listen to them tell their experiences and explain their views.

2. Financial security, so I keep money records straight, plan purchases, and keep a budget.

3. Helping others, so I work in education and support a scholarship program.

4. My health, so I exercise regularly and eat healthy foods.

5. A clean environment, so I recycle and write letters about it.

4. Seek Cooperation from Your Spouse, Friends, and Relatives.

Single parents have many disadvantages in rearing children or teens solo. Yet they do have the advantage of a more consistent set of rules and reactions. Parents with or without partners encounter new problems as teen-rearing becomes *adult*-rearing. Expanding moments of separation become more apparent and the para-dox of *keeping* control while also *giving it away* creates tough moments for all parents.

5. Friends Should Protect Friends.

That's obvious enough, but what happens in *your* home when your teen mistreats you? Who comes to your defense?

Let's look at this conversation with Mom, her son Kevin, and Aunt Eileen:

Kevin: *"I'm going to watch TV now."*

Mom: *"What about your homework?"*

Kevin: *"Later. I've got plenty of time."*

Mom: *"Isn't your history paper due tomorrow?"*

Kevin: *"Mom, you don't know anything about how long that paper will take."*

Aunt Eileen: *"Be careful how you talk to your mother. She's had many years of school. I think she knows."*

Kevin: *"I'll do it when I'm ready."*

Aunt Eileen: *"Well, I can't take you to soccer practice until your Mom says you are ready."*

Kevin: *"You didn't even know about the history paper until Mom brought it up. It's none of your business."*

Mom: *"Don't talk to your aunt that way. She's concerned about you too. Now get to that paper so you can get to your practice on time."*

This struggle may not end here, but Mom and Aunt Eileen, standing up for each other, are not going to take part in Kevin's divide-and-conquer strategy. They stay close, and they don't tolerate abuse from Kevin.

Your best protectors are your own relatives, friends, or

spouse who will come to your aid when you are being mistreated—even by a teenager. Two adults can be stronger than one, and they can provide a model to children and teens about how members of the family should treat each other. *"Say, be careful how you speak to your mother!"* can be a source of comfort to a mom and a help to a growing teen blundering into accumulating guilt. Here's Mom with her friend Erica and her daughter Jenny:

Jenny: *"Mom, where's my tennis racket?"*

Mom: *"Just a minute, I'm talking."*

Jenny: *"I need it now!"*

Erica: *"Take it easy, Jenny, let your Mom finish."*

Mom: *"Thanks, Erica. I can use that support now and then."*

A teen's attitude comes from many sources, but relatives, friends, spouses and the extended family play a role from the beginning. They can make the effort to help, like Erica and Aunt Eileen, or, if they don't, they can be part of the problem. Here's Jane with her husband John:

John: *"You can't find your keys? I can't believe it!"*

Jane: *"Just a minute. Here they are."*

John: *"I swear, you would lose your head if you didn't have..."*

An adult game of *"I-can't-believe-you're-such-a-klutz!"* can be easily absorbed by the kids, and spouses or adult friends should avoid these "games." No one can watch everything they say, but friends of parents, particularly friends of single parents, should keep in mind the examples they set for the kids. The best help a friend of a parent can give is to show a model of respect for the one doing the parenting.

Mom and Aunt Eileen in the car with Kevin and Jenny:

Aunt Eileen: *"If you're going to look for a new car, you better take someone with you who knows something about it."*

Mom: *"I know something about it. I have three articles right here, I've read 'Buyer's Review,' and know the ratings."*

Aunt Eileen: *"Oh, then you're really prepared. What do you think of these prices?"*

Aunt Eileen starts off a little negative but ends up asking Mom for information. Now, Mom needs to return the favor.

Mom: *"How is the car you have holding up?"*

If significant others are going to help, Mom's (or Dad's) model of showing respect for the significant other needs to be part of your teen's family experience. When Mom respects the opinions of Dad, her example improves the value of the opinions of Dad in the eyes of the kids.

Now, when friends or relatives show confidence in Mom's ability to do anything from driving to making financial decisions, their opinion bears added weight when the kids hear it. *"What do you think about these prices?"* sends a message not only to Mom, as a parent, that her thoughts are of value, but also to any other ears in hearing range.

This is a good reason to sort out conflicts in private—away from your teenagers. Teens always have their "antennae out" and are more interested in what the conversations say about how *the people around them feel about each other* than the content of the argument.

John: *"This car needs some work."*

Jane: *"Why don't you take it in Monday."*

John: *"Me? You're the one who drives it most!"*

Jane: *"I have to get to work early. You just lounge around until 8:30 anyway."*

John: *"Hey, you have a cushy job..."*

Jane: *"Wait, wait, let's get the car fixed, OK?"*

Both John and Jane may think this argument is about car repairs and who should see that it gets done. But a teen listening on the side may not understand or even care about the details of dropping a car off for repairs. Your teen may be listening only to the message about the opinion each person has of the other.

So after a simple disagreement on the car, John may be surprised to hear Jenny say: *"You don't like Mom, do you?"*

John: *"What? Of course I do. Whatever gave you that idea?"*

The misunderstanding teens get from focusing on what seems to be the feelings the adults have for each other can be corrected. But the temptation to imitate what they have heard will linger on and that can only be corrected by future examples from you and from the Ericas, Johns, and Aunt Eileens in your family's social world.

All parents need the other adults around the family to show a positive model and message for teenagers to hear. Moms and Dads do not need friends or relatives around who show the teenagers how to abuse their parents. That kind of friend or relative should be asked to begin changing their attitudes...or begin leaving.

Most encounters in parenting are first-time experiences. Even parents with many children are usually surprised at what the next one does. Parents need companion parents to create a situation that is both their sounding board and their think tank. And we need the assurance that others have problems similar to ours.

Whether you are on your own or in partnership, a Parent Support Group can be a great help. Start a small parents group today. Even a reluctant spouse will develop some new ideas and attitudes from a discussion group. A few calls will produce other parents who are willing to be a part. Agreement on parental strategies is *not* a requirement. The opportunity to sort through common problems is the important part, and you will probably discover everyone is partly right.

For opening topics at meetings you could start with one of the steps or exercises in this book. Other topics suggested by individuals could be a part of each meeting so that each meeting covers immediate concerns. The exercise at the end of this section can be a good starting point.

Friends in a support group see your teen less often than you do. They can help you with new insights. Gradual changes taking place in a teen going from 12 on up are easy to miss. We often think of our teens as being about the same when changes are actually taking place every week and month!

6. Waning Parental Influence

The parent support group can help a mom or dad who, not recognizing growth, continues old limits on responsibilities and opportunities. Timely changes would strengthen their son or daughter's always-fragile self-worth. Parents can lose influence just by neglecting their teen's expanding areas of interest. So a teen's complaint of "nothing to do" should be taken as more than just a complaint about the lack of amusements. It could reflect a need for useful activities that are respected in his limited adult world. One fast way to alienate a member from a group is to not allow them to contribute when they are ready to do it!

A strange effect of sexism in our culture is that girls sometimes survive childhood better than boys because they make an earlier contribution to the family, particularly with the domestic chores. While "protecting" a male from drudgery, parents can run the risk of driving their son to find other activities that show he can "do something." Threatened by his feeling of "worthlessness," he will cast around for a way to be proud of himself—what will he find? Will it be a suggestion from his mom or dad? Or something not influenced by his parents and encouraged only by mischievous others?

Some competition for parental influence will come from a teen's expanding circle of friends. Parents feel obligated to hold to limits that are not always popular and so begin with a disadvantage in the competition with their son or daughter's friends. Friends are likely to reward a wide range of behavior and seldom reprimand or punish. The intolerance of peers to deviation from the accepted may seem obvious to parents, but examples of the standards are presented by every peer, making a teen's adjustment to these standards easy.

Your parental advantage is that you know how important *positive* support is, and you can plan heavy doses for good behavior for teens hungry for confirmation that they are doing right. Positive support is the major advantage parents have in the competition for influence with friends who give their support and criticism without much thought. But parents need to be clear about what is worthy of support.

"I think you're wonderful even when your friends let you down" is often an important role for parents, but too much of it can be cruelly misleading preparation for the adult world. A parent support group can be helpful here as well. How are other parents reacting to new fads and habits? What *good* developments are they encouraging?

7. Parents as Teachers, Coaches, Friends, and "Heavies."

Parental roles change with situations as well as with the ages of their teenagers. Parents need to be aware of these changes and avoid feeling "inconsistent" when different roles seem to be called for. Often a teen's confusion over Mom or Dad's changing attitudes can be erased by a frank explanation of their mixture of perspectives:

Jack: *"Why can't we have other cable channels. Everyone else has them."*

Mom: *"They cost more money. And not everyone has them. Parents in my group also say they're too expensive."*

Jack: *"But we're missing all the good stuff!"*

Mom: *"You see plenty of TV with its violence and ...stuff. I want you to use some of your time for useful things—where you learn something."*

Jack: *"If you were my friend, you would get the other channels."* (Sounds like a game of *"If-you-loved-me-you-would-serve-me"*)

Mom: *"Jack, I <u>am</u> your friend, but sometimes I have to be a parent who also looks out for your future. It's not easy doing both."*

Jack: *"Well, I'd be a lot happier friend if I had the other channels."*

Mom: *"Maybe so. But I have to be the parent who watches our money and watches out for your learning, and I want to be a friend, too. It's hard."*

Does Jack understand all this about conflicting roles? I doubt it. But he does understand that Mom is trying to do the best thing even when she doesn't provide what he wants.

Jack: *"All the kids get so noisy at soccer practice. You're the coach, you should tell them to shut up!"* (Sounds like a game of *"You're-the-parent-let-me-tell-you-your-job."*)

Dad: *"Sometimes I don't want to be the heavy. If there's nothing going on at the moment, they can let go a little."*

Jack: *"I try to tell them."*

Dad: *"Hard to control the whole group. Sometimes you should try going off with a friend and just doing a little passing practice until the next drill."*

Jack: *"You're more strict with me than you are with them!"*

Dad: *"It's different. They're not my kids. Sometimes I worry more over how you're doing. To them, I'm only the coach. To you, I'm a parent."*

8. College is Coming, Why Some Quit and Others Stay the Course

In my University of Maryland years as Associate Dean for Undergraduates, I gave a survey to over 500 drop out students who came in to resign. Here is what I learned.

Most students were surprised that only 10 percent of college drop-outs have failing grades. Actually, the biggest dropout factors are wrong housing, acquired bad habits, bad health care and bad time and money management—not grades.

The top factor in dropping out is address. Living too far from campus while working long hours at an off-campus job ranks number one. If college life is limited to a job, traffic, the campus parking lot, and classes, then cutting classes will be seem to be a good solution.

Bad personal habits are the next pitfall. If your usual caretakers are not around, you may feel, "Great. No more critics. I'm free to do what I want." But bad choices here have produced the poor health record of college students. You would think they would be the healthiest part of our population but they are not.

Drinking habits have an extra danger for college women. Fifty percent of women sexually assaulted on campus have been drinking at the time—making themselves more vulnerable—at least in the eye of the one doing the assaulting. The majority of women with unwanted pregnancies in the college-age group report they had been drinking at the time of the "big mistake."

Bad management makes the college dangers list because it's easy to become addicted to a job, to entertainment, computers or partying as well as the more familiar habits of drugs and alcohol. Skipping meals, sleep, or exercise makes getting sick more likely.

When you start feeling bad, review your habits and your overdoses of salt, fat, sugar, and caffeine—they make you sleep poorly and feel tired and depressed.

College Can Be a SNAP

On the academic side, my advice to students and my own daughters boiled down to the letters in "SNAP" which can help the study and class time pay off in grades.

The "S" in SNAP stands for <u>Show Up</u>. Missing class is the best predictor of a slipping grade point average. Also, nearly all students who drop out begin the downhill slide by cutting classes.

The "N" in SNAP stands for <u>Notes</u>. You would think the high school advice of "take notes" would be in every freshman's mind, but when you look around in your college classes you'll see many students who don't take notes.

Notes not only provide valuable review, they keep your attention on the class and give you extra practice if you copy them neatly later.

The "A" in SNAP stands for <u>Active Studying</u>. Many of my students have said, "I can't believe I did poorly; I went through (stared at) all the pages assigned for the test!" If reading is the assignment, get active, take reading notes. Reading notes become a source of motivation and provide bench marks so you can pick up at the right place after the phone, coffee, or pizza interruption. Never turn a page without writing down something.

The "P" in SNAP stands for <u>Plan</u> ahead. Poor time management can be a big pitfall for students on their own for the first time. Look ahead and schedule your study time. Everybody needs party time and you can't plan every minute, but a calendar will keep the priorities in order and, along with the rest of SNAP, you'll be ready for the tests.

For college freshmen, the first two semesters produce more dropouts than all the later years of college put together. After the first semester with big class projects and final exams, the second semester looms ahead. It's a crucial time for parents to send supportive signals to their student.

Samantha called home every week when she started college. Her Mom would respond, "Oh, Samantha, I hope you are well. We miss you so much. Your little sister is so lonely. She keeps asking, 'Is it time for Samantha's vacation yet?'"

These weekly tugs on the guilt strings were intended to let Samantha know she was loved, but she came to my office to fill out the paperwork to drop out and she completed the job.

Samantha's college career was short partly because her parents unintentionally emphasized family events that would make her homesick.

Keep the calls upbeat as much as possible, and the pressure low about jobs, money, and grades.

Most dropouts work too many hours at an outside job far away from the campus. In fact, that's an outstanding difference between successful students and dropouts.

Sons and daughters who juggle busy schedules of jobs and school make their parents proud. But if the schedule gets too crowded with job and commuting, the college experience may be reduced to job, campus parking lot, and classes. No time left for meeting classmates, chatting with professors, or joining in the many campus activities.

Encourage your college-bound son or daughter to live and work close to the campus and work only the necessary hours at an outside job.

Another common reason for dropping out is loss of direction or enthusiasm for a planned major and career. Parents can help here also by talking over the majors represented in the early required courses and keeping the pressure to make an early decision low. One primary advantage of college is learning about the variety of life's opportunities.

Many colleges and universities have 100 or more majors, but few first-time students can name 20! No wonder over 90 percent of freshmen change their major somewhere along the way. Fifty percent will change majors more than once.

Students are often tempted to avoid this decision by leaving college for "a year off." But if college is viewed as a source of information about choices, then staying in makes sense. Little is lost by taking courses to explore the wide range of majors and careers before making this important decision. It's a long way from graduation to retirement.

An additional danger for students comes when their mailboxes fill with offers of merchandise and credit cards. Caution your college student to keep life simple with few obligations to make payments on cars, credit, and clothes.

Habits concerning health (sleeping, diet, and alcohol) and management of time and money, can also be dangerous pitfalls in the college journey.

Most freshmen open a checking account and face the worries of a budget for the first time. They're on their own in budgeting their time, too. Parents of teens with a year or two of high school left have time now to prepare their sons and daughters for the challenges of caring for themselves.

9. Passing Along Your Parenting Style.

Of course you started passing your parenting style along as soon as you started parenting. You encourage some behaviors, model certain attitudes, discourage some habits and support and nurture others. You started making the next generation of parents when you started child rearing in this generation.

When your children are parents, you will coach them and help them. But you have been planting seeds for about two decades, and now they will start preparing yet another generation for parenting.

In these chapters I have advocated a practical approach to child-rearing. The Kids have practiced your routines of conversation, your approach to both learning and teaching, your inclination to show how you like them, and your model and your discipline

My philosophy is that children and adults are more similar than we sometimes think. The most important similarities are that all of us deserve respect and room to learn and experiment.

The successful efforts of both adults and children need recognition and support to keep the progress of learning moving forward. For children, the feeling of self-esteem is still developing and positive reactions from parents are especially needed for children to feel good about themselves.

Both adults and children deserve the same consideration when they make mistakes. Justification for punishment is not strengthened by pointing out the young age or small stature of the victim. Corrections, feedback, and a chance to make amends are still a big part of the parenting job.

Good listening habits are crucial to successful parenting. As the children grow, the communication becomes more complicated and the importance of listening skills grows accordingly.

Along with your successful parenting should come an enjoyment of the nurturing job. Thoughtful and fair strategies will make your role more comfortable. The critical addition is consideration of your own time and your need for support and respect.

Parents need to gather adults around them who will help with the parenting job by respecting and confirming parents' rights. Sometimes Grandma or Grandpa may need to be told, "Mom (Dad), it's harder for me if your remarks suggest to the children that I am not capable." If your spouse or a relative lives with you, it's all the more important that you show each other the respect you expect from the children and that you come to each other's defense and aid.

For the most part, your children will resemble you and the need to be a good role model makes parenting a hard job, but you are their best advantage because you're the one most interested in their welfare and you're close at hand. To raise good kids in these tough times, listen and teach, show them you like them, watch what's going on, model a good example, and cultivate your adult perspective.

We parents have an extra advantage: we learn well from each other. So as a final project, start that parenting group as suggested in this last exercise.

10. Ground Rules for a Parent Support Group

Parent Support Groups can provide a comfort and a good sense of direction with proper ground rules. They might also serve as a sort of extended family for your teen, adding a wider circle of positive adult influences and role models in his or her life.

At the first get-together, the group should take up the following ground rules and come to an understanding, if not an agreement, on how each issue will be handled.

For example, what should be the policy for telling stories, heard in group sessions, about your teen and relating stories about other parents' teens heard at group sessions? Other concerns should be:

1. Controlling Air Time.

What is fair share?

How will we police the air time?

Air time on a hot topic.

Balancing topic time and social time.

2. Concerning the Topic.

Selecting topics

The group is not an individual therapy session.

The group is not a couple's therapy session.

3. Concerning General Rules.

Degrading the kids, even your own, is not allowed.

Members act on their own responsibility, for example, in dealing with the schools, and do not take action in the group's name.

Splitting the group, sometimes when the ground rules are ignored and radical changes are necessary for your teen's sake.

Suggestions for Discussion for a Single Parent in the Parent Support Group.

How do other members of the group maintain their roles as adult and parent? How do they avoid using their teen as a weapon against their former spouse or a sounding board for emotional problems? How can they remain strong, reliable, cheerful and loving for their own teen? Is it true that no matter how conscientiously you help a teen understand the divorce or separation, at times, he/she will think it's his/her fault? How have others talked this over with their teen?

We want to keep our lives as stable and predictable as possible for our teens. How are other members of the group handling new adult relationships?

How do other members of the group avoid making an enemy of their former spouse and avoid competing with him/her? How do they work out the best interests of their teen with him/her? How can parents help their teen know that both his parents love and care about him?

How do most parents schedule family meals at home?

What other books are good on children and teen behavior? Can other parents recommend books that have effective techniques for managing key issues?

How have others involved themselves and their teens in civic, church or community activities? Could the group also provide an extended family network for its members? Maybe some could.

A Brief Last Word

You are the best qualified person for your parenting job. You're the one most interested in the welfare of your teenager, and you're close at hand every day. To enjoy parenting, stick to good habits, show a good model, listen, and cultivate some close advisors to discuss problems and solutions. We humans are busy with our complex lives, but we have an extra advantage: we learn well from each other.

In these twelve steps, I have advocated a practical approach to child/adult-rearing. My hope is that you will enjoy parenting more and enjoy the time spent, not as an obligation to be fulfilled, but as daily moments with a friend you love and like

Parents and their sons and daughters should be friends. Not in the sense of enjoying the same music or having friends in common, but through enjoying time together and supporting the strengths and successes of each other. You are developing a relationship and a life-time friendship.

Friends should support the best in each other. Our attention sweeps the common ground between us looking for sparkles to highlight. We like the behaviors we draw out of each other. Like a friendly searchlight, we seek the best in ourselves and our friends.

Some people have another focus. Their search overlooks the good we offer and zeros in on vulnerable spots. We pull back and risk very little. We know what they're looking for. We cover up.

When encountering old friends or new, aim your searchlight carefully. What are you looking for?

The successful efforts of both adults and their teenagers need recognition and support to keep the progress of learning moving forward. In the teenager's case the feeling of self-esteem is still developing, and positive reactions from parents are especially critical.

The justification for punishment is not strengthened by pointing out the young age of the victim. The unpleasant disruption caused by punishment is no advantage ether. A chance to make amends or practice a good alternative would be a better use of the time.

Parents should gather adults around them who will help with the parenting job by respecting and confirming a parents' rights. Sometimes grandma or grandpa may need to be told: "I need your respect and help with the kids. It's harder for me if your remarks suggest that I am not capable."

If your spouse or a relative lives with you, it's all the more important that you show each other the respect you want from your offspring, and that you come to each other's defense and aid when it's needed.

Teens copy better than they listen. The dominating factor in how they turn out is your example. This is a large responsibility to keep in mind.

All the steps and suggestions in this book take time. Helping a teen cross over his teenage years to adulthood requires time—for talking, planning, and soul-searching. Talking keeps the understanding and friendship healthy. Planning presents a clear view of the important behaviors and keeps the incentives logical and fair. And the soul-searching is for discovering the times to give over more responsibilities to a growing-up person.

**The best thing
to spend on
your kids
is time.**

Staying Cool and In Control

Also by award-winning author Dr. Roger McIntire

What should you say to your kids at supper? How should you react to their less thoughtful remarks? How can you deal with tantrums?

This book is a treasure of practical advice for parents challenged to keep a steady disposition, manage fair discipline, enjoy the job and stay lovingly close to their child.

Parental solutions and strategies are offered through vignettes, dialogues, and examples on every page. They cover the daily challenges from eating problems to cell phones and from social problems of pre-schoolers to the swirl of violence and sexual suggestions on television and computer.

Dr. McIntire's book provides effective, practical and proven answers to these challenges. His books are published in eight languages.

Available as an e-book. Soon to be available as an audiobook on Amazon.com.

Summit Crossroads Press also publishes...

$\mathcal{A}$manita Books, SCP's fiction imprint

features The 90s Club cozy mystery series
by Eileen Haavik McIntire

* *The 90s Club & the Hidden Staircase*
* *The 90s Club & the Whispering Statue*
* *The 90s Club & the Secret of the Old Clock*

The 90s Club at Whisperwood Retirement Village discovers murder and mayhem bubbling beneath the luxurious lifestyle at Whisperwood. Club members, aided by a suspiciously wild kitty cat named Malone, turn up clues like tricks in a bridge game and risk their lives to bring criminals to justice.

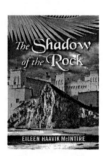

Also by Eileen Haavik McIntire: Two historical adventures—*Shadow of the Rock* **and** *In Rembrandt's Shadow.*

First-Person History Series

Memoirs and autobiographies tell personal stories of experiences living through major events of the 20th century.

On My Own: Decoding the Conspiracy of Silence by Erika Rybeck

Return to the Shtetl by Dorothy Sucher

The Twentieth Century Through My Eyes by Isadore Seeman